Dear Ashish, recomm...
the digital journey ... ...dia's
most valued bank. ... ...st
you. Happy Reading. Chaitanya Kotadia

HDFC BANK 2.0
FROM DAWN TO DIGITAL

TAMAL BANDYOPADHYAY

FOREWORD BY
NANDAN NILEKANI

JAICO PUBLISHING HOUSE
Ahmedabad Bangalore Bhopal Bhubaneswar Chennai
Delhi Hyderabad Kolkata Lucknow Mumbai

Published by Jaico Publishing House
A-2 Jash Chambers, 7-A Sir Phirozshah Mehta Road
Fort, Mumbai - 400 001
jaicopub@jaicobooks.com
www.jaicobooks.com

© Tamal Bandyopadhyay

HDFC BANK 2.0
ISBN 978-93-88423-35-9

First Jaico Impression: 2019

Page design and layout:
Special Effects Graphics Design Company, Mumbai

Printed by
Thomson Press (India) Limited, New Delhi

To my wife Rita aka Babu for being with me, always

Foreword

In early 2015, I noticed the dramatic changes that were happening in financial services due to simultaneous trends in technology, regulation and markets. The rise of the smartphone, India's unique ID system Aadhaar, and payment innovations from the National Payments Corporation of India(NPCI), like Immediate Payment Service (IMPS) and Unified Payments Interface (UPI), were creating a new branchless distribution channel.

The Reserve Bank of India's decision to license many new banks dedicated to payments, was to bring in fresh, technology-savvy competition. And, the rise of platforms like Uber, fuelled by vast amounts of capital, were creating new data-based business models, which did not face the traditional pressures of making profits.

I connected all these dots in a presentation I made at a The Indus Entrepreneurs "Leapfrog" Conference in Bengaluru on 21 August 2015, on the imminent disruption of institutions like banks. It was called 'Are We at a WhatsApp Moment in Finance?'

In the 'start-up' city of Bangalore, the dominant narrative then was that these rapid and diverse changes in the environment would move too fast for incumbents, creating opportunities for agile challengers. I took a straw poll of the delegates, and the overwhelming vote was that the digital newcomers would overcome staid incumbents in the financial sector. Our young audience, however, had not taken into account HDFC Bank and Aditya Puri!

Unbeknown to the delegates of the Bangalore conference, the HDFC Bank MD had already made a visit to Silicon Valley, almost a year earlier in September 2014, to see the developments and innovations in technology and understand their impact on the banking sector. He came back convinced that HDFC Bank had to move fast and take advantage of this digital disruption. Aditya and HDFC Bank had been known to spot trends, and then execute plans at relentless speed, scale and with proper risk controls. This book narrates the transformation from being a start-up in 1994 to striding like a colossus across the Indian banking sector in a little over two decades.

Tamal Bandyopadhyay is one of India's most respected writers and columnists on finance. He tells the exciting tale of how HDFC Bank has transformed itself, especially in the past few years with its digital journey. It chronicles how India's most valued lender faced its most profound challenge— turning itself into a digital bank.

During his Silicon Valley visit, Aditya saw how the fintech companies—the new kids on the tech block—were getting into fund transfers, mobile banking and shopping. They could build products that could give quick loans, and provide a lot of convenience and a slick user interface to customers on their phones.

But Aditya realized that most of the fintech players were Over the Top (OTT) applications that sat on top of the traditional banks network, and their customer base and merchant relationships. They were sitting on top of the banks by using Application Programming Interfaces (APIs). A similar phenomenon had happened in the telecom sector where OTT applications like WhatsApp had sat on top of the telecom network and taken away the messaging traffic.

Aditya and HDFC Bank decided that they would rather disrupt themselves than be disrupted. And while they could provide far more convenience to their customers, they also realized that with full digitization they could reduce costs in their operations. It was truly a win-win situation.

Their strategy was to provide speed, use technology to do credit and risk management at scale, improve the consumer experience and apply Artificial Intelligence (AI) to massive amounts of data for prediction and decision making.

It was also important that the bank combines global trends in technology like smartphones, AI, the cloud, etc. with the state-of-the-art infrastructure that India had built as digital public goods—Aadhaar, e-KYC, Unified Payments Interface (UPI) and other elements of the India stack.

Before the digital leap, by November 2013, the bank had come up with 'missed call banking'. This was a simple way for customers to reassure themselves that their balance in the bank was safe. Customers keep checking their balances every now and then. Providing this as a free service on a phone was the first priority on the bank's agenda. While it had been done in India before, HDFC Bank was the first to implement it at such a large scale.

The early innovations at HDFC Bank included sending money over the phone with an app called 'Chillr'. The app had started with the payment platform from National Payments Corporation of India (NPCI) called IMPS, which provides instant electronic bank transfers through mobile phones and internet banking. Subsequently, with the launch of UPI by NPCI, HDFC Bank pivoted to this next generation interoperable payment platforms and provided payment services to platforms like Google Pay.

The bank has also used AI for many applications like chatbots, commerce bots and humanoid robots. Its chatbot, the Electronic Virtual Assistant (EVA), now handles 6,00,000 queries a month; it has completed 8.7 million interactions since its launch. AI is now being used in every part of the bank.

It has also moved to convert its internal 'systems of record' to 'platforms' so that any application or user could get access to a common set of capabilities through APIs.

This has enabled the bank to launch new products quickly that could be targeted across the country, at both urban and rural customers. For example, the 10-second loan is a genuine innovation that has enabled the bank to reach both existing and new customers, anytime and anywhere. This product, based on the principle of 'paperless, presence-less and cashless', is a great example of combining the traditional strength of the bank in credit underwriting and risk management with the latest technology. Today, around 30% of HDFC Bank's personal loans come from this product, with no increase in delinquency.

HDFC Bank has taken this innovative approach to car loans, loans against securities and loans against mutual funds. With increased data about small business coming after the implementation of the Goods and Services Tax (GST), and its technology backbone the GST Network (GSTN), similar products could well be rolled out for small business lending as well.

As a part of digitization, in 2015, the bank introduced a marketplace platform called SmartBuy, where everything would be available in one place. This functions as an aggregator, hosting links to various sites catering to shopping, travelling, etc. Customers have the advantage of discounts and reward points. Besides, they do not need to take the trouble of going to multiple sites for different products and services. Over a period of time, the platform has been integrated to allow the customers to compare prices as well. They can also purchase online and take delivery from a physical store, showing an e-voucher. There are approximately 3,000 to 4,000 merchants providing these services. The first bank in India to do so, HDFC Bank clocked ₹40 billion from this in 2018. The technology is simple and can be replicated, but it is able to leverage its huge merchant base.

The bank has also moved quickly into digital payments. Traditional PoS devices are being replaced with digital PoS machines that combine card payments with new generation payment systems like UPI and use Quick Response (QR) codes. This flexible architecture also enables HDFC Bank to target new markets for digital payments beyond merchants, like schools, colleges and hospitals.

HDFC Bank's transaction volumes are astonishing. On average, more than 20 million cheques are processed by the bank every month for a value of ₹1.5 trillion to ₹2 trillion. The electronic payment numbers are much bigger. The bank processes more than 50 million transactions in a month through the Real Time Gross Settlement (RTGS), National Electronics Funds Transfer (NEFT) and Electronic Clearing House (ECH)/National Automatic Clearing House (NACH) avenues combined, valued at ₹45 trillion to ₹50 trillion.

The value of transactions in trade finance is almost ₹800 billion a month and transactions in the capital markets have reached ₹500 billion per month – almost 50% of the market share. The retail asset instalment loans issued during an average month reaches ₹110 billion. Moreover, the digitization drive has meant that the movement of documents has been slashed dramatically and this has saved around 2 million sheets of paper every month. The cost-to-earnings ratio shrank to approximately 40% from 49% between 2012–2018. Expenses have grown at a slower pace compared with the revenue earned.

HDFC Bank is not the only bank in India which has understood the significance of digitalization. There are others such as ICICI Bank, Axis Bank, Kotak Mahindra Bank and a few other private banks, and even India's largest lender, the government-owned State Bank of India, are making rapid strides in this space but to HDFC Bank's credit, it has been a leader, and moving at a faster pace and with efficient implementation. Unlike in traditional banking products where HDFC Bank learns at the cost of others and does not play the role of a pioneer, in digital banking, it has been the pioneer. For instance, even as the Reserve Bank of India gave licences to 11 payments banks, HDFC Bank has already taken a leadership position in payments.

HDFC Bank has navigated the difficult transition from being a bricks-and-mortar bank to one which offers banking through both physical and digital channels, for a seamless experience for the customer. The future will, of course, be fraught with competition. With UPI, we are seeing many players in the payments space like Google, PhonePe and Paytm. E-commerce has seen the arrival of global giants like Walmart and Amazon. There will be no 'winner takes it all' markets, and every victory will be hard-fought. Only the paranoid will survive.

The gale of digital disruption has impacted every industry. The print media's revenues have been decimated by the rise of digital advertising. Physical retail is dealing with the onslaught of online retail, which in turn is using its data to provide automated retailing in the physical world. The entertainment industry is seeing their customers 'cut the cord' to go to new direct to consumer internet-based channels. The automobile industry is facing the simultaneous challenge of electric vehicles, autonomous vehicles and ride-hailing platforms. In the memorable words of the internet pioneer and venture capitalist, Marc Andreessen, "software is eating the world".

But HDFC Bank has shown that with an agile leadership which has foresight and flawless execution at speed and scale, even a giant bank can take on the nimblest of start-ups and become a market leader and pioneer. It is an object lesson on how incumbents in many industries can respond to the digital disruption that is staring at them!

Tamal combines his financial knowledge, eye for detail, and an excellent storytelling style to create a vivid portrait of India's most valued bank and its path to the future.

Nandan Nilekani
Co-founder and Chairman of Infosys and
Founding Chairman of UIDAI (Aadhaar)

Preface

It's just been seven years since *A Bank for the Buck – The New Bank Movement and the Untold Story of the Making of India's Most Valued Bank* was published. Why then, would there be an update so soon?

The institution will mark its twenty-fifth year in 2019, but such celebrations are not really part of the culture at HDFC Bank. So much has happened at the bank (and in the broader industry) in the interim that it wouldn't be overstating the case to describe these years as transformative rather than evolutionary.

India's most valued lender has been turning itself into a digital bank, and not in a superficial manner, but by driving fundamental change. All this is taking place at warp speed— around 85% of all its transactions were digital in 2018.

In the 1990s, talking about banks as dinosaurs, Bill Gates of Microsoft famously said, "We need banking, but we don't need banks anymore." A quarter century later, a bank is relevant and will continue to be so if it is willing to reinvent itself.

The *HDFC Bank 2.0* journey began four and a half years ago, with MD Aditya Puri's trip to California in September 2014.

He saw how the financial technology (fintech) companies were getting into fund transfers, mobile banking and shopping. They could provide loans much faster than their old-world rivals and were building better financial products for customers. But Puri also saw that they weren't really reinventing the wheel—they were just much more efficient at using existing platforms. Their genius lay in developing sophisticated APIs—rules, commands, functions and objects for building software applications. And these apps were finding a home on every smartphone.

So he asked his colleagues: "Why don't we disrupt ourselves instead of waiting to be disrupted by fintech companies? Why can't we give a loan in 10 seconds? Why can't we invent something to transfer money in just a click? Why can't we reduce the friction in the banking system? Why can't we reduce the cost to revenue ratio by 5% over three years and 7% over six years?"

HDFC Bank aspires to become a financial marketplace. At another level, it is transforming itself from a life cycle bank (catering to the financial needs of a customer from cradle to grave) to a lifestyle bank (one that a customer will use instinctively, almost without thinking, to perform any task). It wants to be India's Alibaba or Netflix when it comes to banking.

The narrative isn't chronological but chapters are arranged to follow a particular theme because that's the best way of understanding this journey. My objective is not merely to write the bank's history but to tell the story of the making of a successful bank in India, born after economic liberalization, and reinventing itself continuously to expand its reach and remain ahead of the competition.

The book is divided into three parts—The Digital Journey, The Flashback and The Puri Legacy. The first four chapters cover the digital journey, which is still a work in progress. The next four are about the making of the bank—how it was conceptualized, how the team was built and the start-up fervour of the initial days. Senior managers went around in helmets, supervising construction of the bank's headquarters, and its branches, and training sessions were held under a tree at a textile mill compound in central Mumbai.

The chapters that follow discuss the business philosophy of the bank and how that makes it different from rivals in terms of product innovation, cost of funds, risk management and so on.

Chapters 13 and 14 are about two mergers, the first instance of a friendly union through a share swap and the biggest such exercise in India's banking history, respectively. Again, the emphasis is not on financial ratios and data but on the inside story—the nuts and bolts of how they got done.

HDFC Bank, despite being a highly successful venture, couldn't escape the regulator's wrath, having been penalized on a few occasions. Chapter 15 dissects what went wrong, how the bank got into a mess and the safety valves it created to avoid such incidents.

'The Common Sense Banker' tries to analyse what makes Aditya Puri, the longest-serving Managing Director (MD) of any bank globally, different from his peers.

In conclusion, I look at why this bank has been successful. It's not that it hasn't had problems—in terms of boardroom fights with the promoter over policies and skirmishes among senior executives—but despite these it has succeeded. The answer lies in the chapter title: Whose Bank is It Anyway?

While the first four chapters have been added recently, the rest have been recast with new information to make them contemporary and relevant. Some of the chapters have been extensively rewritten, incorporating the latest information and updating all data.

HDFC Bank does very ordinary things which yield extraordinary results. With this book, I have attempted to tell the story of HDFC Bank in the context of the overall banking space in India, which has been changing dramatically with the introduction of new products, newer ideas and technology. And, of course, the pile of bad loans is forcing the industry to look at loan appraisal and risk management in a different light.

Since my focus is the story, I haven't used excessive data unless it helps to illustrate the story. Many of the anecdotes in this book aren't in the public domain, and in that sense this book is the untold story of the making of India's most valuable bank.

I started reporting on the banking sector about a year after HDFC Bank was born, but I discovered several incidents narrated in this book only while working on this project. They have been impeccably sourced, even though in some cases the people involved don't want to be named.

This book is based on hundreds of hours of interviews with bankers, central bankers, policy makers, corporate executives, consumers and investors in different parts of India and overseas. Most of the interviews were conducted in person and a few on the phone and over video. For the data, I depended on information available in the public domain such as stock market notices, documents filed with regulators in India and abroad and the bank's balance sheets.

Some of the conversations narrated in this book may not be exactly the way they happened because they were not documented and I have had to depend on people's memories. I have lightly edited these in a few cases for effect, but by and large they are a faithful representation of what happened.

I have tried to maintain an informal style of narration. For instance, I have used the first names of people mentioned in the book unless more than one person has the same first name, as that would have created confusion. So, Deepak Parekh is called Deepak, but Deepak Maheshwari and Deepak Satwalekar have been referred to by their surnames. Similarly, Neeraj Swaroop is called Neeraj but for Neeraj Jha, I have used his surname. D. D. Rathi of the Aditya Birla Group is well known by his surname and hence I call him Rathi, but Ishaat Hussain of Tata Sons Ltd. is Ishaat, and not Hussain.

The key lesson from the HDFC Bank story is that freedom

for professional managers, non-interference by the board and the promoter and a passion for success are more important than ownership. HDFC Bank illustrates this formula better than any other bank in India. It strives to reinvent itself periodically. This book is an attempt to capture that.

Tamal Bandyopadhyay

Acknowledgements

When Akash Shah of Jaico Publishing House approached me with the idea of revisiting the 2012 book on HDFC Bank, I was excited. The past five years have probably been the most electrifying in Indian banking—dominated as it has been by the deteriorating health of quite a few banks, particularly government-owned ones, under the burden of bad loans. Then, there's been the birth of two universal banks. Besides, there are two new sets of banks—small finance banks and payments banks; the regulator's relentless push to clean up balance sheets; record-setting frauds; investigative agencies keeping a close tab on senior bankers; bank CEOs being stripped of office and even arrested; and, of course, the technological leap in banking.

I approached Aditya Puri, MD of HDFC Bank, with the proposal of rewriting *A Bank for the Buck* to chronicle the bank's digital journey and found him equally excited. He instantly extended all the help.

I thank the bank and its executives, past and present, for their unstinted support. They spent time with me, patiently explaining complex banking technology matters. Mehernaz Rustom, Executive Assistant to Chief Financial Officer (CFO), Sashi Jagadishan, organized many of the meetings that were essential to the writing of this book. I am not naming every individual I met as the book is, after all, about them.

I thank Nandan Nilekani (he does not need any introduction), for being extremely kind and encouraging in writing the foreword to this book.

Dhairya Shah, a chartered accountant who is doing his MBA at IIM Ahmedabad, and Yash Surana, another young chartered accountant in Mumbai, helped me with the transcription of interviews and research while former colleagues—who wish to remain anonymous—took a first look at some of the chapters.

Several bankers, policy makers, corporate executives and investors I met while researching this book spoke to me off the record and many did so on the record. All of them were generous with their time as they told me their stories, putting things in perspective and all of it adding up to a complete portrait of the bank. I wish to thank them for their contributions to my knowledge and all the help they lent in creating this book.

The author photograph is by Aniruddha Chowdhury.

Last but not at all the least, my son Sujan was of immense help in identifying many silly errors in the script and the ever-faithful pet, Gogol, kept me company as I burnt the midnight oil.

I

The Digital Journey

1

The Silicon Valley Trip That Changed the Bank

"It was the best of times, it was the worst of times, it was the age of wisdom, it was the age of foolishness, it was the epoch of belief, it was the epoch of incredulity, it was the season of Light, it was the season of Darkness, it was the spring of hope, it was the winter of despair, we had everything before us, we had nothing before us..."

The opening sentence in *A Tale of Two Cities* reflects Charles Dickens' view on the French Revolution. In some sense, this sums up Aditya Puri's belief in digital banking: Digitalization and disruption are intertwined. Whenever there is change, people tend to panic but if handled right, it can turn out to be for the best.

HDFC Bank Ltd. saw this transformation ahead of others.

At the beginning of the century, the bank had three generations as its customers—one that grew up listening to the radio, another that grew up watching television and a third for which mobile phones and the internet were a way of life.

The era of invisible networks has created a new market with the customer at the centre. Information, specifically actionable information, rushes through the network in a torrent. Customers can pick and choose what they want from a vast base of service providers around the globe. This has blurred the market as there is an apparent overlap of products from insurance companies, telecom companies, finance companies and platform companies. Both geographical boundaries as well as the cost of services have collapsed.

There has also been a secular shift in mobility, computing, telecommunications and AI, leading to a dramatic change in business models and opening up enormous possibilities. Amazon, Netflix, Google and Facebook have used this change to create new business models that offered structured products to customers and, in turn, swept aside traditional companies that just relied on their brands and distribution networks to sell products. Simply put, embrace change or become obsolete.

Aditya wanted to understand this model that would overthrow the old ways of doing business. He wasn't about to accept the fact that the world class bank he'd built would just disappear. He was not one to rest on his laurels while that happened.

A Close Look at the Disruptions

Aditya decided to travel to California to take a close look at the disruptions that were being discussed.

In September 2014, Mastercard Inc., a leading global payments and technology company that connects consumers, business, merchants, issuers and governments around the world, organised the trip for Aditya, then chairperson of its advisory committee for the Asia-Pacific region.

It was one of the rare occasions when Aditya was visiting the US not to meet the investors. The agenda of the trip was to understand the changing landscape of the financial services sector. The buzz phrases those days were: 'Silicon Valley will eat your breakfast and lunch', 'banks will be reduced to pipes', 'people won't need banks but only banking', and so on.

Mastercard helped Aditya link up with a few big financial technology (fintech) companies operating in the payments space, giving loan approvals faster than old-world rivals, virtual relationship management and advisory, e-shopping and building better financial products for customers.

For Aditya, the key lesson from these meetings was: These companies were not reinventing a bank, they were just riding on the platform of the banks with sophisticated APIs—a set of rules, commands, functions and objects for building software applications, popularly called apps.

As usual, Aditya did not take notes but at the end of each day (he was there for four days) he would call Sashi (using someone else's cell phone) and tell him how the world was talking about disruption and India could not escape this wave.

> "The fintechs were not in the process of transforming into financial institutions; they were riding on top of the banks, disrupting their business. Why don't we disrupt ourselves instead of waiting to be disrupted by fintech companies? Why can't we give a loan in 10 seconds? Why can't we invent something to transfer money in just a click? Why can't we reduce the friction in the banking system? Why can't we reduce the cost to revenue ratio by 5%–7% over five–six years?"

These were his questions.

The key was not competition but collaboration and white labelling products. A white label product is a product or service produced by one company (the producer) that other companies (the marketers) rebrand to make their own.

Aditya's ideas were evolving around one theme: If HDFC Bank was at the top in the physical space, why couldn't it be the leader in the online space?

Vision for HDFC Bank 2.0

After an 18-hour flight back, Aditya went straight to his office to hold a meeting as he wanted to "kick everyone's ass" and prepare them for disruption.

Around 20 people—senior management and business heads—were in the boardroom on the sixth floor of HDFC Bank's headquarters in central Mumbai, Bank House. A bleary-eyed, jet-lagged Aditya said there were four kinds of fintech companies responsible for disruptions in the financial services space—loan dotcom companies processing loan approvals at the speed of light; payment companies such as Alipay and ApplePay; wealth advisories using mathematical algorithms to advise customers based on their risk profiles; and finally, the payment wallets.

Aditya said that all the hype over fintech or tech companies taking over the business could be true but they would still have to ride on top of a banking network. If a bank owned the network, how could a third party viably sell OTT products on that network? The network, merchant and customer belonged to the bank. Could somebody take away their business by merely promising a good payment experience? He also believed that HDFC Bank had all the elements and the right technology in place and should rapidly transform itself into a digital bank.

He cited one of his conversations with Jamie Dimon, the CEO of JP Morgan Chase, the largest of the big four American banks, who said that disruption was bound to happen. Aditya told him HDFC Bank was prepared to ride that wave on its own.

The strategy of the technology companies was to ride the banking platform. They were trying to have an application and offer services in a more convenient manner without changing the fundamentals.

Aditya's message was clear: Why don't we disrupt ourselves,

---

instead of allowing a third party to do that? He told the group heads that they would have to look at changes, absorb them and strategize on their businesses.

He was clinical in his approach, asking everyone to set a date for conceptualization and implementation of action plans. No one should be living in a cocoon, he said, with typical Punjabi bluntness.

No Option

Senior executives didn't have a choice—either they could be a part of the transformation or they'd have to exit. It wasn't a pleasant meeting and neither was its aftermath for some people. Those who couldn't deliver on promises or failed to handle the pressure had to move on.

Everyone was given targets, focussing on four aspects:

- Reduce the turnaround time and ensure their products were the best in the industry;
- Change the credit and risk management processes for greater efficiency;
- Revolutionize the marketing procedures for a frictionless experience for customers;
- And, learn and apply artificial intelligence to the huge amount of data at the bank's disposal.

The next chapter will take a closer look at the transformation of the bank and the progress made on some of the products. Before that, let's rewind a bit and take a look at the building blocks that had been put in place much before Aditya's Silicon Valley trip.

Two key persons had been involved in the bank's transformation–Nitin Chugh, Country Head, Digital

Banking, and Munish Mittal, Group Head, IT, and Chief Information Officer.

While many of his colleagues were probably recovering from New Year celebrations on 1 January 2013, Nitin was praying with his family at the Krishna Janbhoomi temple in Mathura. He got back to his car and saw several missed calls on his mobile from Aditya's office.

When he called back, Aditya said he wanted to transform HDFC Bank into a digital bank and that Nitin should start working on the project. For Nitin, the call was like prasad from Lord Krishna.

The Digital Banking team was formed over the next fortnight. As Head of Digital Banking, Nitin was given a string of portfolios ranging from internet banking to mobile banking and digital acquisition. Also among his responsibilities were the outbound phone channel (which communicates the most with customers) and the corporate salary portfolio (as the salaried class would be the first to adopt digital means).

Nitin was no stranger to technology. After all, he had an engineering degree from National Institute of Technology Kurukshetra and experience in selling computer and photocopying machines. Still, this was a new role. He was to head the department from a business perspective and work alongside then Technology Head, Anil Jaggia, and other group leaders to create the digital bank.

Nitin, then working as Regional Branch Banking Head for the Northern Region based in Delhi, started travelling to Mumbai often to meet his team members. He would report to Rahul Bhagat, Group Head, Retail Liability Products. After a series of presentations and discussions with Aditya and other group heads, the blueprint was ready by August 2013.

Missed Call Banking

The focus was to understand customer behaviour and come up with innovative ideas. By November 2013, the team came up with their first product—'missed call banking'.

The focus of the bank at that time was on the rural markets where customers were not using internet banking, mobile banking or apps. Analysing their behaviour, it was found that much like people around the world, rural customers want to just reassure themselves that their money is safe in the bank; for this purpose, the customers keep on checking their balance every now and then.

Checking the balance is a global phenomenon. Bankers across the world try to simplify the process. This was the first item on the team's agenda.

They introduced a series of services that could be invoked by calling a toll-free number. 1800 270 3333: Checking the balance. A text message would be sent with the balance. There were other numbers for the rest of the services:

1800 270 3344: HDFC Bank mobile application link
1800 270 3355: Last three transactions
1800 270 3366: Ask for a cheque book
1800 270 3377: Ask for an account statement
1800 270 3388: Ask for an email statement
1800 270 3311: Ask for credit card related information

The service, initially meant for the rural population, was soon offered to all. Though it was not new or technologically advanced (it required a simple interface for the registered number to connect to the bank and retrieve the balance) and had already been introduced by a few government-owned banks, HDFC Bank was the first to implement it at such a scale.

It was an effective marketing tool for inducing customers to open accounts. Branch staff prepared stickers and pasted them on the back of customers' handsets so they could remember the number. Almost one million people started using it within three months of introduction.

The team initially didn't want to call it 'missed call banking'. After much research, they had come up with 'toll free mobile banking' but found it too long. It was never officially named but the informal name stuck. About 4 million people use 'missed call banking' every month.

Bank Aapki Mutthi Mein

Aditya wanted a digital strategy rather than just introducing digital products and services. Being a life cycle bank, it wanted to start early with customers through a careful onboarding process, get them to start using products and services, build capabilities around intelligent marketing analytics and then, over a period of time, do much of their banking with it.

The meeting after Aditya's Silicon Valley trip was a turning point, which Nitin calls the *'Muhurtam'*. Once he and Corporate Communications Chief, Neeraj Jha, were in Aditya's cabin discussing a possible tagline for the digital bank. While they all agreed that digital banking would empower the customers, Aditya liked a line in the press release, *'Bank Aapki Mutthi Mein'*. One of Nitin's team members had used the term 'Go Digital' as the subject of an email. They combined the two and found the tagline—'Go Digital: *Bank Aapki Mutthi Mein'*.

The campaign was launched in Varanasi. Perhaps, because it was Prime Minister Narendra Modi's constituency. Nitin said it has been an old market for the bank and also a melting pot for all segments of customers, including traders and weavers. There were six branches in Varanasi and all of them had high transaction volumes. At the annual dinner in December at his

Lonavala bungalow, Aditya announced that Nitin would go to Varanasi on 16 December 2014, to launch the digital bank.

Nitin bought an iPhone 6 to display the applications at the first-ever press conference that he would address on a boat on the Ganges. It was to be followed by another meet with the media at the Gateway Hotel Ganges.

He was nervous but Aditya, who was in Delhi at that time, sought to put him at ease over the phone. Nitin, the Corporate Communications team, a local branch manager and the media boarded the boat, which was decked up with helium balloons that were to be released at the time of the launch. There were also a few customers, representing different segments of business and trade.

Nitin was supposed to hold the placard with the tagline and then the balloons were to be released. Everything went as per the schedule and he started speaking in a mix of Hindi and English, when one of the housekeeping staff on the boat used a lighter to free a bunch of helium balloons that hadn't got released along with the others. There was a minor explosion, leading to mild panic when it seemed that the boat was on fire.

Back at the hotel, Nitin made his presentation and demonstrated the services on his new iPhone. The launch received some attention from the national media but, for the local papers, it was a big hit.

In retrospect, Nitin feels the minor explosion at the launch was a good omen. From 44% of overall transactions in March 2013, digital transactions grew to 55% in March 2014, 63% in March 2015, 71% in March 2016, 80% in March 2017 and 85% in March 2018. HDFC Bank has successfully transformed itself into a digital bank—transactions via phone banking have been reduced to 1%, while the share of branch banking is at 8% and Automated Teller Machine (ATM) transactions are at 6%.

The Innovation Team

HDFC Bank had already deployed analytics but after Aditya's Silicon Valley trip these began to be used in more meaningful ways. It also created an Innovation team. The first hire was Rajnish Khare, Chief Innovation Officer, Citibank in India.

The job of the team was to come up with new ideas, look at the existing workflows of the bank, the areas where it can innovate and go out and connect with innovators outside. After starting with fintech as the theme, over a period of time, AI and robotics took over.

At a parallel level, the Digital Marketing team started running a command centre to monitor various tweets, messages, references on social media sites—not only those pertaining to HDFC Bank but of the competition as well.

The first experiment of the innovation team was a tie-up with a Kochi-based technology company Backwater Technologies Pvt. Ltd., which approached HDFC Bank with its app called 'Chillr'. The Unique Selling Proposition (USP) of the app was being able to send money via the phonebook. It had found mention in Nandan Nilekani's 'Are We at a WhatsApp Moment in Finance?' presentation.

In August 2015, Infosys Co-founder and Founding Chairman of UIDAI, Nandan, said India was witnessing a 'WhatsApp' moment in the finance sector due to emergence of payments banks, e-sign, the Immediate Payment Service (IMPS) and other technology-related revolutions.

While delivering a keynote address on 'Disruption in Financial Services' at TiE LeapFrog 2015 in Bengaluru, Nandan said, "...in 2009 there was a WhatsApp movement in telecom. My analysis is, in 2015 there is a WhatsApp movement for finance in India... Change is coming on many fronts...new licences, smart phone Aadhar identification, e-sign, payment banks, etc. Some of it is regulated, some of it is technology, some of it is design, and some of it is market".

The promoters of Backwater Technologies, who were in their late 20s, had approached many other banks but HDFC Bank was the first to respond. It took a few months for testing and technical integration before the app was launched in February 2015. Nitin went to the studio of RadioOne (FM 94.3) with RJ Hrishikesh to promote the app.

Launched in Bengaluru, it immediately caught media attention. But many believed it was an HDFC proprietary app and that perception made other banks turn their back on using it. The company suffered because of this as it could not scale up the business.

In fact, a large bank said that unless several other lenders started using the same app, it would not use the utility as it didn't want to be perceived as using HDFC Bank's app. In 2017, when it was on the verge of being shutdown, Backwater Technologies approached HDFC Bank to buy it out. Although the app was generating revenue, the bank chose to pass and it was acquired by Swedish caller identification app Truecaller.

The app had started with IMPS, which provides instant electronic bank transfers through mobile phones and internet banking. In March 2017, it moved on to the UPI, a unique Indian interoperable payments system. That ensured customers of at least 50 banks gained access to Chillr. Over a period of time, it offered a range of transactions, including bill payment, mobile recharge, topping up of Ola and Book My Show wallets, among others.

HDFC Bank said it had always been revenue positive on Chillr but the promoters of the company found it difficult to scale up as they were spending a lot on customer acquisition and couldn't source additional funds.

Let's Explore the Young Minds

Partnering with start-ups has always been part of the digital strategy. Although start-ups cannot disrupt the bank with their OTT products, why can't the bank offer better and newer services by partnering with them? The promoters of Chillr would operate from a place known as Startup Village in Kochi, which was co-incubated by the government of Kerala and some big corporate names, including Kris Gopalakrishnan, one of the seven founders of Infosys and now Chairman of Axilor Ventures Pvt. Ltd., a company supporting and funding start-ups. At the Startup Village, the bank saw young minds experimenting with all sorts of products. Quite a few of them are currently working with HDFC Bank.

If the Startup Village could have so much talent, there must be plenty more across India was the rationale. This idea led to the birth of digital innovation summits in February 2016.

Typically, HDFC Bank decides on a theme (such as customer experience, analytics, blockchain, etc.), invites applications with ideas around the theme, shortlists 30–40 teams, conducts a two-day summit in the office and the jury, consisting of senior bank executives across disciplines, selects the top five teams that can work with the bank.

In September 2018, the bank engaged with around 40 start-ups, at various stages of evaluation. It does not invest in the projects but works alongside the start-ups and mentors them. It has also started approaching the 50 top colleges in the country (including some of the IIMs and IITs) and partnering with their students on innovative ideas.

Monday Meetings

Every week for almost a year since the launch of the digital initiative, there wasn't a single Monday when Nitin did not meet Aditya at 9.45 a.m. in his cabin and update him on plans. The meeting could end in half an hour or stretch beyond lunch with other group heads joining and discussing customer reactions to new products.

For Aditya, it has always been about what customers are saying as much as what his staff tell him. He believes that customers and employees should be equally involved in the digital drive.

He would often ask Nitin how many processes had been simplified. In how many processes has the bank reduced turnaround time? If they could sanction a loan in 10 seconds, why couldn't they reduce the turnaround time of activity that requires one hour? The relentless focus has been on reduction of turnaround time for every activity.

In 2015, the bank also organised a series of town hall meetings across India to explain to employees the digital transformation and how they should be involved in the journey. There were days when in the morning Aditya and his team were in Indore, in the evening in Bhopal and back to Mumbai by late night.

Typically, such meetings would have a few anecdotes narrated by Aditya and the employees in the audience would share their digital experience. For instance, one would say how a Tauji (a senior citizen in Haryana) sent money to his grandson in Mumbai through Chillr with the assistance of a branch employee. Then, there was the kebab seller in Kolkata who had faced problems with collecting bills from customers as they would just drive away. Chillr transformed the way he did business by allowing to collect money along with orders. Meanwhile, a labour contractor in Manesar was giving wages to his workers on Chillr.

A Mass Movement

Aditya's Silicon Valley trip had led to a mass movement and everybody wanted to participate, contribute and come up with new ideas for the digital transformation. The concept of Virtual Relationship Manager (VRM) emerged following insight into analytics.

Aditya also realised that when a customer living in Malabar Hill, an upmarket residential neighbourhood in South Mumbai, or buying an expensive car did not have much in his or her bank accounts, it implied that HDFC Bank was not the person's primary bank.

A normal analysis of their bank accounts would throw up data on income but the bank wouldn't be able to sell different products to them. So, VRMs were assigned to such individuals, based on their location or other attributes. The VRMs are different from the local branch relationship managers and operate from centralized locations. The bank has currently around 4,000 VRMs, managing 6 million customers. (More on this in Chapter 4)

From Chillr (which was discontinued on 30 August 2018) to digital innovation summits—this was the first phase of the digital journey. In the next chapter, we'll look at the second stage.

2

From Robots to an Agile Office

The second stage of the digital journey was engagement with the next set of fintechs who were not into product development (like Chillr) but into AI, machine learning and the Internet of Things (IoT).

The evolution of the Electronic Virtual Assistant (EVA) is a case in point. HDFC Bank launched EVA on its banking website in October 2016. However, at the 2017 Digital Summit, Senseforth AI Research Pvt. Ltd. convinced the bank that it had a better product that could answer questions with more accuracy than HDFC Bank's chatbot. Senseforth is a humanlike conversation platform powered by AI. It can address queries, resolve issues, and perform tasks.

The bank worked with Senseforth's team and relaunched EVA, which was handling 6,00,000 queries a month by November 2018. Till this time, it had completed 8.7 million interactions since its launch.

HDFC Bank also worked with another company called Niki.ai in Bengaluru and launched its commerce bot on Facebook messenger. Users can search for HDFC Bank OnChat, register their mobile number and start recharging, paying utility bills, book a hotel, etc. The person doesn't need to be an HDFC Bank customer as the payment gateway is integrated. Payments can be made with any other card or payment mechanism.

The next obvious step is to give users the option to bank with HDFC Bank, based on the number of transactions.

The Interactive Robot Assistant (IRA) is another experiment with AI. It's a humanoid that interacts with customers and, at the same time, can navigate them to branch counters. The bank has two such robots. The first version was launched in January 2017 at its Kamala Mills branch in Mumbai. Later, it was shifted to the Palarivattom branch in Kochi. The upgraded version was launched in April 2018 at the Koramangala branch in Bengaluru.

Though both the robots are mobile, the major upgrade from IRA 1.0 to 2.0 is speech recognition. Customers had to interact with the earlier version using a touch screen attached to the robot. However, there was greater customer acceptance for IRA 1.0 (which had feminine characteristics) than IRA 2.0 (which had a male form).

Are Robots a Gimmick?

Are such robots a gimmick? Nitin says the robots are a technology demonstrator for the bank. They don't attract customers to the branch but those who visit the branch come across a novel, unique experience. The plan is to deploy such robots in 15–20 branches over a period of time.

For the bank, AI is fast becoming all pervasive—right from HR for onboarding new employees to portfolio management of customers; from credit and risk to customer acquisition and cross-selling.

Junior level candidates are screened by video interview. They are judged on the basis of responses they give to the questions posed by an app. The app judges them on vocal responses, eye movements, etc. and selects candidates based on the bank's parameters.

As far as marketing is concerned, AI is being used for programmatic advertisement bidding—for various forms of media. Though HDFC Bank has been a pioneer in AI and robotics, it has still not completely got into Robotics Process Automation (RPA). Robotics automation is all about applying intelligence so that machines can learn and start creating patterns, deciphering data and getting an insight.

EVA will become an example of RPA over a period of time by including certain workflows to process certain products of the bank.

There are Failures

Not that every digital plan has succeeded. For instance, HDFC Bank explored working with automobile maker Mahindra & Mahindra Ltd. for developing a mobile banking app that could be hosted on the infotainment system of a car for some basic banking transactions. The experiment, popularly known as Integrated Voice Controlling Banking app, did not work. At the moment, it is not a priority for the bank but can be revived.

Similarly, smartwatch banking is something that could not be scaled up. Nitin admits its failure but is bullish on its potential as a banking interface. The bank had launched the 10-transaction banking app for Apple Watch in July 2015.

In the bank's digital journey, Nitin and Munish complement each other to the point that they can even switch roles: Munish can represent business and Nitin technology. This means, if one can't attend a call with one of the strategic partners because of another meeting, the other will go instead.

In fact, when Backbase, their Netherlands-based technology partner, invited them to their annual customer connect event in Amsterdam in November 2017, Nitin and Munish jointly presented the keynote address—a rare occasion when business and technology complemented each other.

Agile Office?

This will be the new culture at HDFC Bank. The digital journey has also changed the way its executives work. For instance, the business heads from Bank House at Lower Parel visit the Kanjurmarg office in an east-central Mumbai suburb at least once a week and work with the Technology team to come up with innovative projects.

This is very different from the so-called agile office that Dutch banking group ING introduced in the summer of 2015—the first bank to do so, emulating companies like Spotify, Netflix and Google. The office logistics were changed to appreciate the customer's journey in the new omnichannel environment where everything had to be seamless.

ING revamped its entire architecture to do away with elevators (so that employees could interact with each other while going to their respective floors) and conference rooms. Meetings were held at the pool table or beer bar. In such an office environment, cross-functional teams are expected to work on innovation, while sprawled on bean bags.

At least one HDFC Bank office—Bank House, its corporate office in Bhubaneswar (the bank's corporate offices in every Indian state is called Bank House, like its headquarters in Mumbai)—has no cabins but pods like phone booths where employees can hold conversations. There is no emphasis on hierarchy—senior managers and executives all sit together to brainstorm over ideas. The cross-functional teams have members from finance, IT, compliance, operations, business solutions group, among others, who meet once or twice a week for half a day to check the progress of all pending projects. This is expected to be replicated across the bank over the next few years.

The agile methodology has its own advantages in terms of team-work, quick turnaround time and generation of innovative ideas. However, the bank does not call it agile; it's called the HDFC Bank way of working.

What's that? The HDFC Bank way is to implement agility culturally and not structurally. All the teams that the bank creates share a common cause, come together on a project figuring out what to do, how to do it—it's more of a culture than an organisational structure.

The bank will soon have an in-house team of software coders (currently outsourced), and user specialists for User Interface (UI) and User Experience (UX). They will help the bank in redesigning products and processes, using design-thinking principles.

From Chemistry to Software

After his BSc in 1987, Munish wanted to carry out research in chemistry, his first love, but his mother insisted that he take up a job first. He left home for Ludhiana (where his uncle lived) to look for a job. His cousins were in the hosiery business.

Unable to find a job, he accompanied his cousin on a business tour across India. His forte was his ability to speak English fluently and convince the customers. The 45-day tour saw them double the business normally done during the annual trip. His cousin was keen to have him as a partner in his business but Munish's mother was not willing to invest in a business run by family members.

After small stints with JCT Electronics Ltd. at Mohali, Punjab, a regional computer centre run by the Department of Electronics, Electronic Systems Punjab Ltd., a subsidiary of Punjab State Industrial Development Corporation, in 1994, he was part of the IT department of Bank of Punjab Ltd. as a junior executive. At that time, the ATMs of most banks were offline. He was working on a project to make the ATM system of Bank of Punjab online at its main branch in Chandigarh. The ATM chest's door got locked and couldn't be opened.

An engineer from ATM maker Diebold HMA Pvt. Ltd. from Chennai was trying to help him by drilling through the chest door and cutting open the cylindrical shaft that had broken loose and fallen off.

Both of them worked until late evening without success. Then Munish realised that every time they tried to drill a new hole in the steel cylindrical shaft, it rotated and changed its position both horizontally and vertically the moment the drill bit touched the shaft. The centrifugal force was pushing the shaft up and around.

Munish told the ATM engineer to put the drill in, the shaft went up and he pulled the door open! This engineer advised Munish to join HDFC Bank.

The First Meeting

The engineer gave his CV to C.N. Ram, then Head of IT at HDFC Bank. When Ram asked him to come to Delhi, the first question Munish asked Ram was whether he would be reimbursed for the trip. He took a bus from Chandigarh to Delhi and met Ram in the Hindustan Times House branch on Kasturba Gandhi Marg, New Delhi.

At HDFC Bank (he joined in August 1996 in Mumbai), his first mandate was to set up a retail technology platform. By then, the bank had decided to focus on retail banking and was using Finware, made by Citicorp Information Technology Industries Ltd. (CITIL), which later became i-Flex and was acquired by Oracle—as its retail core banking system. For implementing the centralized ATM switch which would drive the network across the country, Munish selected a software called Base24 from ACI, then headquartered in Omaha, Nebraska, (it has now shifted to Naples, Florida), reputed as the best in the business.

Munish believes that the journey towards the digital bank

of today started in May 1997 when telephone banking was introduced in retail core banking and every ATM went online with a centralized switch. Early this century, HDFC Bank was the first to set up two-way disaster recovery with online real-time replication at the storage level.

He attributes the making of the digital bank to Aditya's vision and Ram's tech prowess during the early stages.

Within a couple of weeks of joining the bank, while leaving office (Sandoz House), Ram noticed Munish's sulking face. He stopped by and told Munish if he thought he had made a mistake by joining the bank, he shouldn't come from the next day.

Munish looked up and showed Ram his torn shoes; he could not find time to get them stitched. Munish was living at the bank's guest house at Seven Bungalows, Andheri West, then. "By the time I reach the guest house, the cobbler has left for the day," he told Ram. "Skip office tomorrow, repair your shoe but never sulk," Ram retorted.

Wading through knee-deep water in the Mumbai monsoon, Munish reached the bank's data centre at Chandivali to do the first transaction when the bank introduced real-time SMS-based mobile banking in 2001. He paid his utility bill and got a real-time SMS on his cellphone with an immediate debit from his account. At that time, he was living at Mahakali Caves, Andheri East.

In 2004, HDFC Bank had a consumer loan book of roughly ₹10 billion. That was the time when the bank put in place a state-of-the art workflow and imaging-based digital loan origination system with de-duplication of applications to check fraud (entity resolution system using advanced analytics based match codes) as well as advanced modelling based-application, behavioural score cards and a business rule engine.

For Munish, digital means analytics, mobile, cloud and social networking. Two important elements—social and cloud—were missing in 2004 and instead they had mobile and messaging. The bank had all the systems—depository, debit card, direct banking channel, point of sale (PoS), and merchant acquiring—by then and had also created an enterprise retail data warehouse.

In 2006, the bank set up India's first database marketing analytical customer relationship management practice. HDFC Bank was also among the first to launch the banking application and the securities application on smartphones in 2010–11.

After Aditya's Silicon Valley trip, Munish, Nitin and Manmath Kulkarni, Head, Core Banking Technology Product at CITIL, one of HDFC Bank's largest primary strategic partners in the digital journey, revisited the technology architecture of the bank. Combining business, application technology and hardware architecture, they handed it over to Aditya in a document.

Digital banking is all about omnichannel banking: Connecting all channels of communication—call centre, contact centre, mobile app, smartphone, SMS, missed call, ATM, PoS and branches.

Platformification

Before that came 'platformification'. It had laid the foundation of Service-Oriented Architecture (SOA)—the application programme interface or API banking in the middleware layer—which started in 2008. It was modernized between 2014–2016 and helped the bank set up an omnichannel portal on top of the platform.

What is platformification?

Anything that's created once should be reusable to create derivatives of digital products across multiple channels.

This is an entity resolution platform that uses advanced mathematical algorithms and operates in-memory to arrive at name, address, and other demographic detail matches.

The platformification also comes from the ability to publish web services which are consumed by numerous loans and credit card origination systems, even from across the bank's wholly-owned, Non-Banking Finance Company (NBFC) HDB Financial Services Ltd., which offers a range of loan products, both secured and unsecured, besides Business Process Outsourcing (BPO) solutions to the bank.

Since HDFC Bank already had Customer Relationship Management (CRM), analytics and database-marketing, it only had to create a platform for the branches, personal bankers and relationship managers to provide an overarching view of what was going on across the country. This platform was for sales force automation, customer interaction management and service request management.

HDFC Bank's technology architecture is such that whatever is created is usable for everything. This advantage is due to platformification which provides a universal, holistic approach. CRM, analytics, data warehouse, API—any business can use the same environment to create a digital product and service customers. Most banks have adopted specific solutions for individual tasks.

For customers, HDFC Bank is a one-stop shop—payments, savings, investment, loans, shopping are among the choices on offer. Soon, they will have gamification as well. The customers can choose the location, the device, and the time to conduct banking at their convenience.

Offering conversational banking using a chatty EVA is a kind of gamification. For instance, it might greet a customer by name: "Good Morning Asmita, you need to top up your fuel tank as you are already a week overdue. Shall I put in a reminder for you in your calendar for this evening?"

If the bank's customer dreams of riding a Harley Davidson and his current salary is ₹30,000, instead of spending the entire salary in servicing the bike loan, HDFC Bank helps him plan the buy, customizing his savings every month in such way which does not affect his monthly spending. If the bike is a goal in three years' time, the bank helps him save by starting a recurring deposit every month. He can top up the recurring deposit whenever excess money is available to achieve the dream faster.

Augmented reality is also a sort of gamification as it offers fun-filled engagement. Just point your phone in any direction and the app will tell you where the nearest ATM is and whether it has cash. If a customer is getting married and wants a destination wedding in Goa, along with a certain kind of music during the mehendi ceremony, the bank will be able to organise all that through the HDFC Bank platform by ensuring subscription to one's choice of music capsule Netflix/ Amazon Prime/iTunes, for that matter.

Of course, the customer can do the same thing by approaching a provider separately but the sheer convenience of doing everything through one digital window will persuade her to use the HDFC Bank app. The bank aims to foster loyalty and reward customer trust with discounts and loyalty points. For the bank, the reward is in the form of a broader customer relationship and more business.

More on this in the next chapter.

3

The Bank is a
Financial Marketplace

In the initial stage of the digital journey, the target was the urban market but later HDFC Bank decided to attack the semi-urban and rural pockets as well. Behind all these, the objective was to expand the business and bust the myth of the so-called base effect, which slows down a big bank's growth rate.

The bank's employees took a while to understand what Aditya wanted. When the boss told them to bring down the cost-to-revenue by 5 percentage points, the team came back with an estimate of 0.25%. But Aditya wasn't looking for a marginal change—they weren't really getting the point. He wanted nothing less than transformation through digital.

For instance, if he was talking about a 10-second loan, it meant the entire process being completed in that time—the customer's application, the approval (with the help of an in-built credit scoring model) and money credited into the account. It took six months after Aditya's first meeting on his return from Silicon Valley to bring about fundamental changes in the way HDFC Bank was working.

It was not an easy task as there was complacency after creating what the employees believed was the best bank in India—it had the least bad assets and enjoyed steady growth that outstripped all its rivals comfortably. Aditya kept saying that whatever they had created was history and now they would have to reinvent the bank and themselves. Targets were set daily with three goals—customer convenience, competitive pricing and reduced costs.

The exercise involved an intense effort with most senior managers working without a break between September 2014–February 2015. These six months marked the beginning of HDFC Bank 2.0. Aditya was ready to take the responsibility for anything that went wrong but anyone who didn't respond to the call of duty would eventually look for other opportunities although the bank never explicitly asked them to do so.

The bank had a large pool of data at its disposal. The task was to convert this into actionable information to achieve goals. This would require a change in the technology platform.

The bank had unstructured data obtained from customers on where they shopped, partied, ate out, holidayed, etc. Subject to privacy norms, it wanted to be in a position to turn this into knowledge of everything about every customer, not on the basis of its relationship but relying on the information the bank had. How they worked on this was explained in the previous chapter.

The 10-second Push

Arvind Kapil was the first to come up with this innovative product. He introduced the concept of a 10-second loan for the bank's existing customers that was launched in April 2015. Existing customers (about 30 million) were given a credit score based on the transactions, payment records and internal and external credit history. The Credit team said about one-third of customers could be given pre-approved loans of up to ₹1.5 million.

For a seamless experience, they integrated the front end and back end. The selected customers would be given an opportunity to fill in a few details, get an OTP and the money (loan) would be transferred to their accounts within 10 seconds—the world's fastest loan approval and disbursement.

Let's hear the story from Arvind, Country Head, Unsecured, Home, Mortgage and Working Capital Loans.

According to him, there were constant debates in the bank about how to get the product to consumers in the fastest and most convenient way—how to empower them through the do-it-yourself route.

Arvind recalls a meeting in early January 2015 with a customer in Chennai who was running a large agro products supply chain. The customer was convinced about the bank's products but was reluctant to seek a loan because of the vast quantity of documentation and multiple visits to bank executives involved. He asked Arvind whether he could get a loan sitting at home without having to call the bank.

That was the story of most customers—happy with product offerings but not comfortable with the paperwork and multiple executives being involved in the process that starts from sanction of a loan to its disbursement. That was the inspiration for the 10-second personal loan product.

A senior IT executive in Delhi who had been banking with HDFC Bank for a long time once asked Arvind why would a customer seeking a loan need to provide so many documents—salary slips, PAN, address proof, and so on. "If you already have access to my salary account and all other cash flow statements, why do I need to prove it with paperwork?"

An Unchartered Territory

That set the ball rolling. Arvind started connecting the dots and working towards a seamless product for both the customer and the bank. It was unchartered territory. Initially, the process would be limited to 30 minutes. They were following a bottom-up approach and started thinking of ways to tackle the challenges on loan approval as well as disbursal.

The bank used to undertake income-based lending that

required income tax returns. How would they do this online? Another important aspect was handling the risk. This meant that they had to be super careful but, at the same time, come up with an innovative product. Since the customer would not provide any information, they had to draw it from data they already had such as bank statements, credit/debit card transactions, information about funds flowing into the account, etc. Of course, this could be possible only if HDFC Bank was the customer's primary bank.

The team used advanced analytics to parse this information and compare it with current lending patterns. They prepared an algorithm to give debit scores to customers. However, though they found sufficient correlation between the debit score and the prevailing lending patterns, the Risk team was worried about how well the algorithm would perform under difficult circumstances.

Arvind appreciated their concerns and wanted to walk the path of digital lending in a measured way. He had to convince each of the Risk team members of the feasibility and necessity of this product. There was discomfort primarily because of the online nature of the transaction. So, a hybrid product—part-online, part-offline—was proposed initially with a 20-minute waiting time for the disbursal. After all, letting go of the touch and feel of credit underwriting was a big step forward.

However, in reality, the bank was not diluting its credit underwriting standards; it was advancing them and applying them to a larger database. Between the Risk team and the Product team, a compromise formula was worked out: Let's launch the product in a phased manner. It was seamless and frictionless, an end-to-end digital approval-to-disbursal process.

In the initial phase, it was meant only for select salary account holders where the Risk team had conducted various algorithmic and analytical tests. The product was launched on the bank's net banking website on the evening of 30 April 2015.

The First Loan

The first loan was made at 4.18 a.m. on 1 May 2015, to a 25-year-old process associate in a BPO in Jaipur who was working a 10 p.m.–5 a.m. shift. "Talking to him we found out that as his working day never matched banking hours, so he found it very difficult to apply for a personal loan. While checking his balance online, he found the offer, clicked hoping to see a form and was surprised to get money in his account almost instantly," Arvind says.

Day One saw 215 customers availing the offer for a 10-second personal loan online. The loans were generally ₹0.3–0.4 million (capped at ₹1.5 million). The team clocked a loan disbursal of almost ₹3.5 billion in the first month without any advertisement.

The initial customer response was encouraging. During the early days of the product launch, Arvind's team frequently called up customers to understand their experience on whether the product was meeting requirements and living up to expectations. As the bank gained confidence, it kept customising and personalising the product offering and ticket size, keeping in mind its relationships.

How Does it Work?

How does the interface work? A customer logs onto the bank's net banking website. If the customer is eligible, there is a loan option available at the top. The customer fills in some information (some fields are pre-filled), authenticates it using two levels of verification and the amount is credited to the customer's account within 10 seconds.

Arvind claims that in reality, the amount is sent to the account within 5–6 seconds. The USP is that for a customer, a loan cheque is available and encashable 365 days a year, 24 hours a day. By November 2018, 34% of the bank's personal loans were booked during non-banking hours.

How does it happen so fast? The Credit team of the bank considers every customer of the bank as a potential loan customer and, after analysing data (which is continuously updated), awards a credit score on the basis of an algorithm. All such customers are 'pre-approved' for a specific loan amount at a certain rate. The bank then informs the customer of this loan availability online. Once the customer confirms the loan requirement at a click, it gets disbursed immediately.

For the customer, the entire process is online but there is a lot of work at the back end where Credit and Risk teams are involved.

The product is a culmination of the bank's underwriting prowess and risk understanding, buttressed by a mass of customer data stored in a data warehouse explaining transaction and payment pattern and credit behaviour. There is no paperwork; the documentation is done online via OTP.

The product encapsulates the bank's uninterrupted learning in retail lending over two decades—customer identification, credit underwriting, documentation and customer service. It started with salaried customers and self-employed people were added later. More categories will be added with the Goods and Services Tax (GST) in place, bringing transparency and more people into the tax net.

The biggest hurdle for catering to small businesses remains non-availability of reliable information within the banking system. While credit bureaus have greatly helped in identifying customers with 'intent to pay', banks continue to struggle to get customers with 'ability to pay' in the absence of streamlined business transactions through the banking system. The new tax regime will help increase routing of business transactions.

The personal loan segment of the bank clocks around ₹60 billion in disbursements every month, the 10-second loans have one-third share of this. Customers are mostly

30–40 years old. The delinquency rate is on a par with loans disbursed physically.

The bank's paranoia for risks has increased as it trades the digital path. For risk management, it has created a new credit risk underwriting framework christened P27, or the power of 27, as it is fondly called inside the bank. It incorporates the 'ability to pay' income score and cascades it with the score of the credit bureau as well as a behavioural score of spending habits or past repayments and then mashes it up with the social score, catching an individual's internet consumption patterns.

The campaign, Kil-Bil (Kill the Bad, Build the Good—inspired by the American martial arts film written and directed by Quentin Tarantino), is another interesting initiative introduced to engage the front line teams to use data and insights to improve credit underwriting and portfolio quality.

All about Analytics

Risk management, based on analytics, is in the DNA of HDFC Bank. At the turn of the century, at the Retail Lending head office in Kamala Mills, Lower Parel, Rajesh Kumar, Head of Credit Policy, felt something was missing as he tried to cope with growing volumes of the retail loans. Traditionally this was managed through a touch-and-feel assessment, for which he relied on the experience of seniors like Prashant Mehra, Regional Credit Head, and his excellent network of connections to get customer references and feedback.

Though the bank had plans to set up its data warehouse, Rajesh felt the need to bring in greater standardization and deeper insights into the portfolio to pick up advance signals of distress as the business started scaling. He had heard about a fresh hire from Indian Institute of Management Calcutta, Ashish Abraham, working in the Fraud Detection Unit in Delhi and wondered whether his quantitative background could be used. He convinced Ashish to leave Delhi and join him in Mumbai to start the analytics journey.

Initially, both were groping in the dark and trying to make sense of the vast data at their disposal. Once, they got a hang of the numbers, they started building metrics and templates which could be used to look at the data more meaningfully.

Over the course of the next few months, they completed work on a debit score, which could be computed on bank account information for cross-selling loans to the depositors. This was a first in the industry at the time, where a model was being built on bank account information to asset credit risk. That was the foundation of the bank's cross-sell infrastructure.

During the next few years, Rajesh and Ashish hired promising MBA graduates and statisticians from across the country to form the Analytics Unit, which began to build more and more statistical models.

Being new to such tools and techniques, the Product and Policy teams took time to re-align their thought processes and continuously asked for validation. As a risk-averse bank, priding itself on its quality of assets, there was some hesitancy in trusting these models to carry out risk assessment.

It took years of testing, showcasing results and multiple presentations at Bank House to build the confidence. But once the team was convinced of the efficacy of the models, the bank adopted the new tool to cut down turnaround time and costs.

However, as the business expanded, the risk management started becoming more and more complex. That was when the bank started making its first large scale investments in technology architecture for analytics.

As the demand grew, so did the hunger for data, because more data meant more insights. The unit started an exercise of combing through troves of data across systems to glean any additional insight into customers which could be used in improving the cross-sell offers and making them more attractive for customers. Models were built which would derive insights from anything—ranging from credit card transactions to customer addresses. The unit generates an average of 60–80 million scores a month.

One of the high impact products that the Analytics Unit was involved in building was the 10-second personal loan. It has been running for almost three years and is yet to see a meaningful competitive product from the industry. Disbursing unsecured loans in this manner is not an easy task for a bank, especially one which has always been conservative in its outlook. A few key ingredients have made this possible.

The members of the Analytics team have the right blend of specialization in decision sciences as well as business experience, gained from continuous interactions with the members of the team that run Credit Policy and Products.

The senior management of HDFC Bank, even up to the board level, had always been involved in the mechanics of the execution and usage of the models and risk frameworks like P27 underlying in the risk architecture.

The bank could also trust its 'detection and braking' system. It has a rigorous Through-The-Door (TTD) sourcing and automated portfolio monitoring system which throws up the smallest anomalies or adverse trends in every segment of its loan book, and errors, if any, quickly come to light and feedback loops to carry out necessary corrections work rapidly.

The Analytics Unit is actually like a start-up with geeky young kids and cool coding tools operating within the bank. It has built the models and infrastructure ready to consume almost any data available in digitized form. As a result of this, HDFC Bank is not only able to leverage its large customer database but also feels light on its feet as a small fintech company with an ability to deploy advanced technological solutions on its large customer database.

Other Innovative Products

The success of the 10-second loan encouraged other business heads to come up with more innovative products. Ashok Khanna, Country Head, Secured Loans (Vehicle), introduced a 10-second car loan, based on a similar model in which HDFC Bank tied up with dealers to ensure disbursements using e-vouchers. Parag Rao, Country Head, Card Payments Products, Merchant Acquiring Services and Marketing, proposed the concept of an instant virtual card.

Credit and debit cards are electronic modes of payment although their sourcing could be physical. So, changing to digital does not affect the building blocks of the business. Customers want to interact digitally but for the bank, the core philosophy remains the same.

This means even the digital card requires a person to set limits, providing ways to ensure the transaction doesn't fail, seamless integration, etc. The first experiment was to provide a virtual credit card in just 10 seconds by applying online.

The second experiment was with the marketplace platform—to increase the usage of the payment gateway and banks' products on e-commerce websites. HDFC Bank already had a big chunk of the merchant business. It had a 40% market share, including credit and debit card payments at shop counters and a 50% share of the online payment gateways and e-commerce websites accepting payments.

The Bank is a Financial Marketplace

As a part of digitisation, in 2015, the bank introduced a discount platform called SmartBuy, where everything would be available at one place. The objective was to offer its huge merchant base to customers and the merchants, in turn, would offer discounts to customers, bringing down product prices.

The discount portal offers a host of services—ranging from shopping to travelling. This functions as an aggregator, hosting links to various sites catering to shopping, travelling, etc. The bank cannot provide those services because of regulatory restrictions but it can connect all of them.

Customers have the advantage of discounts and reward points. Besides, they do not need to take the trouble of going to multiple sites for different products and services. Over a period of time, the platform has been integrated to allow the customers to compare prices as well. They can also purchase online and take delivery from a physical store, showing an e-voucher. There are approximately 4,000 merchants providing these services.

The first bank in India to do so, HDFC Bank clocked ₹40 billion from this platform in the fiscal year 2018 without any significant advertisement. The technology is simple and can be replicated but its secret weapon is the huge merchant base. Even a localised product such as Amritsar *aam paapad* is sold through the bank's portal. It may look into offering high-quality wine and even matchmaking services if a matrimonial site wants to list itself on the SmartBuy platform. Unlike e-commerce sites Amazon and Flipkart, it does not charge a commission for distribution.

The bank is now experimenting with financial products on SmartBuy, ranging from loans to splitting product prices into Equated Monthly Instalments (EMIs) and products of other banks as well. It is also creating a category specifically for international brands.

Parag believes that if both sides of the business are very large and if these two parts transact with each other, then it becomes a closed group—something similar to Apple's ecosystem.

What's in it for the bank? The answer is an increase in the volume of transactions using its card and payment gateway. There is a boost to the merchant acceptance business as well. Another important aspect of creating such a product is ensuring customer loyalty.

Superior financial services aren't enough; the platform has to be perfectly implemented, allowing a customer to navigate from one tab to another without a hitch. The bank wants to equip its customers with the ability to compare prices and products on various e-commerce platforms and navigate these through its own website.

Customers thereby get the cheapest price, discounts and reward points. The bank makes money on every payment made but the business plan hinges on customer retention and the balance they maintain in their accounts.

Globally, the model is followed by Discover Global Network which has a closed-loop network that gives it insights across payment network participants such as Diners Club International, PULSE and other global alliance partners. This is used to make better decisions and new products.

'Zapp Up' the Payments System

SmartBuy was integrated over time with the bank's payment application called Payzapp, which helps customers store card data on the bank's network and avoid having to plug this in on every transaction. The product was inspired by PayPal Holdings Inc. (whose founders include Elon Musk and Peter Thiel), which operates a worldwide online payment system that supports online money transfers and serves as an electronic alternative to traditional instruments such as cheques and money orders. The bank was not sure whether consumers would use the payment wallet and hence SmartBuy and Payzapp were integrated.

Next in line was a digital move on the merchant acquiring side. The bank had deployed 490,180 point of sale (PoS) terminals at 409,929 merchant outlets as of 31 March 2019.

The digital wave is all about using the mobile rather than the machine, deploying the internet in the most effective manner. The question was how to provide digital integration?

This led to the rise of digital PoS devices. These could accept payments using QR codes, UPI and the BHIM (Bharat Interface for Money) app. The PoS was interoperable and could accept any mode of payment. Parag calls this "practical digital innovation"—the bank could have launched a separate application for doing this but it did not want to burden merchants and instead decided to integrate it in the original PoS.

After this, the digital drive was taken to schools, colleges, universities and hospitals. Popularly known as SmartHub, the platform is an answer to the problem of long queues and spending time paying fees at such institutions, for instance. The platform helps institutions collect fees online and, at the same time, assists them in creating a website of their own, markets this initiative to the parents of students, integrates it with Enterprise Resource Planning (ERP) or SAP and provides reconciliation statements. This is how HDFC Bank expanded its footprint beyond merchants.

The next set of target customers were the small paan shops and kirana stores who couldn't afford PoS devices. The bank successfully pitched the SmartHub idea to them. Now they could accept payment from customers digitally through any channel. UPI is integrated with the banking application as well as payments platforms SmartHub and Payzapp.

The BHIM app launched by the government doesn't dilute the bank's net banking application as BHIM is an integrated and interoperable platform, specifically designed for customers whose banks cannot invest in electronic applications, such as rural cooperative banks.

Design Your Own Nike Shoes

Progress on the digital front was spectacular but the bank was hungry for more. A Nike ad with the tagline 'Make yourself' gave Aditya the idea for 'loans against securities'. He believed the dematerialized or demat accounts of customers could be linked with savings accounts, enabling them to create their own limits and credit accounts instantly.

In 1999, HDFC Bank was not only busy working on Y2K-related changes to its systems, but also launching new and innovative products in the market. (Y2K relates to the tweaks that needed to be made to ensure that systems could cope with the shift to the year 2000.)

Loan against shares was one such product. Incidentally, HDFC Bank was probably the first to introduce Initial Public Offer (IPO) financing for individuals. While for loan against shares, a customer pledges to the bank the shares one holds, for IPO financing the bank steps in to support the new share applications with a moneyline. The process was paper-based as Depository Participants (DPs) were still getting used to demat shares. It started with select customers and the business grew steadily.

By 2016, the loans against shares portfolio crossed ₹20 billion. The progress of technology had been so dramatic during this period that the bank was encouraged to design a solution integrated with multiple applications within the organisation as well as the National Securities Depository Ltd. (NSDL) and the Central Depository Services Ltd. (CDSL).

It worked with both the depositories to create a complete online digital solution for customers who sought loans against equity through their demat accounts with the bank. It already had the expertise to process such loans. The change was required to leverage this expertise in the digital world and engage NSDL and CDSL as the business is highly regulated. It started conceptualizing the product in 2016.

Over several weeks, multiple iterations and numerous late-evening discussions over samosas, the team arrived at the most optimal solution through integration of multiple applications within the bank with the systems of NSDL and CDSL.

As most digital solutions employ Straight Through Processing (STP) to speed up transaction time, it was imperative that each leg of the operation was completed in less than one second and the overall process was completed within a few minutes. For the customer, it is an end-to-end self-service solution that's paperless with no manual intervention—a first for the bank as well as the depository participants, globally.

Loan against Shares

In May 2017, the bank started marketing this product as one that allowed customers to create their own Loans Against Shares (LAS) online. It takes about three minutes from starting the application to getting the overdraft limit set in the account. Apart from opening an LAS account and setting overdraft limits, a customer having an account with HDFC Bank can also release shares already pledged for the facility and replace shares by pledging new or additional approved securities.

After that, on the product table was Loans Against Mutual Funds (LAMF). There are regulatory limits on loans against shares as these are considered capital market exposure of a bank. However, mutual fund holdings in debt instruments are not considered capital market exposure and hence there is no limit on the amount that can be given as loans to customers.

When HDFC Bank started exploring the opportunity, it zeroed in on Computer Age Management Series Pvt. Ltd. (CAMS), the Registrar and Transfer Agent (RTA) for multiple Asset Management Companies (AMCs). This time, loans were to be given even against mutual fund units held in non-demat form.

By October 2017, it got a grip on the transaction flows

but hit a road block. As it had started its journey on a digital platform and frozen its net banking solution, the product had to wait for the digital platform to be ready. Instead of waiting, it started exploring a different approach. The team asked for 90 days to develop, test and implement the product. The solution was ready by end of January 2018. By November 2018, 75% of all loans against shares and mutual funds were digital.

Change of Guard

Amid all this, there was a change of guard. Anil Jaggia decided to leave the bank in 2015. He joined Avendus Capital Pvt. Ltd. but only for a few months. Bhavesh Zaveri took over as head of both Operations and Technology. Their working styles differed but both had the same tech vision.

By this time, Aditya's digital push was at its peak. The initiative included consolidation of technology platforms and digital customer channels; launching new digital channels and products; bringing automation to newer areas of banking— all revolving around the key theme of 'customer centricity'.

The rate at which technology was changing, it wasn't a question of keeping ahead but one of catching up. Balancing new technology adoption with the safety-first philosophy of the bank was a tricky business.

"We never would have imagined two decades back that banking and social interactions are going to have commonalities and we will be finding these similarities through technology," Bhavesh said. "We are not a technology innovator; that is not our play. Rather we try to use innovative technologies from our partners. We seek to partner with the right technology vendors."

The partnership with Murex S.A.S, a French technology company with global repute in providing trading, risk management and processing solutions in the capital market, foreign exchange, derivatives, and debt securities space, is an interesting one. One December morning in 2015, Murex Asia Pacific CEO Guy Otayek, along with his Sales team, met Bhavesh and his colleagues in the fifth-floor conference room at Bank House to kick off the discussion.

The implementation started after senior management teams of both sides flagged off the project in Mumbai in October 2016, marking the beginning of the bank's digital consolidation initiative for the treasury business.

Changing the Way the Treasury Works

For the bank, this project was the biggest treasury initiative in the past decade. It was also one of those projects close to the heart for Bhavesh and Ashish Parthasarathy, who has been heading the bank's Treasury since 2009 after Sudhir Joshi retired. Paresh Sukthankar, the bank's former Deputy Managing Director and arguably the best risk manager in the Indian financial system, was also engaged in keeping the vision clear and direction steady.

A core 40-member project team was constituted with members from all stakeholders. They were sent to Singapore to understand the features of the software. Sending such a large team overseas on a knowledge expedition was something unheard of in HDFC Bank. Bhavesh managed to convince Paresh to approve the trip as an exception.

The first phase of the project was completed on a date pre-decided 20 months before. When the products went live on 12 February 2018, the Murex team uncorked a champagne bottle for the bank team at the treasury dealing room at Bank House. Another celebration followed at the bank's Kanjurmarg office that houses its Operations and Business Technology Group.

The Murex application—a single integrated platform—has

many benefits. It replaces multiple applications in treasury with a single robust application, reducing some of the risks associated with multiple system. It also enables pricing and valuation of derivatives transactions.

The philosophy of HDFC Bank is to find technology partners for long-term relationships. Naturally, the bank thinks a great deal before partnering any technology company. "We spend time and make efforts in picking our technology partners. And once this is done, we stick to the relationship," Bhavesh said.

Though the core banking partner might have changed hands and names—from CITIL to i-Flex Solutions India Ltd. to becoming part of Oracle Corp. as Oracle Financial Services Software (OFSS) Ltd.—the partnership with the bank is still going strong even after two decades.

Overall, has this been a smooth journey? What about the future? Well, there are many challenges. The next chapter discusses those and the way forward.

4

From Life Cycle to Lifestyle Bank

Here is a story that Bhavesh loves to tell.

There was a Parsi gentleman who used to visit a small restaurant in a quiet corner of the lane. He had begun patronising the café during his college days and maintained that habit over decades. The restaurant became like an extension of his family—he was familiar with the waiters, savoured the special tea, relished the *bun-maska* and enjoyed the service. Then an office complex opened nearby and the restaurant started getting more and more customers. With patrons pouring in, the Parsi gentleman began seeing the quality of the tea deteriorating and the service became abysmal. After putting up with it for a while, he just stopped visiting the restaurant.

"The point is, we have tonnes of volumes coming in with the growth in business, and not necessarily in a certain pattern, but we can't compromise on the service quality. If that happens, the customers will leave," says Bhavesh.

The challenge before the bank is managing growth in transaction volumes without compromising on quality of service.

HDFC Bank's transaction volumes are astonishing. As on 31 March 2018, it had 43 million customers. On average, more than 20 million cheques are processed by the bank every month. The electronic payment numbers are much bigger. It processes more than 50 million transactions in a month through the RTGS, NEFT and ECH/NACH avenues combined.

The bank continues to have 50% market share in the value of transactions in capital markets. The retail asset instalment loans issued during an average month reaches ₹110 billion. These are just a few examples.

Coming up with innovative products is difficult but selling them is even tougher. It is necessary to instil confidence in the front end that the bank has an attractive range of products. Many still prefer going to branches. Convincing them to go digital was a task in itself. Front-end executives started approaching customers, giving them demonstrations of the digital drive, showing them how transactions were secured.

In the second stage, customers were tracked to ascertain that they had indeed migrated to the digital platform. As much as 80%–85% of the fixed deposits in the bank have now gone digital, reflecting the transformation in customer attitude.

From Large Companies to SMEs

The focus of the bank was on corporate clients in the beginning. It was a strong force in cash management and had very good relationships with the top 200 companies by 1998. It wanted to leverage this relationship to provide secured convenient banking products to customers.

Corporate internet banking, which is now routine, was then an innovative concept. 'Digital certificates' and 'public key infrastructure' were phrases that were bandied about but rarely applied. HDFC Bank scouted for a technology partner that could co-create a solution. It found Solution Net Systems, Inc. as partner and developed its own infrastructure to issue digital certificates to corporate customers and became the registering authority as there were very few such entities in the public domain at that time.

The Public Key Infrastructure (PKI) system enables users to securely exchange data over the internet and verify the authenticity and identity of the other party. A digital certificate, part of the PKI, is an electronic 'passport' that helps in authentication of the identity of the sender.

The bank launched its corporate internet banking product in 1999. Christened ENet, this platform started with basic account enquiry facilities but large corporations such as Reliance Industries Ltd., Tata Motors Ltd., Tata Steel Ltd. and Mahindra & Mahindra Ltd., among others, kept pushing the bank to add more and more features to the platform.

It developed almost everything customers asked for—that was the unique selling point. And what started for high-end corporate customers was later extended to accommodate mid-sized companies, small merchant establishments, stock brokers, mutual fund houses and so on.

As part of the digital transition, the bank is now working on migrating ENet into a new corporate internet banking platform. Here too, choosing the right technology partner is the key, entailing a painstakingly detailed evaluation process.

According to Bhavesh, with this transformation project, the bank should achieve the next level of digital banking for its corporate customers—to provide a state-of-the-art and most up-to-date experience in terms of ease of banking and availability of products and services.

Saving 2 Million Sheets of Paper

Has the bank benefited? The digitization drive has meant that the movement of documents has been slashed dramatically and this has saved around 2 million sheets of paper every month. The cost to earnings ratio shrank to approximately 40% from 49% between 2012–2018. Expenses have grown at a slower pace compared with the revenue earned.

The change is attributed not only to the digital products but also to the thought process. Besides, the move to digital created a new customer acquisition channel. It also helped in freeing the bank staff from their routine chores as customers are availing loans with just a click.

Have people lost jobs after the bank embarked on the digital drive? HDFC Bank has capacity models in place for its front-end and back-end infrastructure. The manpower capacity is worked out on the basis of quantitative modelling, using time and motion study. With the advent of new technology, once customers started switching over to digital, the employee requirement declined.

Simply put, by going digital, the bank is able to get incremental sales productivity from existing staff by improving the turnaround time and getting end-to-end process through Straight through Processing (STP). This means while the business has continued to grow at the traditional rate, the addition to head count has not kept pace.

That this shift would happen, was brought home to Aditya at an investor conference in Hong Kong in 2015. A Scottish portfolio manager at a large fund, which manages insurance money, cited the examples of Westpac Banking Corporation and Commonwealth Bank of Australia. She cautioned that people don't want to give way in the face of digital transformations and would continue to do what they were doing. If that happens, costs don't come down.

Aditya saw her point and decided to identify excess capacity. Very few were asked to leave but business heads were asked to not replace natural attrition, especially at the lower levels of the organisation. Attrition at the top and middle level has traditionally been low on account of long-term incentives like stock options. So, from a peak head count of 92,000 people in July 2016, the number dropped to 84,000 in March 2017, which has since risen to 94,000 as of 31 March 2019.

Future of Bricks-and-Mortar Branches

What is the future of traditional channels such as branches and ATMs? Is the feasibility of the bricks-and-mortar model under threat?

On an investor call, Aditya said he did not have the answer but HDFC Bank was trying an experiment with the channel. It has reduced branch from 2,000–3,000 square feet to 800–1,200 square feet. That has meant lower costs and fewer employees. The result: They are breaking even faster.

HDFC Bank is adding 100–150 branches a year against as many as 500 a year at its peak. It also has metrics to judge the efficacy of an ATM.

Between 10 November 2016 and 30 December 2016, ₹15.41 trillion worth of currency notes of denomination of ₹1,000 and ₹500—about 86.9 % of the total notes in circulation—were withdrawn, the third demonetization drive in India since 1946. After demonetization, the profitability of many ATMs has dropped on account of low cash requirement due to digitalization and charges for using cash machines in excess of a certain number of transactions. Customer behaviour has changed and cash transactions have declined, leading to a few ATMs going out of business and hence being closed.

Before demonetization, it had 12,054 ATMs (in October 2016). Since then the bank has closed down some ATMs and relocated a few but the branch footprint is still being expanded.

While HDFC Bank adds hundreds of thousands of customers through its digital route, its branches will continue to welcome the customer, walking in to fund initial cash deposit into freshly opened digital bank account. The idea is to combine assisted digital, self-service straight through digital with human touch-aided relationship banking so that the trust element—key to the banking business—is not compromised.

A VRM powered and assisted with artificial learning technologies will handle a bulk of the customer service requests even as a hot-line option for customers will remain to get into a live voice or video chat with customer service representatives.

In 2007, HDFC Bank launched 'Classic on Phone'—a remote relationship management programme, which was the origin of VRM. It was a success but it could not be scaled up as the customer was not yet ready for it.

By 2015, the scenario changed and the high net worth customers were keen on availing services digitally, without it intruding on their time as would be the case with personal visits. The Phone Banking team was given the job of testing the waters. Thus, the Virtual Relationship Management programme was born.

It started with 500 VRMs in 2016 and by the end of 2018 at least 4,000 such managers were serving 6 million customers. The offering is through a human interface on the phone, catering to transaction and product needs of the customers with the help of an assisted digital journey.

Aditya is convinced that VRM is going to be the future and it can be among the largest revenue generating businesses for retail banking. He wants the VRM team to triple the revenue in the next 24–36 months. Aditya's mantra for the VRMs is fairly simple—"Make use of available information (within the bank) of the customer, to have a meaningful conversation (this is the keyword) and provide services and need-based products in such a way that it leads to a positive change in customer's relationship with the bank." The focus is on conversation; not just selling.

The bank has started leveraging the 'computer vision' to extract the PAN number from a scanned PAN Card on the mobile phone and pre-fill the 'transaction request' form for convenience and is also verifying the signatures on the cheque the customer has issued using machine learning algorithms.

However, an alert supervisory over-sight with strong maker-checker mechanism keeps the bank reasonably figital—a fusion of physical infrastructure and digital architechture, blending the offline and the online spheres.

Let me demystify the maker-checker mechanism. It has its origin in the so-called 'four eye' principle which means no transaction can be put through the system by only one individual, it needs two. The breach of this can cause a disaster. The biggest banking fraud in India, unearthed in government-owned Punjab National Bank (PNB) in February 2018, illustrates this.

In this case, the origin was misuse of SWIFT messages. Banks across the world use SWIFT (Society for Worldwide Interbank Financial Telecommunications), a messaging network for securely transmitting information and instructions for all financial transactions through a standardized system of codes. Here, to ensure safety, six eyes are required. The maker keys in the message in the system, the checker checks it and, at the third stage, the verifier transmits it after he is convinced of its genuineness.

What Next?

The bank has tied up with Netherlands-based Backbase to create the Backbase Omni-Channel Banking Platform. The state-of-the-art digital banking software solution unifies data and functionality from traditional core systems and new fintech players into a superior digital customer experience.

The aim is to provide customers the full financial experience instead of merely delivering products. The underlying motto is that if a customer wants to shop, pay, invest, trade, borrow, the only option in their mind should be HDFC Bank.

Aditya says it is positioning itself as the Indian Alibaba. Founded in 1999, Chinese online giant Alibaba Group

Holding Ltd. provides consumer-to-consumer, business-to-consumer and business-to-business sales services via web portals, as well as electronic payment services, shopping search engines and cloud computing services.

The next wave will see the lender partnering with an array of fintechs globally that can plug into HDFC Bank's system and offer their products and services to customers. This will be by way of an API that connects to the front end of the bank. Simply put, the mobile banking platform will act as a one-stop solution for anything and everything that a customer would look for.

The plans of HDFC Bank are such that the bank wants to scale it up to have even Amazon, Google on its platform and offer them to customers through its website or app and also offer its products and services on the platform for merchants, e-commerce players and corporate banking customers. This, HDFC Bank believes, is 'banking at the edge'.

A digital bank, with self-service and computer vision to extract and process data from scanned images on the mobile device, and straight through API generating real time account number in core banking, can potentially add millions of new customers a month on their short taxi ride from home to the airport on the way to a holiday destination.

HDFC Bank, I understand, is rewriting its applications and recalibrating platform to become 'Cloud Native'—which means these become elastic and can expand and contract automatically in sync with the workload.

Omnichannel

The omnichannel vision first came up in 2013 when it began to gain traction in the market. However, the bank did not go ahead with the project as it wouldn't be able to achieve this on its own. Instead, it made some changes to the user interface in terms of screen layout on the website and mobile app.

The idea cropped up again in 2016 when HDFC Bank was in the process of revamping its mobile application. It was looking for a redesign of the UI when Munish suggested that the omnichannel experience project be revived. Over the next few days, the team held discussions and brainstorming sessions on the pros and cons of such a project.

Aditya gave them the go ahead but also told them to search for a strategic long-term partner; he did not want to deal with multiple small vendors. Such a partner was found in Tata Consultancy Services Ltd. (TCS). However, the business side of the bank wanted to change the application and give customers a better experience while the Technology team wanted a platform.

At that point, the CFO, Sashi Jagadishan, stepped in and suggested that the bank revive its omnichannel project with Backbase. The team had already researched Backbase and was convinced it was the best in the space. They went back to their drawing board to transform all the digital channels.

Munish, Ashima Bhat (Finance), Ajay Kapoor (Head of Business Technology Group) and Nitin went to Amsterdam (Backbase's headquarters) in June 2016 for a due diligence of the project. At the end of the trip, they sent an email to everybody from a coffee shop saying they had looked into all the elements and the bank should go ahead with Backbase for the project.

Once back, they decided to have TCS as the system integrator and their partner for all the digital banking arrangements.

In Digital 2.0, the bank wants to make everything automated—a person clicks and searches for something related to money and the bank's products pop up, the website navigates them to the product and within 10 seconds they have access to the product. The bank wants to develop an algorithm that can use all the data it gleans to gauge every little need of customers.

Social media, mobile, analytics and cloud, popularly known as SMAC, are the foundation of any digital banking initiative. HDFC Bank's next few years of transformation agenda and strategy is based on cloud. "We will build an infinite scale, we will move up from 1.5 billion monthly transactions at the rate of 5,000 transactions per second to 3 billion transactions a month in 18–24 months and probably 6 billion in next 36–48 months," Munish says.

Cyber Security

The digital platform of the bank creates 'infinite' lanes super 'internet' highway for transporting billions of data packets, digital vehicles, billions of customers' digital transactions such as money transfer and bill payments and e-commerce shopping payments. They pass through dozens of toll gates using 'FastTag' in an authenticated secure manner but at the speed of light.

Cyber security in Digital 2.0 means 'frictionless experience' through a seamless authentication of a digital certificate embedded in the 'trusted processing element that is, the microprocessor within the mobile phone microprocessor', unlocked by the face/touch/voice ID biometric of the customer. It rides securely on the quick access multi-digit secure PIN, which can only be set-up on valid credentials of a customer identification and password over a 'finger printed' mobile phone device.

"This is not science fiction," Munish says. HDFC Bank has already created the solution blueprint and basic public key cryptography platform to implement 'frictionless' payments.

Cyber security in Digital 2.0 also means that the bank takes control as the external attack vectors keep morphing into newer threats every day. It has deployed a multi-layer cyber defence strategy, involving detective and preventive controls with a mix of firewalls, network admission controls, advanced threat protection combat engines to unearth landmines of persistent threats.

Cyber security risk is the key risk for any bank, particularly those that are aggressive in their digital push. HDFC Bank has developed a cyber-security framework, resting on four pillars—protect, detect, respond and recover (PDR2). This model prescribes control to protect the bank from cyber attacks, detects attacks swiftly and responds and recovers from such attacks fast. In other words, it helps the bank achieve cyber resilience.

Cyber security risk is an extremely important banking business risk which could impact financial assets, business continuity, trust and reputation. That is why in HDFC Bank, its Chief Information Security Officer Sameer Ratolikar is increasingly viewed as a business enabling leader.

From Life Cycle to Lifestyle Bank

This will be the next wave which will use robotics, AI and other cutting-edge technology as the bank prepares itself to entirely change the customer experience. From initiation of the transaction to closure, everything will be online. From a life cycle bank (meeting the needs of customers from cradle to grave) HDFC Bank is transforming itself into a lifestyle bank.

Life cycle is opening an account for a customer, provide them with loans and credit cards in a few years, then a car loan and follow it up with a home loan—being the person's primary bank. Now, it also wants to get involved in day-to-day activities of customers. When the customer wakes up and wants to do anything related to money, HDFC Bank should be the default option.

It wants to be a part of everything—paying the grocer, booking a cab, ordering food, booking air tickets and hotels, buying consumer durables and apparel, and paying school fees and advance tax. It should be the one the customers trust to help manage their money, transact and buy everything they need.

The whole concept of the marketplace was based on this factor—it wants to penetrate the mind of the customer.

Aditya has repeatedly said his company is not a bank anymore but a financial experience. He wants to change the theme from convenience to experience. For that, it is launching new products and transforming old ones. In order to transform the user experience, HDFC Bank has partnered with US-based Human Factors International, a world leader in user interface and user experience design consulting. It wants to find out the expectations of customers when it comes to creating a wonderful experience for mobile and internet banking. While making a payment, the customer has various options like NEFT, RTGS, IMPS, UPI, etc. However, since customers are in a hurry and they do not care what the mode of transfer is and keeping in mind that the experience should be seamless, a customer is not required to choose options each time—the system defaults to NEFT, for instance. The customer always has the option to choose a different method.

The new customer experience also involves features such as 'click to pay'. Customers are taken directly to the payment page instead of having to log into their customer accounts and going to the bill payment option.

For example, the website offers the option 'Send Money' rather than asking whether it should be processed through NEFT or IMPS. Similarly, the bank statement now reminds the customers of bill payments and helps the customers do so with a few clicks.

The next digital wave will see the omnichannel experience coming to full fruition through the deployment of design thinking concepts. A form half-filled on the desktop will still be accessible, say after a month on a customer's mobile for continuing the process. This has been in project mode for long and Backbase, along with TCS, is working with the bank to make this a reality.

Doing Things on Their Own

There was a time when people liked to go to a bank branch, interact with humans and withdraw or deposit money. Now, they want to do things on their own but also need someone to discuss and help them out. That is why the bank is developing a Conversational User Interface (CUI). This will be launched in 2019.

HDFC Bank has moved from merely collecting data in the initial years to using that information to provide a seamless experience and various services through AI. The Technology team talks of intelligent banking through AI, blockchain, IoT (Internet of Things) and experience-led interactions. It has to be intuitive, conversational, contextual, relevant and hyper personalized.

For all practical purposes, HDFC Bank in the near future will have three banks under one roof—the digital bank, which will also have the brick and mortar model; the virtual bank supplementing the digital bank; and a digital-only bank, a la Atom Bank, the UK's online-only bank.

By 2020, HDFC Bank wants to provide every customer with a digital banking assistant—a banking concierge of sorts making transactions, interacting with the bank and even advising customers investment and expense management.

By that time, HDFC Bank will be 26 years old. How did it start? I will narrate the story of its birth and early days from the next chapter.

App Flap

As I am about to finish writing this chapter, HDFC Bank's new mobile-banking app has been taken down from the Android Play Store and IOS App Store after it crashed on 27 November 2018, hours after its launch in Delhi at the bank's Annual Digital Innovation Summit 2018.

In a packed conference room in one of its branches, Nitin briefed the media on the features of the next-gen mobile-banking app together with a new UI (user interface) and UX (user experience). Its features included biometric log-in with fingerprint and facial recognition for iPhone X users. It also promised a simpler UI.

The unprecedented surge as millions of customers wanted to download the app put a strain on the system, leading to the crash—leaving the bank red-faced. This was a nightmare that tech-savvy HDFC Bank will never forget.

The incident became a hot topic for debate in the media and the bank was subjected to national anger and ridicule, giving its top brass sleepless nights.

Each time the bank's customers tried to access the app, they received a message: "Sorry, we are experiencing high traffic on our servers. Please try again after some time."

Flipkart co-founder Sachin Bansal tweeted: "In this day and age, how can the largest private bank of India do this?!" He also retweeted another tweet that questions how a bank's app can go down in 'the age of serverless technology and distributed architecture/containerised applications'.

First, the bank issued a public apology and then steered its customers to the next best option available at that point. It pulled down the new app, and replaced it with the old version for customers to download and use. On 4 December 2018, it provided an update on the mobile-banking app through a tweet stating that the older version of the mobile-banking app was available in the App Store and Google Play Store and provided the links for downloading the same.

"We had clearly let our customers down. Our first priority at that time was to reduce the difficulties," Nitin says.

Of course, such incidents are not rare in the industry, globally. A few days after the HDFC Bank event, Halifax, a British bank (a wholly owned subsidiary of Lloyds Banking Group) and one of the most popular banks for online banking, had problems. The bank's official Twitter account said: "Is the Halifax website down for you right now in your area on Monday December 17, 2018? Leave your status below and check back here for updates from the PR team and other Halifax users reporting similar outages in their town or city."

Another British bank, Santander UK Plc., in November 2018 confirmed that its online banking services were suffering issues. In a server update to Express.co.uk, a spokesperson for the high street bank said: "We are currently experiencing intermittent service issues with our web and mobile banking services and our call centres."

An *Express Online* report from 30 November 2018, says, "Santander is down with the online banking site and app not working for hundreds of users. Independent website Down Detector has received a surge of Santander down reports today—which is payday for many in the UK. The outage monitor has received a peak of almost 1,300 reports of Santander down today. Out of those Santander down reports 45 per cent related to internet banking and 40 per cent were to do with mobile banking."

These are just two such instances in the recent past. As I hand over the manuscript for printing, the bank plans to re-introduce the new app soon.

Nitin says, "It's an app on which we have worked hard to create for our customers an experience they'll relish. It was working fine and had no bugs; just that the response was overwhelming. We knew our (customer) numbers, but never realised what they meant in reality until we woke up to read a report in *The Times of India* titled 'Mobile app matters more than branches'." Indeed, this is the digital India that banks are waking up to.

II

The Flashback

5

One Day in Malaysia

On a Thursday morning in February 1994, the telephone rang at Citibank House in Jalan U-Thant, a tony neighbourhood dotted with the world's embassies in Malaysia's capital Kuala Lumpur. Amrita, the eight-year-old daughter of Aditya Puri, the CEO of the Malaysia operations of Citibank N. A., answered the telephone. The caller was a man gaining tremendous influence in India's financial industry. He wanted to speak to her father.

"Papa, a Mr Parekh is on the line," Amrita yelled. Aditya had just finished his breakfast and was adjusting his tie. He was rushing for a meeting with Shaukat Aziz, Head of Citibank's Asia-Pacific region and another man of tremendous clout who would, a decade later, become the 17th Prime Minister of Pakistan in General Pervez Musharraf's government.

But Aditya had to take this call.

Deepak Parekh was an old friend. He was more than an old friend. He was the Chairman of Housing Development Finance Corporation Ltd. (HDFC), India's lone mortgage company founded by his uncle Hasmukh Thakordas Parekh, a veteran banker. Aditya had known Deepak since his days as a management trainee with automaker Mahindra & Mahindra Ltd., his first job after graduation. Aditya's buddy Bharat Shah, later a colleague at Citibank, was Deepak's cousin.

Bharat had a group of close friends with a common passion—bridge. Investment banker Hemendra Kothari, builder Dilip Thakker, Aditya, Deepak and a few others, all powerhouses who would meet for dinner every fortnight and often go over to each other's homes. "As a young kid, Aditya used to fix our drinks and stand behind the bar," Deepak told me.

Aditya got to know Deepak better while he was heading Citibank's institutional banking business for India, Sri Lanka, Nepal and Bangladesh, based out of Mumbai.

After a brief exchange of pleasantries, Deepak told Aditya he would be in Kuala Lumpur that weekend, and invited himself over for dinner. Deepak was, in fact, going to Mauritius to attend a board meeting of the Commonwealth Development Corporation. The normal course would have been to fly from Mumbai (then Bombay) to Singapore and from there to Mauritius. Instead, Deepak decided to make the detour from Singapore to Malaysia. "I told him I'm coming but I didn't tell him why," Deepak said. That would have to wait until dinner.

Citibank House in Jalan U-Thant is a sprawling old bungalow, built before Malaysia got its independence, spread over one and a half acres and decked with a swimming pool and a volleyball court. Forty-something Aditya was a rising star at Citibank—one among 50 executives worldwide chosen by the bank's Chairman and CEO, John Shepard Reed. This 'gang of 50' would be critical for the US bank's future. The chosen ones were given options, separate from the usual equity options—golden handcuffs, as they would privately say.

Aditya's Mercedes drove Deepak and buddy Bharat, who had tagged along from the airport, to his house in the evening. They sat by the poolside, sipping single malts, and Aditya's wife Smiley, like a good hostess, made sure the *kebab*s were succulent and the *papad*s crisp despite the liberal sprinklings of shredded onions and green chillies.

Deepak was there to tell Aditya that HDFC was shortly going to get a licence from the Reserve Bank of India (RBI) to run a bank. And that he was looking for a CEO.

Before approaching Aditya, Deepak had spoken to Bharat,

who was working in Singapore. Bharat used to report to Aditya
in Citibank in India. But they weren't boss and subordinate;
they were friends forever.

Whenever Bharat travelled to Malaysia on work, he would
invariably stay with Aditya and spend the evenings by the
pool. Aditya did the same whenever he was in Singapore.
Deepak wanted Bharat to help him rope in Aditya as the new
bank's CEO.

Deepak had decided that Aditya was the one capable of
building his vision of a world-class private bank in a newly
liberalized India, an institution comparable with the best
global banks. Aditya, of John's 'gang of 50', would be his man.

Bharat told Deepak to speak directly to Aditya. But he
offered to accompany Deepak to Malaysia. At Citibank
House, with Bharat by his side, Deepak eased into his pitch:
"You run around the world a lot," he told Aditya. "Now come
back to the country, do some real work, build a bank."

Aditya was by no means gullible. He was earning about
$100,000 annually, about ₹3.15 million (going by the rupee–
dollar exchange rate at that time), a tidy sum in those days.
Then, there were the bonuses, the regular options and the
special options he was entitled to as one of John's chosen 50.

Their conversation at the poolside continued:

"What bank?" Aditya asked Deepak.

"We are getting a licence to set one up."

"That will be your bank."

"No, it will be your bank. I won't even be on the board.
It will be run by professional management and you will head
that."

"Do you know how much I get here?" Aditya asked
Deepak.

"*Arre baba*, you have earned enough. Now do something
for the nation. You've worked enough for foreign companies.
Abhi aake desh ke liye kuch karo." [Now come and do
something for the country.]

"Come on Deepak," Aditya insisted. "You need to tell me what's in it for me."

"You will build an institution," Deepak told him. "I can't match your salary. But we will give you stock options. You will do well and earn much more than what you are earning."

Smiley was curious about the unusually animated and earnest discussion among the three men. In one of her rounds while topping their plates with *pakoras*, she finally got the drift, "You three will run a bank!" she exclaimed.

After some more of Deepak's hard persuasion, Aditya agreed to consider the offer, provided he was promised a good share of the stocks. His math was simple: If the bank was successful he would make good the losses he would suffer by leaving Citibank, and he would have built an institution.

There was another reason perhaps to return to India—to be with his father, Tapishwar Puri, who had been the aide-de-camp to India's first Air Marshal, Subroto Mukherjee. Aditya's dad wasn't getting any younger and returning to India would allow him more time with his father.

Aditya asked Smiley whether she wanted to go back to India. She was and still is his confidante.

Aditya first met Smiley at a party in Delhi when he was doing his chartered accountancy articleship. She was a student at Miranda House, the distinguished residential women's college of Delhi University. They lost touch with each other and went their separate ways. When the time came for marriage, Aditya went looking for Smiley and, within a week, proposed to her.

Before heading its Malaysia operations, Aditya was in Hong Kong, managing Credit and Market Risk for Citibank in North Asia. He had worked in Saudi Arabia before that, returned to India, and again taken a job abroad. He knew that if he returned to India this time, it would be for good. His teenage son Amit was already in India, studying at Mayo

College in Ajmer. Amrita was studying at the American School in Kuala Lumpur.

"I am surprised you are asking me this. Go by what your heart says," Smiley replied.

Deepak told Aditya he was on the board of trustees of the famed Bombay Scottish School in Mumbai, and getting admission for Amrita would be a cakewalk. Deepak even promised to escort Amrita to the school at Mahim.

"I want complete freedom to run the bank," Aditya told Deepak. "No interference."

"You will get it," Deepak told him.

Aditya asked for 24 hours to make a decision. The next day, shortly after Deepak checked in at a hotel in Mauritius, the telephone rang. It was Aditya. "I am on," he said.

Elsewhere in Uganda

Months before Deepak met Aditya in Malaysia, in late 1993, he made a call to S. S. Thakur, former Controller of Foreign Exchange in India. Thakur, after a long stint with the RBI, had joined the United Nations' International Civil Services as a senior advisor, and was deputed from New York to Zambia to advise that country's central bank. Deepak told Thakur that he was soon going to get an in-principle approval from the RBI to set up a bank and that he wanted Thakur to be the bank's Founder-Chairman.

Deepak explained that he wanted a high level of corporate governance and regulatory compliance at the bank, and that he believed Thakur was the top candidate for the job.

Thakur had played a key role in formulating India's Foreign Exchange Regulation Act (FERA) and was involved in implementing it in national and multinational companies. FERA, enacted in 1973 by the Indira Gandhi government, imposed stringent regulations on certain payments that dealt with foreign exchange and securities and transactions involving the Indian currency. Its purpose was to regulate payments to conserve India's foreign exchange resources.

Many dubbed the Act draconian. Its first victim was the American icon, The Coca-Cola Company, India's leading soft drink until 1977. Coca-Cola decided to leave India after the Janata government, citing the new law, ordered it to hand over its formula—a trade secret held in a bank vault in Atlanta for decades—and dilute its stake in the Indian unit.

Coca-Cola, and its closest rival PepsiCo Inc., also American, would return to India 16 years later in 1993, after India opened up its economy.

As Controller of Foreign Exchange at the RBI, Thakur knew Deepak well. He knew Deepak's uncle H. T. Parekh even better. Thakur had helped HDFC immensely during its early days in getting bulk deposits. Not many people were willing to take home loans as it was a new concept in the late 1970s, just after HDFC was formed. Even more were reluctant to deposit money with it. The first public issue of the shares of HDFC bombed and the mortgage lender found it a headache to get a capital of a mere ₹100 million.

It was during this phase of disquiet that the World Bank Group's International Finance Corporation (IFC) stepped in and picked up a 5% stake in HDFC, and even offered it a loan of $4 million. But it was quite the tease, adding a rider that it would release the money only if HDFC could arrange matching deposits in Indian rupees. In other words, HDFC had to mobilize the rupee equivalent of $4 million to draw IFC's line of credit. Although not a big sum as a dollar used to fetch around ₹8.75 in 1978, HDFC found even this extremely difficult to mobilize.

Retail deposits were out of question in those days. In fact, in the first decade of HDFC's existence, till 1988, while hundreds came to borrow, no one trusted the company with their money. HDFC had to depend on bulk deposits. There were many FERA companies—locally incorporated companies with foreign equity holdings in excess of 40%—that raised money from the market but couldn't remit the funds as the RBI was never prompt in clearing their applications. HDFC sensed an opportunity there.

Hasmukh-bhai, as the founder of HDFC was widely known, got himself a list of tea companies in Assam that had raised money from the public and were sitting on the funds, as the RBI was being slow in clearing their applications for remitting the money overseas. He wanted these companies to deposit their monies with HDFC till the RBI gave its nod. But there was a hitch. By the rules of the book, these companies were allowed to keep their funds only with banks, not with mortgage companies.

Thakur, convinced by Hasmukh-bhai's argument, changed the rule and allowed these companies to deposit their monies with mortgage companies as well. And that is how HDFC started getting FERA deposits and, more importantly, was able to draw from the IFC loan.

Deepak knew the story well, and thought it was a good idea to have an ex-RBI insider as his bank's first chairman. He got Thakur's number in Zambia from a contact in the RBI and called him. "Mr Thakur, I would like you to come to Bombay. I will send you the ticket. Can you come for a couple of days?"

Thakur flew to Mumbai and met Deepak. He heard him out. It was a bold and tempting offer. But to resign from the prestigious United Nations job was a tough call, especially when he was earning a handsome tax-free package.

Deepak offered Thakur shares of HDFC. Thakur eventually agreed to the offer, though not because of the shares as, in those days, not many really cared for HDFC's stock. "I took up the assignment in spite of the monetary loss," Thakur told me, "because it was a challenging task and they were very sincere in their approach."

Thakur joined HDFC Bank Ltd. as Founder-Chairman on

2 January 1994 at Ramon House in downtown Mumbai, where the mortgage company was headquartered till January 2014 when they shifted the headquarters to HUL House on the same road (H. T. Parekh Marg in Churchgate, Mumbai). However, its registered office continues to be Ramon House. He occupied the cabin of H. T. Parekh on the fourth floor of Ramon House after Hasmukh-bhai passed away in November 1994. At the time of joining, Thakur was in his early sixties.

"A couple of months later, the RBI issued a new rule which said that if a bank has a managing director, its chairman must be a non-executive chairman. [I had] no regrets," Thakur, now 89, had told me at his office in Express Towers at Nariman Point, Mumbai's financial district. He was the Chairman of HDFC Bank till 2000.

The Pune Warrior

Deepak's third choice was not a banker but a corporate executive and a close friend, Vinod Yennemadi. Vinod had worked with at least half a dozen companies, local and foreign. Deepak got to know him while doing his chartered accountancy in London in the 1960s. Deepak was a regular visitor to the YMCA Indian Student Hostel, at 41 Fitzroy Square in London, where Vinod was staying.

After completing his chartered accountancy, Vinod joined Shell International—at Burmah-Shell Oil Storage and Distributing Company of India Ltd.—in 1971 at a princely salary of ₹2,000 a month. He worked with the group till it was nationalized in 1976 (and renamed Bharat Petroleum Corporation Ltd. the next year).

Vinod's next job was with the Rama Prasad Goenka (RPG) Group. He became the Finance Director of a small firm of the RPG Group, a subsidiary of Asian Cables Ltd. Following this, he joined Mather & Platt Pvt. Ltd., a company that produced fire protection systems and submersible pumps, as Finance Director.

Manohar Rajaram Chhabria of the Dubai-based Jumbo Group bought over Mather & Platt Pvt. Ltd. and took an instant liking to Vinod, but Vinod did not like the new owner's ways. He left the group to join Baba Kalyani—known for his auto parts company Bharat Forge Ltd.—as Finance Director of Kalyani Steels Ltd. in Pune in 1992. And that is where Deepak met his old pal Vinod after years.

On a Sunday morning in the first week of February 1994, Deepak told Vinod that HDFC was applying for a banking licence and he was reasonably sure he would get it. "What are you doing in Pune? Come back to Bombay and join me and set up the bank," he told Vinod.

Vinod wasn't keen. "From 1971, I have been on the other side of the counter, asking for money," he told Deepak. "I have never been a banker myself. What will I do with your bank?"

Deepak didn't buy his argument. After all, Deepak hadn't been in the housing loans sector before he joined HDFC. He had worked with Ernst & Young, Precision Fasteners Ltd., ANZ Grindlays Bank and Chase Manhattan Bank—none of them a mortgage company—in New York and Mumbai until his uncle brought him to HDFC in 1978.

At the age of 34, Vinod took a 50% cut in his Chase Manhattan salary to join HDFC as Deputy General Manager. "You needn't worry, you'll learn," Deepak told Vinod.

On 4 April 1994, Vinod joined the bank. He was the first employee on the bank's payroll. Thakur had joined the bank before him, in January, but he was on a contract. Vinod didn't want to join on 1 April, All Fools' Day, and as 2 and 3 April covered the weekend, he had to wait a few more days. HDFC had a five-day working week.

Testing the Waters

Before taking the plunge, Aditya decided to send his wife Smiley and daughter Amrita to India for a month to test the waters. Deepak had taken care of Amrita's school admission but Aditya wanted to see whether his wife and daughter would find it easy living in Mumbai—a lively and spirited city but also humid and difficult—after having lived privileged lives abroad. He didn't want to regret the move later.

After a month, when Aditya came to India to see how they were doing, at Smiley's sister's house at Bandra's Pali Hill in Mumbai, he was hugely relieved to see Amrita grooving to the popular Raveena Tandon song 'Tu cheez badi hai mast mast' from the Hindi film Mohra. For her, that was possibly a practice session. Later, Amrita would act in Anil Kapoor's Aisha along with Sonam Kapoor, Mukesh Bhatt's crime thriller Blood Money and UTV's Kai Po Che!

Citibank was not willing to accept Aditya's resignation till he firmly told Shaukat he would not change his mind. He got no official farewell. He took a Singapore Airlines flight to India and, from the airport, drove straight to Ramon House to meet Deepak. By then, Thakur and Vinod were already on board and the key elements of the first team that would run the bank were in place.

For Deepak, half the battle was over. He had got the people he wanted—a bright young banker with a vision, a former central banker who knew the rules and regulations of banking like the back of his hand, and a trusted friend who was thorough with the intricacies of the corporate world. "This bank cannot fail," Deepak told himself the day Aditya landed in Mumbai.

What's in a Name?

There was still one detail nagging Deepak. He was not comfortable with the idea of lending the 'HDFC' name to the bank, as that would mean anyone running the bank would also have to be an ambassador of the long-nurtured HDFC brand. Will they stand for the value and ethos HDFC symbolized? He was worried that if the bank didn't do well, the HDFC brand would get sullied.

A conservative Deepak had one name in mind: The Bank of Bombay. His logic was faultless. The bank was the only one among a group of ten new private lenders allowed to have its headquarters in Mumbai. The others were asked to have their registered offices outside the large metro cities, keeping in sync with the RBI's focus on spreading banking services across the nation through the slew of new private banks. ICICI Bank Ltd. had its registered office in Baroda, Gujarat; Centurion Bank Ltd. in Panjim, Goa; Global Trust Bank Ltd. in Hyderabad, Andhra Pradesh; IndusInd Bank Ltd. in Pune, Maharashtra; and UTI Bank Ltd. (the first bank to get a licence, later renamed Axis Bank Ltd.) in Ahmedabad, Gujarat.

But the acronym for Bank of Bombay—BoB—clashed with an established public sector bank, Bank of Baroda. As an afterthought, Deepak suggested Bombay Bank. Neither name worked for the others.

Thakur prepared a list of two dozen names. His personal favourite was Everest Bank of India, to symbolize the height the bank would reach one day. Other suggestions included Greater Bank of Bombay and Bombay International Bank, many of them revolving around 'Bombay'. But the majority wanted the name to be 'HDFC Bank'.

HDFC was already a household name in India. Its board was not sure how effectively the bank would function and they didn't want to risk their reputation by officially adopting the new entity. There were many brainstorming sessions to break the deadlock.

Deepak Satwalekar, Managing Director of HDFC, was possessive about the HDFC brand. After all, the bankers were all outsiders. How would they view the value system at HDFC and its brand? "Until their credentials are established clearly, I am reluctant to lend the name," he told his colleagues in private.

"Why don't we call it Bombay International Bank?" Satwalekar suggested to Aditya over lunch one day. "You can call it that," Aditya told him, "but I will catch a flight and go back to Kuala Lumpur. I am not interested in any Bombay International Bank. If it's HDFC Bank, I am here. Otherwise, forget it."

Aditya got support from his chairman. Thakur reasoned that the Unit Trust of India (UTI), the Industrial Development Bank of India (IDBI) and the Industrial Credit and Investment Corporation of India Ltd. (ICICI) had lent their brand names to their banks and if the HDFC brand name were not given to the bank, it would require a lot more effort to build the bank's brand. Hasmukh-bhai saw the point and, finally, so did Deepak and Satwalekar. The outsiders had the final say.

The HDFC insiders had one condition, though: If HDFC's shareholding in the bank dropped below a certain level, the mortgage company could ask the bank to change its name. The final agreement on the name doesn't have any clause on charging a royalty for lending the brand name, something that the diversified Tata Group does with its many subsidiaries.

Plan B

The shrewd strategist that Deepak is, he didn't leave anything to chance. He drafted a plan B, as he does for any situation— the reason why, along with Aditya, Deepak was also in talks with Mehli Mistry, another long-time Citibanker, for the top job.

Mehli was with Citibank in Saudi Arabia but quit the job and returned to Mumbai when Citibank decided to pull out from a Saudi Arabian bank named Samba, the acronym for 'Saudi American Bank' (the name was changed to Samba Financial Group in 2003). It was established in February 1980 with the takeover of Citibank branches in Jeddah and Riyadh, in accordance with a local law that forced all foreign banks to convert their branches to affiliates with Saudi nationals acquiring at least 60% ownership. Mehli was heading Samba at the time.

Mehli informally agreed to the proposal and Deepak even told one of the new recruits, Harish Engineer of Bank of America Corporation, to update Mehli on RBI regulations. Harish did have a few sessions with Mehli at Ramon House but he could not come on board because of taxation issues.

Mehli was a US citizen. This meant he would have to pay taxes on income both in India and in the United States of America (USA) and HDFC Bank was not willing to pick up the tab. Deepak kept him on hold for a few weeks till he was convinced that John's blue-eyed boy Aditya would agree for the top job.

The parting with Mehli was amicable and there was no bad blood. Mehli went on to become the head of Grindlays' India operations, which was sold to Standard Chartered Bank PLC in 2000.

Deepak declined to be on the bank's board, despite being closely involved in creating it, primarily because he was on the board of a number of blue chip companies that any bank would want to do business with. Had Deepak joined the bank's board, HDFC Bank could not have done business with these companies as India's banking laws prohibit a bank from lending money to a company whose director is on the bank's board. Essentially, Deepak could not remain on the boards of the blue chip companies and the bank at the same time.

It was a prudent decision to give up directorship of the bank and remain on the boards of Glaxo India Ltd., Siemens Ltd., Hindustan Unilever Ltd., Indian Hotels Co. Ltd., Mahindra & Mahindra Ltd. and Castrol India Ltd. He could use the relationships with these companies to the bank's advantage.

Also, the RBI still doesn't like the CEO of one finance company to be on the board of another finance company as that may create a conflict of interest. There is no written law on this, though.

Three representatives of HDFC were nominated on the bank's board: Deepak Satwalekar, Nasser Munjee and Keki Mistry.

Deepak chose not to be on the board but Thakur, Aditya and Vinod could always lean on his broad shoulders. In the initial stages, he was the bank's face to the regulator, investors and even consumers. Nobody grudged that.

Banking is in Deepak's genes. His grandfather, Thakordas Parekh, was the first employee of the Central Bank of India. His father, Shantilal Parekh, had spent about 40 years in the same bank till he retired as Deputy General Manager. And before founding HDFC, his uncle, Hasmukh-bhai, had headed ICICI, the development finance institution that spawned ICICI Bank, HDFC's closest private sector rival.

Deepak was not on the board of the bank but for several years he did not miss a single meeting—always attending as a special invitee.

Initial Package

One can well imagine why Aditya had strong reservations about taking up this assignment if one takes a look at his initial package at HDFC Bank—₹100,000 per month, plus ₹20,000 dearness allowance along with actual medical benefit and ₹50,000 leave fare concession.

Thakur's salary was ₹1.5 million per annum. A company-leased accommodation, a car—a Premier NE-118—for official use, gas and electricity, ₹2,500 a month as entertainment allowance, ₹1,500 for servants and gardeners, ₹1,500 for soft furnishing, ₹1,000 for books and periodicals and two club memberships were common for Aditya and Thakur. Indeed, this was far better than packages at public sector banks, but it was nowhere near what was paid to Aditya's counterparts at foreign banks, which would be HDFC Bank's main rivals.

Money would come their way as the bank and the stock did phenomenally well. But at that point none of them had any fantasies about compensation, only dreams about creating a bank with a difference.

6

Raising a Toast

The idea of floating a bank came to the HDFC bosses in 1987, a few years before the banking regulator decided to open the sector to private companies. For the mortgage company's tenth anniversary on 17 October 1987, Satwalekar, then its General Manager for Finance and Planning, prepared a paper for the board on non-mortgage opportunities for HDFC.

Satwalekar, who would eventually climb the ranks to become the Managing Director of HDFC and later head its life insurance venture when India opened up that sector, was convinced that a pure-play housing financing business alone would not fully justify the strengths and capabilities of HDFC.

He listed a number of businesses HDFC could venture into: Commercial banking, mutual funds, insurance, property funds and private equity. Satwalekar wanted HDFC to begin securitization of home loans as well. He believed banking was a critical building block for any business which may want to grab the opportunities which would arise *whenever* (not *if*) India chose to open up her constricted economy.

In principle, the board agreed that HDFC needed to get into these activities. When the RBI began discussions on allowing new private banks to open up, after the P. V. Narasimha Rao government liberalized India's economy in 1991, the HDFC top brass was very excited. On 22 January 1993, the RBI finally issued guidelines on the entry of new private banks.

For over two decades, since the nationalization of 14 large banks in 1969, followed by another six in 1980, no private bank had been allowed to set up shop. During this period, public sector banks had expanded their networks extensively, adding numerous branches, often in remote areas at the behest of political bosses, and catering to the socio-economic needs of the masses in a highly regulated industry where the central bank dictated interest rates and directed credit flow.

Within two decades of nationalization, government-owned banks accounted for 91% of the bank branches in the country and 85% of the total business done by the sector. The rest was shared by a handful of foreign banks and old private banks. "A stage has now been reached when new private sector banks may be allowed to be set up," the RBI, India's central bank, said in its historic declaration in 1993.

Down with Lazy Banking

The RBI's objective was to introduce competition in the sector and force banks to be efficient and more productive. Bank employees—from tellers to managers—were in great demand in the marriage market in those days. A bank job gave a person status and dignity, though banks had nothing much to do in the tightly regulated industry. Technology and product innovation were unheard of. A bank's primary job was to mobilize money from individuals and lend most of the money to companies. Of course, 40% of the loans would go to the so-called priority sector of farmers and small-scale industries, a rule that stands today even though the composition of priority sector has changed.

Those were the days of lazy banking. Banks could, of course, blame the regulations, which did not allow much scope for dynamism. Because of the very high pre-emption in the form of the Cash Reserve Ratio (CRR), or the portion of deposits that commercial banks need to keep with the RBI, and the Statutory Liquidity Ratio (SLR), or the compulsory investment in government bonds, bankers were left with very little money to lend. Banks do not earn any interest on CRR. Besides, no bank was listed and so there was no pressure from investors to perform.

In this seller's market, the concept of customer care did not exist. A branch manager was happy being confined to his or her glass cabin, where promoters of companies and corporate professionals would come to pay their homage. Barring a few exceptions, most bank chiefs saw their primary job as making sure the balance sheets grew every year.

RBI guidelines made it clear that allowing the entry of private banks was a part of the financial sector reforms to provide competitive, efficient and low-cost financial intermediation through the use of technology. The new banks were to have a capital of at least ₹1 billion and their shares had to be listed on the stock exchanges.

A little before this, India had introduced new asset classification norms as part of its prudential regulations. Banks could no longer get away with accumulating bad loans—which were piling up as a result of poor credit appraisals and monitoring as well as political pressure to favour certain industrial groups. Then, there were the so-called loan *melas*, or waiver for loans given to farmers, again dictated by politicians.

Banks now had to set aside money to make up for any such souring assets. Of course, this resulted in some early glitches. The provisioning requirement eroded the profitability of many banks and the government had to step in and infuse capital in phases to keep them alive. Till today, this phenomenon of banks piling up bad assets, setting aside money to provide for them, and being recapitalized by the taxpayer's money continues.

Simultaneously, the Parliament amended the Banking Regulation Act of 1949 to lower the government's absolute ownership in state-run lenders to 51%, despite resistance from the powerful trade unions that controlled the industry in those days. The RBI, on its part, arranged a hefty World Bank line of credit for upgrading technology in select public sector banks. India's banking industry was on the edge of a re-invention.

"Why Do We Need a Bank?"

It wasn't easy for Deepak to convince the board of HDFC to take the plunge into banking. Hasmukh-bhai, by then Chairman Emeritus at HDFC, was blunt. "We don't know anything about banking. Why do we need a bank?" he asked.

There were more questions about their reasons for starting a bank, their knowledge of banking, who would run the bank, and the kind of liabilities that they were going to create.

"Applying for a bank licence doesn't mean that we are getting it, but what's the harm in trying it out?" Deepak argued. He hired Atul Sud to prepare a draft application and that was the clincher. Atul had just left American Express Co. after serving 13 years as its India Head for Commercial and Investment Banking and Treasury.

The RBI received 113 applications, many of these from large industrial houses. It asked noted economist-bureaucrat Sharad Marathe, the first Chairman of IDBI, to review the applications.

Sharad, who was also the alternate Executive Director representing India at the International Monetary Fund and the Economic Advisor to the Government of India from 1964–68, had been on the boards of several Indian and multinational companies, including Glaxo India where Deepak was a director. While reviewing the applications, Sharad didn't discuss anything with Deepak, but after the RBI released the licences, he told Deepak that HDFC's application was the best.

HDFC Bank was incorporated on 30 August 1994. On

5 January 1995, Deepak got a call from RBI Governor C. Rangarajan's office. The licence was through.

Roughly one in every 11 applicants was given a licence, making it ten overall, including Development Credit Bank Ltd. (DCB), an old cooperative bank that was allowed to convert itself into a full-fledged commercial bank.

Four of the new entrants were floated by established financial institutions. Development financial institutions ICICI and IDBI got licences. So did India's oldest mutual fund, UTI, which teamed up with state-run life insurance behemoth Life Insurance Corporation of India.

Some finance professionals were also given licences to set up banks. Ramesh Gelli, former Chief of Vysya Bank Ltd. and a Padmashree awardee, got the nod to set up Global Trust Bank Ltd.; Darshanjit Singh, son of Inderjit Singh, former Chairman of Punjab & Sind Bank, to set up Bank of Punjab Ltd.; and Devendra Ahuja of the NBFC 20th Century Finance Corporation Ltd. to set up Centurion Bank Ltd.

A few group companies of the Hindujas, backed by the Sindhi diaspora, got a licence for IndusInd Bank Ltd. and the Jains of Bennett, Coleman and Co. Ltd., which runs India's largest media house and publishes the *Times of India* newspaper, got a licence for Times Bank Ltd.

"Are We Risking Too Much of Our Money?"

The RBI was okay with an initial capital of ₹1 billion, but Deepak wanted to have double that amount in capital to make the bank solid. The board of HDFC was not comfortable with the idea as the mortgage company's capital base was just ₹1 billion at that time. There was an intense debate on how much money HDFC should put on the table.

The RBI had capped promoter holding in a bank at 40%. For the ₹2 billion capital Deepak was insisting on, a 40%

contribution meant bringing in ₹800 million into the bank, an amount equal to 80% of the capital of HDFC. This was not a joke, certainly not for the board members. "Are we risking too much of our money?" the board asked.

It was an illustrious board with directors such as former RBI Governor, M. Narasimham, who wrote two seminal reports on financial sector reforms; industrialist Keshub Mahindra; bureaucrat and former Chairman of the State Bank of India (SBI), D. N. Ghosh and former Capital Market Regulator, S. A. Dave.

The board also insisted that since HDFC was new to banking, to mitigate risks its bank would need a foreign partner as early as possible, essentially an investor. A foreign partner was also a necessity because HDFC Bank was an unknown entity in the global banking world. It needed someone who would not hesitate to give it lines of credit. Unless it got these lines of credit from foreign banks, or at least from its foreign partner, it would not be able to grow and help Indian importers who needed dollar funds. The final decision was to sell a 15% stake in the bank to a foreign bank, and keep 25% with HDFC.

The NatWest Misadventure

In search of the ideal foreign partner, Deepak went to London to try his luck with the National Westminster Bank PLC, better known as NatWest, a very large UK bank with a looming presence over the city, literally. It had built the tallest office block in London, the NatWest Tower, in the 1970s, when it overtook Barclays PLC to become Britain's largest commercial bank.

Deepak's itinerary was not thoughtfully designed and was more a toss of a coin: Who he knew and when was the first available flight to get to them. Deepak had been introduced to

Robert Alexander, NatWest's Chairman, through somebody. Alexander took him to meet Derek Wanless, Group CEO of NatWest. Deepak spent a day with them in London.

His next stop was New York, where Deepak called on Bankers Trust, a big American bank. Deepak was on its international advisory board. The day was well spent with the head of International and Foreign Exchange Divisions at Bankers Trust and Charles Steadman 'Charlie' Sanford, Chairman of the Board and CEO. They were quite excited about the new Indian bank.

From there, Deepak flew to Singapore to talk to DBS Bank Ltd. (earlier known as the Development Bank of Singapore Ltd.). The DBS Group was interested but, eventually, it could not go ahead with the plan as the Indian banking regulator made it clear that if the DBS Group were to hold a large stake in HDFC Bank, it would not be allowed to set up a branch in India—something the Singapore bank was keen on doing.

Incidentally, it was the first foreign bank in India which decided to go for local incorporation.

Both NatWest and Bankers Trust were willing to pick up a stake in HDFC Bank. The final choice was NatWest as the response from London came first.

Bankers Trust put pressure on Deepak, whom they knew well.

"Come on Deepak, you can't let us down," Charlie said.

"The only way I can let you come in is by asking NatWest to share their stake with you—7.5% each," Deepak responded. He would have been happy to allow both the banks to come in as HDFC Bank then could have had a British and an American association.

Bankers Trust tried to negotiate with NatWest but the UK bank refused. It wanted a piece of India, as the economy was opening up and the balance of payment crisis had receded. There was big-bang liberalization. By that time, HDFC was 16 years old and growing at a healthy pace as middle-class

Indians had started to dream about owning a home.

So NatWest Markets Ltd., the corporate and investment banking arm of the NatWest Group, became HDFC Bank's partner. The shares were offered at par. But when Deepak and Aditya went to London to seal the deal, they found NatWest had one worry: Who would be accountable if there was a run on the bank?

The NatWest Group had had problems in Australia when one of the banks it had invested in suffered a liquidity shortage. Depositors chased the group to London and asked it for money as it was one of the promoters of the Australian bank, though a minor one.

"We will pick up a 20% stake but don't want to be called a promoter," NatWest told Deepak.

HDFC could still own a 25% stake in the bank—below the RBI's 40% limit for promoters—and allow NatWest to pick up a 20% stake now that the UK bank had declined to be classified as a promoter. Had NatWest agreed to be a promoter, it could not have taken a 20% stake, as that would have increased the combined promoters' stake to 45%, beyond the permissible threshold.

Today, almost everybody in the HDFC Group admits that NatWest didn't add much value, but in the initial days the partnership was a great selling point for the new bank. A multi-part launch campaign milked the partnership in every possible way.

Half-page advertisements in the nation's leading financial dailies in January 1995 positioned HDFC Bank as 'The Action Bank' and said NatWest Markets was the 'Window to the World'. Along with the parentage ('The HDFC Advantage') and commitment to customer care ('Customers Are Really Everything'), the campaign said the alliance with NatWest Markets gave the bank a unique international edge.

North, South, East, NatWest

The advertisement copy proudly laid down information on the NatWest Group: That it was present in 40 locations in 17 countries, had an asset base of at least $250 billion, was one of the largest foreign exchange players in the world, and ran daily transactions of at least $45 billion.

There was also a joint advertisement campaign by HDFC Bank and NatWest Markets in February 1995—'North, South, East, NatWest'. Among other things, it said, "NatWest Markets has now formed a strategic alliance with HDFC Bank to provide a unique service to clients in India. Together with HDFC Bank, NatWest Markets is dedicated to providing clients in India a truly international edge."

The calling cards of HDFC Bank executives also mentioned the strategic alliance with NatWest Markets, just in case they were to meet foreign bankers for credit lines.

NatWest did not give HDFC Bank the international edge it so coveted because the UK bank did not really have a large international presence. It had about $12 billion in assets in the Asia-Pacific region and employed nine hundred people in nine countries, with Hong Kong as its regional headquarters. In 1994, NatWest Markets helped to arrange $3 billion for Asian nations.

From the day it signed the agreement with HDFC Bank, NatWest was worried and did not want to get into a mess similar to that it had faced in Australia. It did not want to put in a penny more. HDFC Bank had to struggle to increase the limits for letters of credit and foreign exchange dealings.

The relationship lasted less than three years as NatWest got involved in a major scandal of mis-marking interest options in London, having dabbled in complicated derivative products it did not fully understand. In 1997, NatWest Markets revealed a £50 million loss. That sum exploded to £90.5 million after investigations, deeply eroding the confidence of its investors and shareholders.

NatWest decided to sell its 20% stake in HDFC Bank—part of its larger strategy to pull out of equity investments in Asia after the Southeast Asian crisis in 1997. The bank's management told HDFC Bank that it had to sell its investment as it needed money. At that time, shares of HDFC Bank were trading at around ₹54 apiece, almost five and a half times the price at which the UK bank had bought them. "I was not a fool to buy back the shares by paying so much more than what I'd begged them to put in just two and a half years ago," Deepak told me.

The only vestige of that association is a clock, signifying the NatWest chimes, gifted by the British Bank. The clock still finds a place in the lobby outside the boardroom on the sixth floor of Bank House, the headquarters of HDFC Bank.

A Mistake

HDFC Bank instead found another investor to replace NatWest.

"That was a mistake. We could have raised our stake to 40% by buying at least 15% of their holding," Deepak says in hindsight, candid in his admission.

NatWest had a long but not-so-exciting history in investment banking. It had made a series of small but costly acquisitions. In November 1995, it bought Gleacher & Co., an American boutique investment bank specializing in mergers and acquisitions. It followed this with the acquisition of Greenwich Capital Markets Inc., a bond house; Gartmore Investment Ltd., an asset management company; and Hambro Magan Corporate Finance, a UK mergers and acquisitions company.

There was a protracted legal battle until finally, in February

2000, NatWest's shareholders accepted a takeover offer from the Royal Bank of Scotland PLC, a fellow UK bank but much smaller in size.

"It was not the greatest [banking group]; [they] had no clue about running a bank in India—what was the point of the partnership?" reminisces Satwalekar about the NatWest tie-up. Even technology-wise, HDFC Bank was superior to NatWest. The UK bank made a cool ₹2.2 billion on an investment of ₹400 million in a short span without adding any value.

"We should be extremely careful about partnerships as at some point in time our needs and their needs will diverge," Satwalekar said, making a larger point. He is quite sceptical about a foreign partner's intentions. The only reason a foreign entity wants to come to India, according to him, is because it needs a foothold in the fast-growing economy.

Historically, most joint ventures in India—particularly in the financial services space—have not succeeded as the foreign partners either wanted bigger stakes in the Indian entities or aspired to have a full-fledged presence on Indian soil. A case in point is the partnership of Goldman Sachs Group Inc. with Kotak Mahindra Group for investment banking. Goldman Sachs stayed with Kotak Mahindra till it understood the Indian market. ICICI Bank's investment banking arm, ICICI Securities Ltd. (I-Sec), faced the same fate and had to part with its foreign partner J. P. Morgan & Co.

Kotak Mahindra bought Goldman Sachs' entire 25% stake in its investment banking and securities outfit in March 2006, 14 years after the alliance, as Goldman Sachs wanted to be in India on its own. J. P. Morgan & Co. pulled out of I-Sec in March 1998, five years after forming the joint venture with I-Sec, holding a 39.6% stake.

Eleven days after getting the licence and forging the strategic alliance with NatWest, HDFC Bank opened its first branch on the sixth floor of Ramon House, the headquarters of HDFC, on 16 January 1995, with fewer than a dozen staff, including Vinod, his secretary Goretti Soares (whom he brought from Mather & Platt) and an administration person who came from Bayer India Ltd.

Deepak inaugurated this apology of a branch, which for all practical purposes was nothing more than an extension counter. T. Chandrasekhar, the loveable property manager of HDFC, did the interiors for the sixth floor. He also organized an elaborate Ganesha puja for the inauguration. That idol of Ganesha—the Hindu god revered as a remover of obstacles and the preferred god to seek blessings for any new beginnings—now adorns Vinod's drawing room at Khar, a western suburb of Mumbai.

A month later, on 18 February 1995, Manmohan Singh, then Finance Minister and the chief architect of India's financial sector reforms, opened the bank's corporate office at Sandoz House on Dr Annie Besant Road, Worli.

Coincidentally, it was also the birthday of Bharat, one of the early recruits.

Deepak Goes to North Block

With a general election round the corner, the bank couldn't have a big function involving Singh to announce its arrival. The finance minister, in fact, was reluctant to come. Hasmukh-bhai knew Singh well but he was not there to invite him. His nephew went to North Block on Raisina Hill in New Delhi— where the Finance Ministry is housed—but the finance minister told Deepak he would not be able to make it because of the upcoming election.

"In that case we won't have any function and won't call the press. You come, cut the ribbon, and have tea with us," Deepak told him. Singh was also aware of the illustrious members of the HDFC board. He agreed to cut the ribbon, walk around, have a cup of tea, but said no to lunch, dinner and the press.

RBI Governor, C. Rangarajan, and his Deputy Governor, D. R. Mehta, who later became India's capital market regulator, were the other dignitaries.

Aditya took Singh around the office. The locker section was in the basement; the banking hall and the Information Technology (IT) hall were on the ground floor; the dealing room was on the first floor. The corporate office, on the second floor, was not fully ready yet.

Singh's brief speech focused on why the government wanted to introduce world-class Indian private banks, the need for more competition and employment and the necessity to expand banking activities across the nation. This is now termed 'financial inclusion'.

Singh was very impressed with the training facilities. "Accent on training is going to be very important to sustain the banking activity," he said.

As the first branch was already open at Ramon House, Aditya could actually show the finance minister how the transactions were done—fetching account details from a server and checking a customer's signature. He also explained why a centralized approach was superior to 'branch banking'. In this system, a customer banks with a bank and not with any particular branch—something unheard of in the state-run banking industry at that time. A customer's signature is registered centrally and any branch can call up the signature on its computer when required for a transaction.

The finance minister was also shown the security features. By that time Deepak had already opened an account and Aditya could show Deepak's signature on the screen and explain how the system of remote access and centralized banking would work.

Singh was mighty impressed by the computers in the dealing room and the way Luis Miranda, HDFC Bank's Head of Foreign Exchange Business, explained the trading system. C. N. Ram, the bank's Technology Head, showed off the ATMs to Singh and Rangarajan, who had been his professors at the Indian Institute of Management, Ahmedabad (IIM-A). ATMs were still a novelty in those days.

The bank had prepared dummy ATM cards in the names of Singh and Rangarajan. While demonstrating how an ATM worked, Ram inserted the card with Singh's name into the machine and punched in the keys. The ATM instantly flashed a message indicating insufficient funds. "You are not the central bank; you can give the FM some money. What's the big deal?" Rangarajan's joke got everyone laughing.

The laughter got louder in the evening. Next to Sandoz House, on the terrace of architect I. M. Kadri's office, the bank threw a party to celebrate the launch. Deepak knew Kadri well. Sharad Pawar, then Chief Minister of Maharashtra, joined the party. Corporate India raised a toast to the birth of a bank that changed many established norms, created new ones, did very ordinary things in extraordinary ways and discovered the distinction between real and perceived risks.

The Lucky 13

VINOD YENNEMADI: The first employee on HDFC Bank's payroll.

HARISH ENGINEER: Harish-bhai, as he is popularly known in the bank, was an early catch.

C. N. RAM: His role in IT was to see how HDFC Bank could make a difference to its customers.

A. RAJAN: Taking a leap of faith, he decided to join the bank.

SHAILENDRA BHANDARI: Staying with Citibank vs. going ahead with HDFC Bank – it was like tossing a coin where both sides seemed equal.

PARESH SUKTHANKAR: His offer letter came on an A4 sheet of paper, with the words 'HDFC Bank (proposed)' neatly typed on the top.

BHARAT SHAH: He was still serving his notice period with UBS when he got drawn into the HDFC Bank project.

LUIS MIRANDA: Thinking not so much about the salary, as about the prospect of working for an Indian company.

SAMIR BHATIA: A company flat on Warden Road and extensive travel to Africa and Eastern Europe – all gone in minutes.

ABHAY AIMA: Abhay had been a fighter pilot in the Indian Air Force before turning banker.

ASHISH PARTHASARTHY: He had prepared Abhay Aima's resume for the Human Resource Department of HDFC Bank.

G. SUBRAMANIAN: As Head of Compliance, he used to report directly to the chairman.

H. SRIKRISHNAN: He calls his son, Satwik, an "HDFC Bank product".

The Launch of the Bank

NEW BEGINNING: Manmohan Singh (then Finance Minister), with Aditya Puri and Deepak Parekh, at the bank's launch in Mumbai. *(Page 102)*

MONEY TALK: Former RBI governor C Rangarajan, along with Manmohan Singh, Paresh Sukthankar and Deepak Parekh at the opening ceremony. *(Page 102)*

WELCOME TO NEW BANK: HDFC Bank's corporate office at Sandoz House, the old logo and the ubiquitous NE-118 given to the bank's chairman and managing director. *(Page 102)*

WORK AND PLAY: Aditya's A team at an off-site meet at Jaipur, Rajasthan. *(Page 139)*

Firing on All Cylinders

SPREADING WINGS: HDFC Bank's ADS listing on New York Stock Exchange in July 2001. *(Page 178)*

BREAKING THE ICE: When some senior executives stopped talking to each other, Aditya made them walk his dogs at Lonavla. They had to talk and share tips on how to walk a dog. After that, it was party time. *(Page 352)*

FINANCIAL LITERACY: All borrowers attend an induction session at a branch where it is explained why they should take the loan and what they should not do with the money. *(Page 262)*

SUSTAINABLE LIVELIHOOD PROGRAMME: Aditya interacting with SLI beneficiaries at Chomu, Rajasthan, in 2013. *(Page 263)*

Digital Diary

GO DIGITAL—*BANK AAPKI MUTTHI MEIN:* The campaign was launched at Varanasi—on a boat in the Ganges. *(Page 12)*

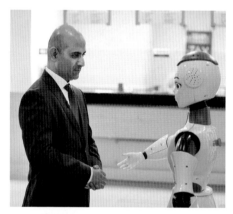

GENDER BIAS!: Among bank customers, there is greater acceptance of IRA 1.0 (which is feminine) than IRA 2.0 (which has a male form). *(Page 22)*

NATWEST CHIMES: The only vestige of the association with NatWest is a clock, in the lobby outside the boardroom on the 6th floor of Bank House, gifted by the British Bank. *Page (100)*

7

The Lucky 13

ICICI Bank, India's second largest private lender, and HDFC Bank, the largest both in terms of assets as well as market value, are as different as chalk and cheese in their approach to banking. Till the collapse of the iconic US investment bank Lehman Brothers Holding Inc. which played a large part in the world's worst financial crisis, ICICI Bank was flamboyant, innovative and quick as a flash when it came to seizing an opportunity. HDFC Bank is staid and waits for opportunities but emerges a winner at the end of the day.

In many segments, HDFC Bank learns patiently from the experiences of others before it steps into a new business, whereas ICICI Bank loves playing the pioneer. The ICICI Bank stock is volatile; HDFC shares are range-bound. The same applies to earnings. HDFC Bank is monotonously predictable on most financial parameters.

But there is one similarity between the two: K. V. Kamath, who succeeded the legendary N. Vaghul at ICICI, drafted the vision for ICICI Bank in 1996 while he was still in Indonesia heading the Bakrie Group; Aditya drew the blueprint for HDFC Bank in Malaysia while he was on a three-and-a-half-month exit notice at Citibank.

Aditya's vision was to create an Indian bank that could compete with the best on global parameters. India's economic liberalization, he believed, would give the new bank a fantastic opportunity. Public sector banks, with over 90% of the branch network in India, had the advantage of distribution; foreign banks had the products. Aditya wanted to combine the products and services of foreign banks with the relationships, funding and distribution networks of state-run banks.

Also, technology and telecommunications were on the cusp of an unbelievable change and outsourcing had become a possibility. A disruption was emerging worldwide. Aditya saw in that a lifetime opportunity.

He gave the chosen 13 employees—the lucky 13—the freedom to bring their own people to the bank, people who would share the same dream and passion. But he had one caveat—not too many people could be hired from any particular bank, as this would make it difficult for HDFC Bank to evolve its own culture.

So Aditya, perched on a broken chair at Sandoz House, in an office still being done up, declared to those being hired that they would be working in the best bank in India. His men, the lucky 13, shared that vision.

People in the industry ridiculed and laughed at them. Aditya told his team they had no choice but to succeed, as that was the only way they could make any real money. He could not afford to pay them great salaries, but made up by way of stock options. And if the bank did well, so would its shares.

Thakur, the bank's Chairman, was the first to join. His role was to frame the policy guidelines, including audit and compliance regulations. Vinod joined the bank in April 1994. The day he joined, Vinod called Goretti, Secretary to the Managing Director of Mather & Platt, where he had worked, to join him at the new bank.

Goretti was only too happy to say yes. She thought it was a golden opportunity to be able to return home every evening by 5.30 to look after her children. She had done her due diligence—HDFC had a five-day week, unlike Mather & Platt, and she would not have to work on Saturdays.

On 1 June 1994, she entered an empty office at Ramon House as the bank's third employee and asked Vinod where she would sit. "The whole place is yours," he told her. However, she was not correct about the five-day week. Indeed, HDFC had a five-day week but not the bank.

By July, the office resembled a Mumbai railway station—new employees were pouring in from all over India and abroad and they were all handing Goretti their bills and tickets for reimbursements. Goretti was also busy typing appointment letters—some on HDFC's letterhead and a few on plain A4 paper.

While still in Malaysia, Aditya would fax the telephone numbers of prospective candidates to Vinod. Deepak, too, was continuously scouting for the right talent.

"Who Will Pack Our Furniture?"

Harish was also an early catch. He was in London on a three-month assignment. Deepak called him to come back to India and work for his bank. "What bank? Aren't you an HFC [Housing Finance Company]?" Harish asked him.

"Come on, I have got a licence now," Deepak told him.

Harish knew Deepak and many others at HDFC because he was a Relationship Manager with Bank of America, where he had spent 26 years. Although he was a corporate banker, his role in Bank of America was quite diverse. He had been sent to London to fix a problem for the bank in relation to business brought in by Non-Resident Indians (NRIs).

By sheer coincidence, the day Deepak called him, Harish also got a call from his Country Manager, Ambi Venkateswaran.

"Harish, why don't you take up an assignment in London and stay there for five years?"

"Had I wanted to stay overseas, I wouldn't have come to London from Los Angeles. I will have to go back to India," Harish retorted, already sold on Deepak's idea.

Harish resigned and Ambi agreed to let him go on one

condition: Harish had to hire his replacement in London. He did that in two weeks and took a flight to Mumbai.

In the earlier part of their lives, Harish and Aditya used to fight for business as corporate bankers. They were working in the same market in India, with the same idea of either displacing the other or introducing new products. Bank of America and Citibank shared a healthy rivalry in the late 1980s and the early 1990s in the top-tier markets.

Harish joined HDFC Bank on 12 July 1994 as its Corporate Banking Head. His wife Sudha thought he had lost his head to leave a high-paying job and a well-settled career. "Why do you want to start all over again?" she asked him. Sudha used to work at Bank of America, where Harish and she met and fell in love.

Harish was 49 years old then, and a father of two. He lived in the Shanu Deep building on Altamount Road in Mumbai. He called Thakur, Aditya, Deepak and Vinod home on a Sunday to help ease Sudha's worries. In their presence, Sudha lost her nerve and asked: "Who will pack our furniture? Where will we stay?"

Aditya promised to take care of everything and told her that when Harish retired, he would have a better house. Eighteen years later, Harish would live in a bigger flat at Breach Candy, an up-market neighbourhood in South Mumbai, overlooking the Arabian Sea.

Harish-bhai, as he is popularly known in the bank, and Anil Jaggia, Chief Information Officer, constitute the baldies club in the bank. Later, Nitin Chugh joined the duo.

"Hang on, Somebody Wants to Talk to You"

The second of the pack was Ram, an expert on information technology, also from Bank of America, in Chennai. Sometime in May 1994, he met Satwalekar, Vinod and Thakur at Ramon

House. He met Deepak the next day.

"You know what", Deepak told Ram during the chat, "I was going to meet a colleague of yours this morning, and I thought it might be very embarrassing for you if he found you here. So, last night I called him and asked him to come in the afternoon."

"What really struck me was that the Chairman of HDFC appreciated the fact that I might be embarrassed if my colleague saw me in his room. It's a fantastic organization," Ram says.

He went home convinced about working with Deepak, and a formal offer letter followed. The job also presented him an opportunity to return to India's financial capital after a three-year stint in the sleepy southern state of Tamil Nadu.

By that time, Ram had spent 12 years with Bank of America, having been its first IT employee in India. His assignment was to establish the systems—grow the organization, set up the connectivity, plug in India-specific banking systems and, later, migrate them to the mainstream global banking systems.

Bank of America at that time used the BankMaster software that was connected to home-grown mainframe-based systems used by the bank worldwide. It had data centres in Singapore, Hong Kong, London and San Francisco.

An electronics engineer from the Indian Institute of Technology (IIT) in Chennai, Ram began his career as a graduate trainee with Tata Iron and Steel Co. Ltd. or TISCO (now Tata Steel Ltd.) in Jamshedpur. He left the company to study at IIM-A before joining Bank of America.

The job was exciting as Bank of America was planning to set up a retail business. It didn't have a retail presence anywhere outside the USA. The bank's India manager, Vikram Talwar, had coaxed the management into doing retail in the country, given the vast potential of the market, and had lobbied intensely with the mandarins in the Bank of America headquarters in Charlotte, North Carolina. But, by the time

Ram and his team could put the systems together, the project had to be scrapped.

The project had envisaged home banking, a precursor to internet banking, and a complete suite of products based on the experience of running those systems in America. The idea was to bring those products to India and customize them.

It took the team three years to construct the systems, but as the project neared completion, Bank of America acquired Seattle-First National Bank of Washington, which had a big retail presence in Asia. This meant Bank of America's retail business in India would fold into that organization. The bank found it would be too expensive to run Thailand, Manila, Hong Kong and Singapore with the same software while leaving out India. So it scrapped the tech project worth $25 million and decided to look for a system that would suit the entire region.

The HDFC Bank offer for Ram came through a placement agency, Personal Search Services Pvt. Ltd. of the Clarence–Lobo PSS Group. "I decided to give it a try as I was fresh out of a project and knew exactly what needed to be done," Ram said.

"I Can't Reveal My Name..."

One day, while at work in the Bank of America office in Chennai (then Madras), Ram got a call from Vinod who merely told him somebody wanted to speak to him, but didn't tell him who.

"I just want to have a chat with you," the caller on the other side said. "I am going to join the bank and just thought we could have a colleague-to-colleague chat. I can't reveal my name at this point as I am still serving in another organization. But you and I will be colleagues in HDFC Bank."

It was a long chat, mostly about Ram's vision for IT and

how the new bank could use technology innovatively.

Ram's vision was clear: Banks had to reach out to customers and automate more to improve their efficiency and effectiveness. The process, rather than being inward, had to be outward. Most banks at the time were automating to improve their own efficiency and any benefit to the customer was only incidental. The banks were thinking about themselves—their consolidation, their risk appetite, their dashboards.

At that time, the telecom sector was the virtual monopoly of Mahanagar Telephone Nigam Ltd., Videsh Sanchar Nigam Ltd., the Department of Telecom Services and the Department of Telecom Operations—the latter two were central government divisions that merged in October 2000 to form Bharat Sanchar Nigam Ltd.

There was no other option but to apply to a telecom operator, wait for the link to be commissioned and then hope that the line would be up and running. And there had to be a backup in the form of 'dial-ups'. But clearly the opportunity was to leverage technology not merely for operational efficiency at the back end but to provide customers greater convenience and superior high-quality service.

Ram told the caller that the way to look at IT was to see how HDFC Bank could make a difference to its customers. He believed that banks should look for more and more products even if it meant doing a lot of the work customers were expected to do.

Ram didn't know he was speaking to Aditya. Neither did he know Aditya would be heading the bank.

Ram first met Aditya in 1985 as a rival banker at the Siemens office at Worli in Mumbai, where he had gone with Harish to meet the business personnel and explain what IT could do for their cash management systems.

Bank of America had a treasury management software that it had deployed in South America. It had imported the software to India and was looking for customers who could use the terminal to automate a lot of their banking work.

Harish introduced Ram to Aditya. Ram found him rather a flamboyant fellow—the way he carried himself, the swagger—very distinctive.

That was almost ten years ago. Ram saw Aditya at Ramon House a few weeks after he joined HDFC Bank. "We were sitting at a table and the architect was showing us designs of the future office at Sandoz House. Aditya was there but I wasn't introduced to him at that time. I still didn't know he would be heading the bank."

Rajan's Quickest Decision

Another catch from Bank of America was A. Rajan, its Head of Operations in Delhi. A science graduate from Bombay University (now University of Mumbai), he had spent almost 20 years with the bank. When he got a call from HDFC Bank in July 1994, Rajan was overseeing a project on business process re-engineering for Bank of America—a process that mimics building a bank from scratch.

Rajan's first meeting with Vinod didn't go that well and he found Vinod a bit daunting. Aditya followed up with a call to him after about two weeks. Rajan didn't know him personally but was aware of the fact that Aditya was one of the three pillars of Citibank during his days in India heading Corporate Banking, the other two being A. S. Thyagarajan, Head of Treasury, and Jaithirth 'Jerry' Rao, who was handling Retail.

"Aditya came on the landline and bluntly said he was ready to take me as Head of Operations and asked me whether I had any questions. I was taken aback," Rajan told me.

Rajan had been given stock options at Bank of America, a special privilege at that time. As a senior president at the bank, he was eyeing an overseas posting. Naturally, he couldn't make up his mind immediately about joining the new venture.

He insisted on the lowdown on the new bank, how it would work, its mission and so on.

Aditya didn't have the patience or the time to explain it all. "All these things can be explained later, for now just tell me whether you're interested."

Rajan told Aditya he would join. "That was my quickest decision ever," Rajan recalls.

Rajan's boss at Bank of America, Louis Pratico or Lou, was a seasoned banker. He tried his best to persuade Rajan to stay as he was anyway learning how to start a new bank as part of his assignment on business process outsourcing.

Ambi, Bank of America's Country Manager, trying to dissuade Rajan, told him there were two kinds of banks in India—the big multinationals, such as Citibank, the Hongkong and Shanghai Banking Corporation (HSBC) and Standard Chartered Bank, that had deep pockets and technology, and public sector giants, such as SBI. "So", Ambi asked Rajan, "from where would this new bank get its business?"

But Rajan had made up his mind, based on a leap of faith. By that time, Harish and Ram had already left Bank of America for HDFC Bank.

During his days with Bank of America, Rajan used to stay in South Mumbai. Vinod, the practical man that he is, identified some flats at Gamdevi in central Mumbai for Rajan, not an address that would make any banker proud. Vinod himself used to stay at Santacruz, a western suburb in Mumbai.

To Vinod's dismay, Rajan rejected his choices and moved into a flat on tony Napean Sea Road. "You foreign bankers are all tough and have high expectations," Vinod told him.

Aditya had not joined yet. It wasn't until a few months later that Aditya entered the Sandoz House office, which was still being renovated. He was given a table and a makeshift partition separated him from the others. Almost immediately, he asked Rajan to make a list of everything a new bank would require. That was Rajan's first task.

For Shailendra, It was like Tossing a Coin

The next to join the bank was Shailendra Bhandari, who eventually went on to head ING Vysya Bank Ltd. He was with Citibank then, running one of its subsidiaries—Citicorp Securities & Investments Ltd. A headhunter called him but Shailendra was not interested in leaving his job. Two weeks later, Aditya called him from Kuala Lumpur and persuaded him to meet Deepak.

Deepak told Shailendra that he would not be on the board of the bank but would fully support it. His intention was to scout for the best talent from the market. Shailendra had worked with Aditya in Citibank in Delhi in the mid-1980s, when Aditya used to handle Corporate Banking and Shailendra, Treasury and Markets. He never worked for Aditya at Citibank, but they knew each other well.

After meeting Deepak and chatting with Aditya over the telephone, Shailendra showed some inclination to join the bank but changed his mind, as he believed Citibank was too good to let go. Aditya advised him to take some time and think it over. He also wanted to talk to Shailendra's wife Reena.

Shailendra and his wife were clear about one thing—though this venture could turn out great, there would definitely be a great deal of hard work and uncertainty. Aditya told Reena this was an opportunity of a lifetime and Shailendra should grab it. "I remember telling Reena that the whole issue was like tossing a coin: staying with Citibank was fine and going with HDFC Bank was also fine. We simply had to decide which option to choose," Shailendra said.

One of the things that eventually influenced him to join the bank was a little fact Aditya let slip in: "*Bharat* [of United Bank of Switzerland AG or UBS] *bhi aa raha hai.*" [Bharat is also coming.] Shailendra knew Bharat well. He joined the bank in mid-August, around the same time that another Citibanker came on board—Paresh Sukthankar.

Shailendra joined as Head of Treasury but was apprehensive about how well he could run a bank's treasury from midtown Worli, where HDFC Bank planned to have its corporate office. Most banks in those days were located in South Mumbai, close to the central clearing house of RBI at Fort.

But the Fort area was expensive, with the rent going at ₹200–250 a square foot while the rate at Sandoz House was about half of that—₹120 a square foot. Shailendra was worried. Bharat, who was on garden leave at the time, along with Aditya, addressed Shailendra's concerns over a cup of coffee at the Oberoi.

It was decided that a small branch of the bank would be kept at Ramon House to remain connected and oversee processing of high-value cheques; Shailendra could manage the operation sitting at Sandoz House.

Paresh Took a 20–30% Pay Cut

Somebody from the bank, and not a headhunter, called Paresh, an MBA from the Jamnalal Bajaj Institute of Management Studies in Mumbai, in July 1994. Incidentally, ICICI Bank's fourth Managing Director and CEO Chanda Kochhar also graduated from the same institute and both of them were toppers—Chanda in 1984 and Paresh in 1985. Paresh had been hired by Citibank through campus recruitment in 1985.

Thakur and Vinod explained the opportunity to Paresh. In a couple of roles, Paresh had worked with Aditya at Citibank—once when Aditya was the Corporate Bank Head of Western India, Paresh was a Relationship Manager; and another time when Aditya was heading Citibank's Institutional Banking Business in India, Paresh was part of the Credit Risk Management team.

The designation at HDFC Bank was Head of Risk Management. The offer letter was not on company letterhead but on a sheet of A4 paper with a neatly typed line on the top—'HDFC Bank (proposed)'—and signed by Vinod, the bank's CFO.

"It is unsettling for the family when you are taking this sort of risk. You could justify it if you were being compensated liberally but this was not the case here. I took a pay cut of about 20–30%," said Paresh, who rose to be the effective No. 2 at HDFC Bank as its Deputy Managing Director, a post that was abolished after he left in November 2018. "We were told that we will get some stock options and the bank will do well. But at that time options were a new concept. And, it was a start-up bank."

So why did he join? "I felt that there was an opportunity to create something special and that we could make a meaningful difference to the way banking had been done in India... We were not born entrepreneurs but we were sure that we would build something world class over a period of time. We wanted to set a benchmark in terms of technology, service levels, risk management and others—world class, not better than others only in the Indian banking industry."

Paresh used to sport a handlebar moustache. He is down to earth and drives a grey Skoda Superb. More like a professor of mathematics than a banker, he loves to explain things to his colleagues instead of simply making a statement. As the bank's Chief Risk Officer, he had once said: "HDFC Bank is what it is not only for the things it has done but also for the things it has not done."

Paresh used to reach office sharp at 9.20 a.m. every day. He would get off his car on the other side of the road and leg it across to save the time taken by the car to make a U-turn to the office entrance.

His role went beyond Risk Management—Finance, Human Resources, Investor Relations, Corporate Communications, Information Security, Sustainable Livelihood Initiative and Corporate Social Responsibility. Paresh, who many believed to be Aditya's heir apparent, drove most strategic initiatives and handled analysts' conferences.

In the bank, he was the favourite sounding board for decisions across businesses and functions as he always brought a different point of view—he was brutally frank, but never abrasive. His other qualities, insiders say, are a great feel for numbers and a strong sense of fairness.

'Mr Cool' in times of crisis, Paresh also led the way in the annual ritual of blood donation, organized by Bhavesh Zaveri, the bank's Group Head for Operations.

Bharat Wanted to Stay in Singapore for Six Months

Bharat, Deepak's cousin and Aditya's chum, was one of the early recruits. He wanted to stay in Singapore with UBS at least for six more months to complete his assignment but Aditya said a firm 'no' as Bharat would need to help them out with hiring people.

He returned to Mumbai in December 1994. Even though he didn't join the bank immediately, Bharat got involved in the project while serving his notice period in India. His wife, a doctor in Singapore, took it in her stride as they had been planning to come back, though after a year, to be with their aged parents. Bharat was made Head of Human Resources and Retail.

Luis Wanted to Work for an Indian Company

Luis Miranda, an alumnus of the University of Chicago Booth School of Business (then Graduate School of Business, University of Chicago), famous for its cutting edge research in economics and finance, had worked with most of the gang— Bharat, Shailendra, Paresh and Aditya, in his Citibank days between 1989–1992, till he joined HSBC.

He hadn't enjoyed his jobs with the foreign banks for the simple reason that the big decisions were taken either by people sitting halfway across the world with barely a clue about what really was happening in India or by expats who had a vastly different view of the world and the local realities.

Luis was keen to work for an Indian organization, but the problem was that professional outfits did not pay a decent salary in those days. And those that paid a decent salary were not professional in their approach.

A headhunter from Personal Search Services told Luis about the new bank being created. (Later, it became a contentious issue as immediately after the headhunter spoke to Luis, Bharat too called him and the headhunter never got paid!) Bharat was still with UBS in Singapore and Aditya with Citibank in Malaysia.

At Ramon House, 33-year-old Luis met Thakur, Vinod, Harish and Ram. Later, when Aditya called him, Luis was quite candid in saying that he wasn't looking at the salary as much as at working for an Indian company. That was the incentive to come on board.

Another attraction was the people he would be working with. Aditya was someone with whom he had had the occasional fight when they were at Citibank, but Luis always found him interesting. On 16 August 1994, he joined the bank.

His wife Fiona met Deepak before Luis joined the bank, at a farewell party for Gerald Clive 'Gerry' Dobby, CEO of HSBC India. The music was loud and nobody could hear what they were saying.

"Don't you think your husband is mad?" Deepak asked her.

"Why?"

"He's leaving a job with HSBC to join a start-up bank! When I left my job at Chase Manhattan to join HDFC, my

mother and wife didn't talk to me for a very long time."
Deepak was teasing Fiona.

Fiona assured him that she wouldn't stop talking to her
husband even for a day. "He and I talked about all these issues
before we got married. We knew that work would be a roller-
coaster ride because there are so many opportunities and one
wants to gather experience along the way," she told him.

From Bandra, Luis and Fiona moved into an apartment
on Malabar Hill that Bharat had arranged for them. It wasn't
ready yet and Fiona had to go to Spain for a friend's wedding.

While she was away, Luis had just one room for himself
with a mattress to sleep on. The kitchen was still not ready,
and so, on his way to work, the new Vice President-in-Charge
of Foreign Exchange at HDFC Bank would stop at Café Ideal
on Marine Drive to have *bun maska*—oven-fresh buttered
bread buns—with scrambled eggs and tea. He would be the
first person in the office, arriving at around 8 a.m. everyday.

After reaching the office, Luis would top off his breakfast
with a *vada pav*—the hugely popular Maharashtrian street
food—outside Ramon House. Being the first person to arrive,
he would collect the newspapers and open up the office.

After reading the newspapers, Luis would spend time
learning to use PowerPoint as there was no work in the
early days. Showing off his new skill, Luis created the first
presentation on HDFC Bank. Many years later, though a lot
changed, slides from that first presentation were still being used
to explain the business model and philosophy of the bank.

The father of one of Luis' friends, who was related to
Aditya, once told him that they could be building a great
Indian bank but their main motivation was money. Luis didn't
buy that. "Yes, we were given stocks, but we never imagined
even in our wildest dreams where the stock prices would go."

Luis hadn't negotiated his compensation package. His only
passion was to work for an Indian organization. The bank
found in him a good ambassador and asked him to influence

others to join the team. But it wasn't an easy task. "It was quite difficult; no one readily wanted to leave their jobs at foreign banks to join a nascent venture. Also, a private bank in India had never really taken off."

"No Salary Hike, No Foreign Trips"— How Did That Sound to Samir?

A career Citibanker, Samir Bhatia was familiar with Aditya's work–life balance—coming to office at 9.30 in the morning and leaving at 5.30 in the evening. Aditya was a sharp guy with a phenomenal grasp of things. He could work with great speed, clarity and understanding.

Samir had never worked with Aditya but knew a lot about him. "Aditya would go through every credit proposal with an x-ray vision and pick out just a few things that were absolutely necessary. There would be no paper on the table."

In August 1994, Paresh, with whom Samir had worked in the Risk Management Unit at Citibank, asked him whether he would like to have a chat with Aditya. By then Samir had put in his papers at Citibank and accepted an offer from ABN AMRO Bank N. V., but had not joined there yet.

"*Kya kar raha hai aaj kal?*" [What are you doing these days?] Aditya asked him at their first meeting at Ramon House.

"*Aaj kal toh main Corporate Banking mein hoon.*" [I'm involved in Corporate Banking.]

"*Kya karna chahta hai?*" [What do you want to do?]

"*Main khush hoon.*" [I'm happy doing what I want.]

"Would you like to build a new bank?"

The prospect of creating a new bank was thrilling. Aditya told him there wouldn't be any foreign trips in a long time because they were building a domestic bank. He also said, "Once you join, I can't give you a salary hike. Whatever salary you were getting, at best I can match that." So much for selling a job to a potential recruit!

Aditya also asked him where he was staying.

"*Warden Road mein rehta hoon,*" [I live on Warden Road] Samir told him, in a Citibank flat.

Aditya told Samir the bank wouldn't be able to allot him a house and he would have to find his own. Samir had a family home in Santacruz where he used to live before moving to the Citibank flat.

"No salary hike, no foreign trips, back to your own house, how does that sound to you?" Aditya asked him.

Maybe it was Aditya's charm, maybe it was his way of communicating or just the excitement of working with a start-up bank—Samir was convinced. "Done. I'm on. But what am I going to do, what's my job?" he asked Aditya.

"First you come and build the bank and then we'll decide *kya karna hai* [what needs to be done]. Right now, we need people to work and you simply come on board."

A company flat on Warden Road and extensive travel to Africa and Eastern Europe—all gone in minutes. But Samir's wife Neela, who used to work for American Express, was fine with it.

Samir was 31 then. "It seemed a completely new thing to do and clearly there was a huge opportunity because there was room in between the foreign banks and the government banks—a massive vacuum in terms of speed of response, the ability to decide faster, fewer restrictions, branches... It was like something big was being built and one simply had to be a part of that excitement," Samir told me.

Samir joined the bank in September 1994—the day Aditya formally came on board. "I saw Aditya walking in... I had heard about his fabulous office in Malaysia overlooking the ocean, and here there was no cabin as such and only one toilet was functional." A unisex toilet as Goretti was also a part of the team!

Samir's job was corporate banking, but for the first nine months he was the project manager for setting up the bank—Vice President of Projects.

Abhay, a Fighter Pilot, Thought of Switching to Farming

Almost all the members of the founding team came from the banking industry except Vinod, who was a Corporate Executive. Abhay Aima had seen both the banking and the corporate worlds. He had worked with Citibank in Treasury but had left, along with his boss Harjit Sawhney, to join Ravi Ruia of the diversified Essar Group, which was trying to forge a joint venture with Paine Webber & Co., an American stock brokerage and asset management company. But that did not take off and Paine was bought by UBS in 2000.

Abhay had been thinking of switching to farming and had taken a few months off work to explore the idea, but the plan did not work as he had problems acquiring land. And so he had to go back to his job.

But now he wanted to be an investment banker. He started negotiating with Shankar Dey, an ex-Citibanker who was with the Indian outfit Peregrine Investments Holdings Ltd. Shankar was happy to take him but Abhay needed to meet the company's CEO, Francis Bruce Pike. In 1994, Francis set up the first foreign-owned Indian investment bank, Peregrine India, where he became Chairman in 1997.

Abhay took an instant dislike to Francis. A historian and journalist, Francis was related to Britain's royal family. His wife India Jane Birley was the half-sister of Jemima Goldsmith, former wife of Pakistani cricketer-turned-politician-turned Prime Minister, Imran Khan, and the daughter of James Goldsmith. Francis did not have nice things to say about India and that made Abhay uncomfortable, though he found

Shankar, who would be his proximate boss, brilliant.

So, when Shailendra, who had been Abhay's boss for some time in Citibank Treasury, checked with him, Abhay was happy to explore the opportunity of working with a start-up bank. By November 1994, Aditya had already joined and the bank was operating out of Sandoz House.

The job profile was not well defined but Shailendra told Abhay that they would find a place for him in the team. Abhay knew Samir, Paresh and Aditya besides Shailendra and thought the comfort of working with people he already knew was critical. He had never worked with Aditya, but there had been chance meetings at Citibank when Aditya was the institutional head and Abhay was in Treasury. Aditya told Shailendra that he didn't have a problem with having Abhay in the team.

The comfort factor apart, the strong parentage of the bank attracted Abhay. "At that time, there were two big brands in India—HDFC and Bajaj [Auto Ltd.]. As an equity guy, I thought they were the best brands in India. The Tatas also have their brand but I think the HDFC brand name has been utilized to the fullest," he told me.

He was made the Vice President of Treasury, reporting to Shailendra, an Executive Director. His cabin was the coldest because it was carved out of the software storage area where the air-conditioning was very strong. By the time he joined, there was no room for creating a cabin elsewhere.

Before his banking days, Abhay had been a fighter pilot in the Indian Air Force. He had spent two years with the Air Force and three years with the National Defence Academy. He had once told Jerry Rao at Citibank that since he could handle a fighter jet on his own, he could also do banking.

"In the Air Force, you actually sign off for the aircraft and technically not even the Chief of Air Staff can tell you what to do because you are in command. I went solo after flying for 11 hours and the Government of India entrusted me with a multimillion-dollar aircraft. So, after three months of training in banking, if you are not as conservative as them, you should be able to give me responsibility," he told Jerry.

A graduate in international relations from Jawaharlal Nehru University in New Delhi, Abhay, a well-built six feet and three inches, always sports an unkempt look with panache. He hates wearing a tie.

Abhay is the only one in the team who smokes cigars, at times, in office after blocking the smoke detectors in his cabin.

Ashish was the Quietest of the Lot

Abhay's colleague at the Essar Group and previously Citibank, Ashish Parthasarthy, also joined the bank. In fact, Ashish had prepared Abhay's resume as the bank's Human Resources Department had wanted a resume and Abhay didn't have one ready. Twenty-six-year-old Ashish joined as Head of Money Markets, basically in charge of the domestic part of the Treasury.

Ashish had worked with Shailendra and Luis at Citibank where he had dealt with Local Currency and Treasury Risk Management, and Shailendra was instrumental in getting both Ashish and Abhay to HDFC Bank. When Ashish joined the bank at Sandoz House in November 1994, a huge board hung outside the Treasury Division with the word 'CASH' written in capital letters. Presumably this was the place where the cash counter of the previous occupant was located.

Ashish is the exact opposite of Abhay. At just a shade above five feet, he is the shortest of the group heads. Quietest of the lot, he drives a Land Rover Discovery Sport.

Another important member of the founding team was G. Subramanian, who came from the RBI to head Compliance at HDFC Bank. Hierarchically, it was not a top-end job but a very critical one as in HDFC Bank the Head of Compliance reported directly to the Chairman and not to the Managing Director. This was an exception that exemplified the bank's strong focus on corporate governance—a tradition that continues.

A Huge Culture Shock for GS

One day in November 1994, Subramanian, GS to his colleagues in the bank, got a call from his boss at the RBI, A. M. M. Sarma, Chief General Manager in the Department of Banking Supervision. "Are you looking for a challenging assignment?" he asked. Forty-seven-year-old GS, a Deputy General Manager, was only too willing. He went to Ramon House to meet Thakur who was looking for a bold and confident person who would be able to withstand the vagaries and temper the enthusiasm of 'foreign bankers'—a favourite terminology of the banking regulator in those days.

When GS called on Aditya, he was advised to meet the others first—Shailendra, Ram and Rajan—in that order. Aditya told him, "I am fine with you joining us but I don't want your wife to accuse me later of being responsible for her husband's heart attack. There will be a lot of stress in a new bank. I suggest you spend a week with us and then decide."

GS took his decision on the spot and didn't regret it till the first offsite of the bank at Lonavala in April 1995. At the offsite, all the group heads were to make presentations on their game plan for the next financial year. The presentation made by GS was on audit and compliance. One of the slides showed Sherlock Holmes with a magnifying glass in hand, bending forward to peer at something on the floor. Luis instantly said: "GS you need to take care; the back side is unprotected and tempting."

That rattled GS. It was a huge culture shock for a man who had spent 23 years at the formal and staid RBI. Aditya promptly came to his rescue. "Luis, GS comes from a different background; let's respect it." That put him at ease. "The way Aditya intervened, I was convinced that I had made the right choice," GS told me.

On his way to Delhi for the first audit of the Delhi branch, GS came across Deepak at the airport. When Deepak got to know why he was travelling to Delhi, he told GS that earlier whenever he used to get a call from Sarma, he would pick up the telephone quickly as he knew that it could be for his views on some banking issues, but now he thinks twice before picking up the telephone as he worries about whether Sarma is unhappy with the way the bank is being run.

Srikrishnan Got the Call on a Diwali Day

On Diwali in 1994, H. Srikrishnan received a call from his ex-boss in Bank of America—not for exchange of greetings. By that time, Rajan had already signed up with HDFC Bank and two of his colleagues, Harish and Ram, had also committed to join. He was looking for someone who could take charge of Operations and Transactional Banking—which was Srikrishnan's specialization.

Son of a Sanskrit scholar in Chennai, a B. Com. graduate, Srikrishnan's first job was that of a management trainee in GEC even before he formally graduated from Chennai's Vivekananda College. Loafing around on Mount Road (now Anna Salai), dotted with fancy offices and tall buildings those days, he used to dream of working in one of those offices, especially Bank of America, which stood out because of the golden signage on black granite. A good written test and typing skills (Srikrishnan could type without seeing the keyboard, considered a unique art those days) came in handy to crack a clerk's job at the bank. In January 1982, he joined the imposing office with granite façade, wearing a tie—the youngest employee in Chennai, earning little over ₹1,000 per month as salary (₹894 plus allowances).

A part time MBA course with Loyola Institute of Business Administration over the next three years, and all-round exposure at the Chennai branch—from front-end operations to issuing letters of credit and guarantees, general ledger book keeping, audit and accounting—helped him secure a position in the Special Project team that would implement automation in four Bank of America branches across India: Mumbai, Delhi, Chennai and Kolkata.

By that time, Bank of America planned to make Chennai its hub for Asia—the term Business Process Outsourcing or BPO was not coined as yet—but the 1992 Harshad Mehta stock market scam changed its plan and India was dropped from the list of priority markets. Many employees were relocated outside India (they called it 'outplacement') and a Voluntary Retirement Scheme or VRS was rolled out for the Indian employees who had spent at least ten years with the bank.

Srikrishnan, one of the administrators for VRS in southern region, himself decided to opt for the VRS—the youngest employee to do so. The Country Administrative Officer, Lou Pratico thought he was kidding but Srikrishnan meant it. By July 1993, he was in Dubai managing the merger of Middle East Bank with its parent Emirates Bank. It was a cushy job—the work started at 7.30 a.m. and by 3 p.m. he was driving back to his luxury apartment in a Honda Civic, for lunch, and to play with his three-year-old daughter Sriya.

Rajan's call made him wonder whether Emirates Bank had anything more to offer, in terms of roles and responsibilities. By that time, his wife Suguna was carrying their second child. Among other things, children's education, helped him make up his mind to accept the offer. He made a few weekend trips to Mumbai to meet the team but had to wait till January 1995 to join as he could not have claimed his bonus unless he was on the pay roll of Emirates Bank till 31 December. On

4 January 1995—his birthday—Srikrishnan, 'Keech' for his colleagues in Bank of America, joined HDFC Bank.

Initially, the family stayed at Holiday Inn, Juhu, till they shifted to Lakshmi Niwas on 16th Road, Khar, in the western suburb of Mumbai with a Premier NE-118 car. The daughter got admitted to St Joseph School, Bandra, and later made it to Bombay Scottish at Mahim, like many other children of HDFC Bank executives, courtesy Deepak Parekh, who was on the board of trustees of the school. Soon his second child, a son, Satwik was born. Srikrishnan calls him an 'HDFC Bank product'.

The package offered by the bank was not 'great' and there were moments he regretted quitting his previous job as there was no formal policy in terms of travel and stay arrangements of prospective senior employees but he stayed calm remembering Rajan's words—"You are a youngster and your rush of blood will be high but you have to be patient and everything will fall in place." There was nothing in writing about the stock options and in the initial six months (until the IPO and stock options were offered formally) like everyone else, Srikrishnan was on a leap of faith.

In the early days, HDFC Bank was full of executives from Citibank and Bank of America. The Citibankers were handling Risk and Treasury while Operations, Technology, Corporate Banking and Payments were done by those from Bank of America.

There used to be frequent get-togethers of the management teams along with their families. Whenever Puri visited Srikrishnan's home, he used to dip his finger in Black Label scotch and put in the mouth of Satwik. The toddler used to wander around the house but would invariably go back to Aditya uncle again and again to suck his finger dipped in whiskey! Srikrishnan's wife Suguna would never forgive Aditya for it!

Now a 22-year-old, 6 feet 3 inches tall, Satwik occasionally enjoys a drink with Aditya uncle.

Vinod, Bharat, Harish, Ram, Rajan, Shailendra, Paresh, Luis, Samir, Abhay, Ashish, Subramanian and Srikrishnan formed the lucky 13—the 'A team'—that launched the bank.

Two other gentlemen who played stellar roles in the making of the bank were Neeraj Swaroop and Sashi Jagdishan, but they weren't a part of the founding team.

And, there were Kaizad Bharucha and Jimmy Tata.

The Thought of Leading a Team Excited Sashi

Sashi, the bank's second CFO, joined the bank in February 1996, after close to a three-year stint at Deutsche Bank AG, first as a Trainee Officer and later a Senior Officer in Financial Control.

When he was head-hunted by the Human Resources Division of HDFC Bank, 31-year-old Sashi had no clear idea about the bank's profile—whether it was a public or a private institution. He knew about HDFC but didn't know how much stake it held in the bank.

His wife Nagsri, who was working for Thomas Cook (India) Ltd., wondered, "You are leaving an MNC bank to join HDFC?"

Sashi had an offer to join Deutsche Bank's Investment Banking Division in Singapore.

"It wasn't money or the organization or the pride of working for a domestic firm but the thought of leading a team that was the most exciting part," he told me. The bank needed someone to head Financial Control.

It was not the CFO's job—Vinod was doing that as an Executive Director. Sashi was made the Manager of Finance. By that time, the bank was 'listed' and getting ready to announce the earnings of its first full year.

"Don't Waste Time Neeraj, Join Me Now"

Neeraj remembers Aditya calling him during the Diwali of 1998. Apparently someone had strongly recommended him to Aditya at a Diwali party. They met over coffee at the Taj Mahal Hotel on Mansingh Road, Delhi, popularly known as Taj Mansingh, in December and without much ado, Aditya offered Neeraj a job to steer the bank's Retail Operations.

At Bank of America, Neeraj was looking after Retail Marketing, Sales and Distribution. Tony Singh was Head of Retail and Neeraj was reporting to him. It was a critical juncture as around that time Bank of America had taken a decision to diversify its retail business in Asia following its takeover by NationsBank of the USA in 1998. The management assured the employees that nobody would be laid off but Neeraj had seen that his colleagues were either losing their jobs or being transferred to other parts of Asia. Bank of America wanted to sell the India business.

It wasn't an easy decision to leave a foreign bank as Indian banks weren't doing much in retail banking. State-run banks didn't have the products and private banks lacked a wide branch network, as did foreign banks. Bank of America had four branches at that time and HDFC Bank had 40. But the foreign banks were trying to overcome the handicap with product innovation, backed by technology. Besides, the previous Retail Head of HDFC Bank, Samit Ghosh, a former Citibanker, did not even last a year because of serious differences with Aditya on business philosophy.

This was Neeraj's first meeting with Aditya. The HDFC Bank boss was direct: "Don't waste time Neeraj. Join me now and do whatever you want—Strategy, Planning, Products." After the one-hour meeting over coffee and cookies, Neeraj accepted the idea of joining HDFC Bank in principle.

Bharat carried the offer letter to him the next week.

"To be honest, I was excited. Partly because of Aditya. The

money was not good—just about what I was getting at Bank of America, but there were also the stocks that later became valuable. The excitement was the job," he told me.

Neeraj had a few ex-colleagues from Bank of America working with him at HDFC Bank. Ram was Neeraj's batchmate at IIM-A. Neeraj was aware of Aditya's reputation of being a quick and effective decision maker. That was very different from what he had seen at Bank of America, which had a matrix organizational structure where a division head typically had a dotted relationship with the local CEO but reported to the global head of business in another geography.

The decision-making process was superior and faster in a single-country organization than in a matrix organization structure that came with its share of checks and balances.

With his two young children, Neeraj moved to Mumbai from Delhi. And predictably, Deepak stepped in to ensure that Neeraj's children got into Bombay Scottish.

At Sandoz House, Vinod asked Neeraj whether he could do without a cabin. So, Neeraj operated from a closed meeting room that was fitted with a round table, a computer, a telephone and a shared secretary. It took almost a year for Neeraj to get his own cabin and a little less time to get a secretary. Neeraj joined as one of the group heads in Retail. The other person was J. K. Basu, who was running Branch Banking. Vinod was cost-conscious and that was the culture of the bank.

Kaizad was a Squash Champion

Kaizad started his career at the Bank of Credit & Commerce International, registered in Luxembourg and founded by Agha Hasan Abedi, a Pakistani financier. When it was liquidated in the early 1990s for its involvement in massive money laundering and other serious financial irregularities, SBI took over its Indian operations and named it SBI Commercial & International (SBICI) Bank Ltd.

Kaizad, the squash champion of Bombay University for two successive years, and also part of the national team at the Asian Junior Squash Championships in Singapore and Malaysia in 1983, was in Trade Finance at SBICI Bank. He was about to join Standard Chartered Bank when his wife and colleague Havovi asked him to explore whether there was any opportunity at HDFC Bank. Around the same time, a head-hunting company too called him.

He joined the bank in October 1995 as a Senior Relationship Manager but after a couple of years he moved to the Risk Management Unit.

Everybody in HDFC Bank talks about his significant contribution to Risk Management across Wholesale and Retail Banking. His Grey BMW 5 Series is the last car to leave the bank's headquarters at Lower Parel. Once, in his annual performance appraisal form, Paresh, his boss, made leaving office early one of the goals for Kaizad. He did follow Paresh's advice, but only for a few days.

Ask him why he needs to sit late every day, his answer is, "In credit risks, the devil is in the details; one needs to be very careful about every document and that takes time."

He has no time to play squash anymore. Often, he is seen at Otter's Club, near Jogger's Park on Carter Road in Bandra—a Mecca for squash—not for squash but for a drink. No wonder, he is growing a paunch!

"If I Could Do This, Why Can't You?"

Jimmy was two years junior to Kaizad at Sydenham College in Mumbai, the first college of commerce in Asia. (Incidentally, Paresh too is from the same college.) Jimmy used to work for Apple Industries Ltd., an NBFC that was into lease finance and term loans.

Jimmy joined the bank in December 1994 as a Relationship Manager (RM) in Corporate Banking. It was tough as Aditya, Harish, Samir and Paresh had all been relationship managers in the past and were demanding. "If I could do it as an RM, why can't you?" was the refrain. But Jimmy proved his mettle with his meticulous scoping of business opportunities for every corporate relationship and driving his team to close deals. When Samir left the bank to join Barclays, the UK bank that wanted to get into retail business in a big way, Jimmy was made the Corporate Banking Head.

The key to the success of HDFC Bank, according to Vinod, was cobbling together a strong founding team. In Aditya's absence, the first meeting of most of the executives was with Vinod. The meetings often were at the Bombay Gymkhana bar over *lassi* or coffee.

"The whole story was around Deepak. That made my life easier. I used to tell them, 'We are planning to set up the first private sector bank in India, promoted by HDFC, and you know we are trying to get the best of professionals.' The only carrot we were offering was stock options. But that was secondary. The real thing was the challenge and independence of setting up a new private bank in India. Not a single guy said 'no'," Vinod told me.

That's what Vinod claimed, but there were a few who said 'no'. Piyush Gupta, who in 2009 became the CEO of DBS Bank in Singapore, was one of them. He was with Citibank in Indonesia when HDFC Bank was being set up. The trio—Aditya (to whom Piyush reported in India in Citibank), Bharat and Piyush—spent a lot of time talking about starting the bank.

Aditya offered him a job before leaving Malaysia. But Piyush, one of the original partners for creating the new bank, chickened out. "I had spent just two years overseas and wanted to hang around for a few more years and create some savings. I told Aditya to carry on."

For investors, HDFC Bank is the most predictable among Indian banks when it comes to earnings, but in the early days, many things happened that were unpredictable and unheard of in Indian banking history—rats chewing off computer wires, a baby crawling on the treasury floor, bottles of wine hidden in the drawers and whatnot.

Finance was laced with fun in the early days.

8

"There's a Baby on the Trading Floor!"

Thakur, Chairman of the bank, joined in January 1994, about eight months before HDFC got the regulator's in principle approval to set up the bank and a year before the licence came. For most of the year, the sixth floor of Ramon House, HDFC's headquarters, was the camp office for Aditya's army. While the commander was in Malaysia serving his notice period, Vinod held fort. As CFO, Vinod signed appointment letters, looked after the logistics and oversaw everything that a new company needed, including drafting the so-called memorandum and articles of association, searching for a new office, and even bargaining to bring down the price of granite for the office floor.

Till about July 1994, only Thakur, Vinod and Ram were in the office. Vinod's secretary Goretti used to order lunch from the executive lunchroom of HDFC. They would be served soup, starters, a main course and dessert, followed by coffee. While this ritual was abandoned when the team grew to about a dozen, other rituals were adopted.

Every Monday, the top brass of HDFC, led by Deepak, would invite all the bankers working on the sixth floor for lunch at the executive lunchroom on the fourth floor. Deepak Satwalekar, Keki Mistry, Nasser Munjee, Renu Sud Karnad and Deepak Parekh would discuss with them the economy, inflation and interest rates over a light yet full-course lunch that started with soup and ended with dessert (mostly cut fruits) and coffee.

For Deepak, the starter often was a discussion on the macro economy. He would invariably come to the main course—the banking opportunities and what the yet-to-be born bank should do. He was very gung-ho and justifiably so, as he had just managed to get NatWest as a strategic partner. He would goad Ram to go to London, see NatWest's modern systems and figure out how best those could be used in India.

Aditya was a man in a hurry. The day he joined, in September 1994, he asked Rajan and Samir to prepare a list of all the things a new organization would need, right down to clips, pins, paper pads and vouchers. In turn, Rajan and Samir asked each employee for a wish list.

Monday Morning Meetings

Later, after the bank began operations in 1995 at Sandoz House, Monday morning meetings became sacrosanct. Aditya would talk about his vision for the bank with the lucky 13. These boardroom meetings and the discussions were not on looking back at what had happened but on looking forward at what could happen. Of course, any significant event that had taken place in the previous week would feature in the discussions, but it was often new ideas on business opportunities, tackling a particular issue or doing things differently that dominated the content.

Starting at 9.30 a.m., the meeting would go on for about an hour or longer on some days. Aditya didn't like to see the senior managers for the rest of the week if the business was running well; he didn't even feel the need to talk to them. Everyone was empowered. But Aditya was ruthless if anybody came late for the meeting. A five-minute delay without a valid reason would invite a rebuke. If someone was not carrying a notepad, he would remember Aditya's cold stare for the rest of his life.

People would operate independently. At the same time, there was a culture of coming together and sharing thoughts and views. The Monday morning meeting was the biggest platform for collective ideation. On other days, communication was mostly through chits and notes (e-mail had not become widespread then).

By October 1995, HDFC Bank had relocated its office to Sandoz House in Worli, making it the first bank to have its headquarters in midtown Mumbai. Until then, all the Mumbai-based banks had their corporate offices either in the business districts of Nariman Point or Cuffe Parade or in the vicinity of Fort where India's central bank, the RBI, has its headquarters.

The emergence of the Bandra Kurla Complex, in the western suburb of Mumbai, as an alternative business district years later, prompted many banks to set up their corporate offices there as the cost of real estate was relatively lower. Many banks moved out of rented places and opted for their own spaces at the Bandra Kurla Complex.

HDFC Bank chose to stay at Sandoz House as the rent there was almost half of what an office space in Fort or South Mumbai would have cost. The bank got three floors and the basement—a total of some 30,000 square feet—in the building, which had just been vacated by Sandoz subsidiaries. It was taken on a twenty-year lease.

The team moved in even before the interiors were done. The desks were rented from the previous occupier. Quite a few of the cabins had windows so small one could just about put a hand through, something a bank teller would have found useful. As there weren't too many chairs, the rule was 'first come, first served'. Anyone coming in late had to stand for the day.

So, the latecomers would invariably huddle in the conference room—a large place with a long table and quite a few chairs—on the pretext of a meeting. More importantly, unlike in the rest of the office, the chairs in the conference room were not broken and the tables were not three-legged. The air-conditioners were rented and painting was considered a waste of money till the bank neared its inauguration date.

As D-day—16 January 1995—approached, the architect issued an ultimatum to Aditya to vacate the place if he wanted the work to be completed on time. The drilling and the hammering and the humongous amount of construction work had anyway made life difficult for most of the bankers at Sandoz House.

Ram remembers an incident before they moved to the new office. "Aditya told me some guy would come and show me a place where we could set up a temporary office. I was dealing with all sorts of vendors then. So when I saw a new guy in the office I thought 'here is the broker, let him wait.' I took around 15 minutes and this guy waited patiently. When I came out and started looking for my car, he said, 'Come, let's go in my car.' It was a Mercedes Benz. He was Ramesh Gowani, the owner of Kamala Mills."

Samir was made Project Manager. And Rajan would wear a helmet and supervise the work when Samir was out.

"Bank Bandh Ho Gaya"

Ramesh was developing an office space at Kamala Mills Ltd., an old textile mill that was still running. Over a weekend, everybody working at Sandoz House was told to report at Kamala Mills the following Monday. In those days, dozens of appointment letters were being couriered every week and in January, just before the formal launch, a large number of people were to join.

The existing team moved to the temporary office but did not realize that a bunch of new employees would be reporting at Sandoz House that Monday. When the new recruits turned up, the security guard told them, "*Bank bandh ho gaya.*" [The bank is closed]

At the makeshift office at Kamala Mills, Aditya's team was wondering why the newly hired employees had not turned up. When they realized what had happened, they began making calls to each of the new recruits, and put up a sign at the entrance of Sandoz House asking them to report at Kamala Mills.

Ashima Bhat, who would later head HDFC Bank's SME (Small and Medium Enterprises) business, had joined the bank only the previous week. She had summered with Citibank during her MBA days, when Aditya was heading Institutional Banking there. When she got to know that Aditya would be heading the new bank, she wanted to join.

When Ashima walked into Sandoz House that Monday, she didn't find a soul. It was 9 a.m. Her mind was a whirlwind of panic: "What have they done? Have they changed their minds and shut the bank? For half an hour, I was shell-shocked. I had left a good job at Ferguson to join them and there was no bank," she recalls. Tears rolled down her eyes.

The bank had not advertised for candidates in the newspapers as the team was not sure how they would handle the applications. In any case, who would look for a job in a new bank? Besides, Aditya wanted people with experience. Through word of mouth, people got to know and started coming in for interviews. Typically, Rajan would interview a person for a position in Operations for about 20 minutes before Harish would come in and ask for the only table available for job interviews.

There was no meeting room at Kamala Mills. So, whenever they wanted to have a meeting, they would just rotate their chairs, face each other and start discussions. It was a start-up in every sense.

Kamala Mills today is abuzz with activity—it houses banks, media outfits, communication agencies, eateries and outsourcing units. Hundreds of cars are parked in the compound and security guards check every vehicle that drives in. In late 1994, the textile mill was still in operation and there was hardly anyone else besides the mill workers.

Training Sessions under a Tree

Since there was no meeting room at Ramesh's office at Kamala Mills, the bank held meetings under a Peepal tree like in the ancient gurukul system.

Luis remembers his first training session on foreign exchange under the tree and Samir remembers the session on corporate banking. When the mill siren wailed to announce lunch hour, workers would troop out in groups only to see a bunch of young bankers sitting round a Peepal tree. Curious, they would surround the bankers to ask them questions. They would not believe that a banking class was on as there was no blackboard or any other prop by the tree.

In the two-floor makeshift office, the bank set up the systems—connecting the computers with a server. It was done through coaxial cables like the ones used to connect a TV with the antenna. The unshielded twisted pair cables are more expensive and normally used in finished buildings. For the bank, the Kamala Mills office was a stopover. The coaxial cables were laid all across the floor and people were furiously testing the systems as training had to be given.

There was a lot of energy and a lot of drama. People would scream, "this is how we want to set this up; savings account could go this way; current account could go that way, letters of credit have to be done like this, " and so on, as if they were discovering banking.

In some sense, this was true as India's public sector banks in those days worked manually. Their chiefs had just started getting computers but the machines were largely used as showpieces because they didn't know how to operate them!

And the bosses' secretaries, who belonged to the unionized cadre, were not allowed to use computers. Trade unions resisted computerization in banks till the first decade of this millennium as they feared the machines would replace them and shrink employment opportunities.

The training sessions under a tree were fine for certain subjects but a proper place was needed for more complicated subjects. So a *gala*—or an industrial shed—was rented at the nearby Kewal Industrial Estate on Tulsi Pipe Road in Lower Parel.

Typically, SMEs operate in such *galas*, which are nothing more than an industrial floor where heavy-duty machinery works. This particular *gala*, measuring about 500 square feet, had four walls, a wide front door and a ceiling from where a dozen fans hung. It had just one toilet.

The bank began training its IT and back-office people at this industrial shed, with the help of internal and external experts. Often during the training, the electricity would go off, but the training would continue by candlelight with the computers powered by a UPS.

A male colleague would always escort a female employee—in the initial days of the bank, there were only a few of them—in the darkness when the electricity supply was cut in the mill area. They were all working long hours and late into the day.

The *gala* at Kewal Industrial Estate did not have any toilet. The men could relieve themselves in the open space away from public glare but the women employees had to take a taxi to the Kamala Mills office to use the toilet.

Aditya was firm that he would not get into the business without the systems and procedures in place. His mandate was that the systems had to be up and he would not have anybody doing anything manually. Rajan, Head of Operations, was also insistent that the bank needed to be run entirely on automated systems.

The wires that connected all the computers in the *gala* were stuck to the floor with tape, but once in a while, someone would inadvertently trip on them and bring down the entire network. Women employees, particularly those wearing saris, had to be careful not to trip on the mess of wires.

Typically, such *galas* were infested with rats. There were times the rats chewed on the cables but no one could figure out why the systems weren't working because the wires were concealed. So while one person would shout out that he could not log in, those not working on the computers would find everything normal, until someone inspected the wires and they would come off as they'd been gnawed by a rat!

At Sandoz House, Ashima was selected to be the prototype woman customer for whom the teller counters were to be designed. The counters had to be of a comfortable height for the typical Indian woman, not requiring her to stretch herself or bend forward too much to submit her cheques or get her cash. The contractor made Ashima work for hours, asking her to stand straight or bend forward and backward or turn right and left so he could get the right measurements.

Srikrishnan was instrumental in organising management off-sites at HDFC Bank. The first session was held at the HDFC Training Centre in Lonavala. With a view to strengthen the team spirit, the entire team travelled in a Pune-bound local train. From their conversations, many people in the train figured out that they were bankers. They were talking so loudly that when they got off the train, a fellow traveller asked them which bank did they work for? While getting down, they said they worked for ICICI Bank!

The theme of the off-site was '200 by 2000'. Each one was to make a business of ₹200 crore(₹2 billion) by the year 2000. While the year-on-year basis operating plans were being rolled out, a vision was drafted for the year 2000. Of course, the achievement far exceeded the target. The next few years saw such off-sites in Jaipur, Kumarakom, Madh Island

and many other places. Such off-sites were part of the family bonding exercise where the executives were accompanied by their spouses and children.

Baby's Day at the Bank

Luis used to bring his daughter Mihika, who had not yet turned one, to the office on Saturdays. He would pull two chairs together for her to sleep. If she was awake, she'd crawl all over the dealing room. "My wife was at home but I loved having my daughter with me in the office. That's me."

Mihika would crawl on the trading floor and try to stand holding on to the sides of the dealing tables, which had exhaust fans at the bottom. That raised a bit of a scare in the dealing room as she would try to reach for the fan blades. Eventually, the office fixed wire mesh over the fans to keep her fingers from getting cut.

Once, Mihika refused to sleep and began bawling. Luis had to make an internal presentation that day. He made the presentation cradling his precious daughter in his arms.

Some of Luis' colleagues, too, would bring their children to the office, though not as frequently as he did.

It was an informal environment that allowed the bankers to bring along their babies. The children have grown but still share a bond. For instance, in August 2010, Paresh organized a get-together in his house at Lower Parel for those children, who, of course, had grown into their teens or early twenties. They exchanged stories about the peek-a-boos in the office and the Christmas parties at Madh Island where Luis used to play Santa Claus.

The initial days also meant hard work, long hours and chaos. The people being recruited were young—for some, it was their first job. The founding team was also relatively young, with many in their thirties and forties.

A bunch of mostly foreign bankers had left high-profile, well-paying jobs, expensive cars and spacious houses in tony localities to drive Premier NE-118s, earn less money and live in smaller flats in the suburbs. Their children went to Bombay Scottish, though, thanks to Deepak.

Tequila Shots in the Evenings

Some of the executives would sneak in a drink at the office once in a while, mostly in the evenings after office hours to celebrate the little successes—the first deposit, the first loan. Luis had a mini bar in his room—mostly a few bottles of wine and beer in a small fridge, meant to be hidden, of course. Many remember the tequila shots they had late evenings to celebrate when the bank got its thousandth customer or when it became a part of a consortium of lenders for the Birla Group.

Aditya is fond of his whisky but prefers to drink at home when he is with his family. Deepak loves Beck's and Heineken beer with his Sunday lunches. His evening preference is Johnnie Walker's Blue Label. He holds the glass but hardly drinks, only taking small sips every once in a while. A smart strategy, especially when he has to hop parties for networking.

Ram doesn't drink. For Paresh, even tea is poison. Rajan finds beer too strong and, given a chance, will dilute it. Vinod, the 'original Brit' as some of his colleagues dub him, is always measured in drinking, like his steps while walking.

They are all very different from one another; they have their whims, fancies, and idiosyncrasies, but have coexisted wonderfully well in professional harmony.

The ATM Swallowed the Managing Director's Card

All of them swore by the HDFC brand. Day in and day out Aditya reminded them that the bank's services had to be perfect and must not sully the parent brand. But there were the odd glitches, and one of these was quite embarrassing. Hardly a week had passed since Manmohan Singh launched the bank when the bank's ATM swallowed the ATM card of Satwalekar, Managing Director of HDFC. Satwalekar was also a director on the bank's board.

But this was an accident. The bank was meticulous in its plans for integrating its ATMs with the overall architecture. It bought an ATM switch to ensure an online real-time interface connecting individual ATMs and the host system.

When a customer swipes a card at an ATM, there are two ways to verify the balance money in the account. One is the online real-time system that checks with the host on how much money is available in the customer's account. The other is the offline system in which details of a customer's account are fed to the host server only at the end of the day. That leaves a bank open to a potential credit risk. A customer can go to a bank branch, withdraw the last rupee from his or her account, then head to an ATM and withdraw money again as the main server wouldn't know until the end of the day that the customer had already withdrawn all the money from his or her account.

Now all banks follow the online real-time system, but in the 1990s even some new-generation private banks had opted for the offline system. They lived with that mainly because the then popular banking software, Bancs 2000 of Infosys Ltd., did not provide for a centralized service.

HDFC Bank opted for a centralized online real-time system both for its ATMs and for its internet banking. This enabled managers to view a single statement for each customer across all channels, regardless of how the bank was accessed. This was its first step towards riskless banking.

HDFC Bank short-listed ten vendors for the software, including TCS and Infosys, the country's biggest software companies. It was left to Ram to make the call.

Ram went to London to study NatWest's system. He came back extremely disappointed. "Those were very ancient mainframe-based systems. It would have been hugely cost-ineffective and inefficient for us to tie our fortunes with NatWest's IT department," Ram told me.

Coming from the bureaucracy of Bank of America's IT department, Ram knew what he was talking about. "It's a nightmare dealing with those people as each country has to make its own plan. You have to make presentations to various committees saying, 'If you do this, I can assure you this much of revenue, and that's the basis on which they short-list you,'" Ram explained. India was always way down in the list for Bank of America because Japan, Korea and even Indonesia were larger markets than India at the time.

Ram was in favour of cutting the cord with NatWest as far as technology was concerned. He was keen on getting a centralized system as it would have been impossible for a new bank to sustain separate systems at individual branches.

"Are you sure?" Aditya asked him. "You are asking for so much money."

Ram was sure. A centralized processing system would pull together data on all the accounts proposed to be opened in different parts of the country to one central place for verification. If the verifications were to be done by the many individual branches, the bank would not be able to ensure a standard application of its rules and regulations.

HDFC Bank was the first Indian bank to have a centralized system. As it opened more branches, the documents started pouring into the central data centre for verification, and many of the applications had to be turned down because the branches hadn't properly scrutinized the papers. The branches, in turn, would contact the customers for additional details or verification of data. The resultant delays in opening accounts frustrated many customers. "We took a firm stand to bring down the percentage of wrong processing to an acceptable level. It was around 20%, we brought it down to 2%," Rajan said.

A centralized system is expensive to set up as a bank needs to buy large servers upfront but, in the long run, it is cost-effective. The bank would not need to add or expand these servers every time it opened a branch.

In 1994, telecommunications in India was far from ideal and reliability was always a concern, but Ram's logic was simple: It had to improve; it could not get worse. So he asked the management to place its bets on a centralized system. He convinced them it was the most convenient way to roll out services, and the fastest because the bank wouldn't have to waste time setting up servers at each new branch. That ruled out Infosys' Bancs 2000 software.

Nandan Couldn't Sell the Infosys Software

Nandan Nilekani, then Head of Marketing and Sales at Infosys, came to Vinod at Ramon House to market his product. Nandan and Vinod knew each other reasonably well. Both are from the same community—Chitrapur Saraswat, a community that originally hailed from Kashmir and moved south. There are only 25,000 of them, fewer than the Parsis, scattered all over the world.

Ram, Vinod and Thakur went to Bengaluru at Nandan's invitation. Infosys had just built its campus at Electronic City in Bengaluru, India's Silicon Valley. It was listed in 1993 and, by 1994, its turnover was ₹300 million. The company had some very interesting people, hired from the nation's largest lender SBI, to advise it on the features a bank would look for in software. Nandan demonstrated Bancs 2000 to the trio but it did not meet the requirements of HDFC Bank. Plus, it was not centralized.

Nandan eventually became Chairman of the Unique Identification Authority of India (UIDAI), the government agency that is assigning digitized and centralized identification numbers to each Indian resident, similar to the social security numbers in the USA. Nandan was CEO and then Co-Chairman of Infosys before he took up this assignment.

"Infosys didn't get it. And we never got the Infosys account," Vinod told me.

Ram considered some international systems instead, including Fidelity Information Services' mainframe-based Systematics, though he was clear that in India a company would need a UNIX-based system because support would always be a problem for the mainframes. Mainframe systems were reliable but expensive and the support cost was high as most of the people who were trained in mainframes preferred to go to America, Japan and Germany to work on the systems there. That's where they got their money. HDFC Bank would have had to pay handsomely to retain such people for support services. It would not have been worth it. Ram had first-hand experience of that at Bank of America.

The other issue was that International Business Machines Corporation, commonly called IBM, was the dominant mainframe vendor and it would have been tough for a start-up to deal with it. UNIX was less proprietary and had many vendors.

The bank knew exactly what it was looking for and how to go about it. There was consensus on two critical aspects: the system had to be centralized and had to be based on UNIX, even if that meant spending tonnes of money.

MicroBanker, a fully integrated online banking automation system, developed by CITIL, a Citibank subsidiary, fit the bill, but CITIL was not willing to deal with HDFC Bank. A small outfit, CITIL thought, would not be able to afford the system. CITIL was expanding operations in Africa and Europe and was not too keen to sell the software to a start-up Indian bank.

While CITIL reluctantly made a presentation on the system, Citibank intervened before a deal could be signed, saying that selling MicroBanker to HDFC Bank could give the Indian bank more muscle as a competitor. Aditya had to call Rajesh Hukku, CITIL Head, to play ball and he relented. CITIL later became i-Flex Solutions Ltd. (now Oracle Financial Services Software Ltd.).

MicroBanker was designed for corporate clients and had almost nothing for retail banking, except that if someone were to open an account with any branch, however remote, it would show up in real time in the central database. Ram's team had to build the interface for ATMs and internet banking, and, of course, train colleagues at the industrial shed at Kewal Industrial Estate, often by candlelight.

A great business model, a bunch of talented people and high-end technology made for a cocktail of sure success, but even all these ingredients would not have yielded results had the bank not been cost-conscious.

Spend Less, Spend Smart

Vinod drove costs like a miser. For most of his colleagues, especially those coming from multinational banks, it was a shock to be asked why they wanted to stay in a hotel till their flats were ready. He was stingy in allowing senior executives to buy furniture for their flats; he preferred they took furniture on rent. It would take months to get the CFO's nod for even buying curtains.

The same philosophy worked for the bank branches. The first branch was fancy, bejewelled with marble and granite. But the bank realized that customers did not want fancy branches:

They expected to transact and get out, with the least hassle. The decorative granite was a sheer waste of money.

HDFC Bank did not really believe in offering customers a banking experience; it just wanted to ensure a fast and efficient transaction—nothing more, nothing less. When one is a start-up operating from rented offices with rented furniture, one can't splurge money, which is why HDFC Bank had its training centre in a *gala* though it had the cash for a better location. This became the bank's culture—'spend less, spend smart'.

"Even on lease documents [for flats], people used to make fun of me. Cost control is extremely important and we executed it seriously. I used to do interiors of branches at ₹800 per square foot. The equivalent amount spent by Citibank and Grindlays would be at least ₹2,500," Vinod told me. "The bank doesn't say 'don't spend' but it questions the reason behind every spending. If you need it, you will get it, but give me the cost benefit of doing it."

"Coffee in Office? Bring Your Mugs"

"There used to be paper cups for tea and coffee. We banned them in 1997. We said each one will have to bring his or her own mug from home. We were probably spending about ₹5 million a year on the cups across India. If you don't do it at the initial stage, it will be difficult to curtail costs when you become a large bank with thousands of branches," said Sashi, the bank's second CFO.

People did ask: "Why are you doing this?", Is it such a big thing?", "You have gone bonkers.", "You are being penny-wise, pound-foolish."

"If you do it now with so many thousands of people, even if they take four to five cups a day, it is a staggering amount of wasteful expenditure. So we nipped it in the bud," Sashi says.

There were many such decisions—hard and unpopular. For instance, traditionally, most banks in India offer lunches to all their employees at the end of every fiscal year on 31st March and at the end of every half-year on 30th September. HDFC Bank followed this ritual only for the first couple of years.

The lunches had become a tradition in the Indian banking industry where accounting was done manually and people had to put in extra hours for closing the accounts at the end of September and March. But the fully computerized HDFC Bank didn't require any great effort from its employees for closing the accounts.

Another tradition the bank shunned was presenting calendars, diaries and Christmas and Diwali cards to its customers—not to talk of corporate gifts. Well, not entirely true. Of its 40 million customers, a few thousand rich individuals get diaries, if the bank's management approves the budget for it. The bank also does not believe in retreats, annual strategy meets or partying.

Biscuits Banned from Meetings

HDFC Bank even stopped giving biscuits with tea at meetings. The only exception was for board meetings, where biscuits are still served. It also does not offer subsidized lunches at its canteen. Each employee has to pay for the food.

Even senior bankers cannot treat anybody to a round of beer without Aditya's permission. Every liquor bill from across India and across the hierarchy comes to Aditya and Paresh (till he quit) for clearance. There is no prohibition on liquor but it is the bank's policy to keep a check on the money being spent. Aditya has the last word on any foreign travel too.

After Vinod retired, the person who drives the cost-control exercise is Sashi. In this role, Sashi often had professional skirmishes with Anil Jaggia, Head of Information Technology—

the largest cost centre in the bank. After years of resistance, Sashi allowed the use of BlackBerrys in late 2008, provided employees bought the BlackBerry device at their own cost. The monthly usage charge for each employee, even for official use, was capped. Before the BlackBerry days, employees were all given a cheap Samsung mobile handset and the monthly charges were capped under a corporate plan.

A firm believer in practising what he preaches, Sashi is most spartan with spending in his own department. One of his team members, Saurabh Jambhekar, had to celebrate a tenth birthday party for his calculator before Sashi yielded and permitted him to replace it.

On 14 January 2011, Saurabh sent this e-mail to some of his colleagues:

> *On this day, exactly 10 years ago, I was delivered the Thakral Casio, the calculator that cost some ₹1,000. Sashi's reaction then was nothing short of sensational for a newcomer. Purchase of calculators was banned by Fincon [read: Financial Control Unit] from then on, for several years, and that's now part of Fincon folklore. Poor Mr [Deepak] Majithia had to bear with the PC-based adding software for several years, until he managed to pick up one on the sly from some unsuspecting team member's desk.*
>
> *Over the years, my calculator has travelled to various offices before coming back to Bank House...I have never managed to lose it and it remains one of my prized artefacts...*
>
> *Please join me in wishing my Thakral Casio a happy birthday.*

Sashi seamlessly took over the CFO's role when Vinod retired and masterminded the transformation of Fincon into the bank's nerve centre and the vital driver of the bank's MIS-based performance monitoring system. MIS refers to the 'Management Information System'. The Fincon team works closely with each business group or support function and tracks hundreds of operational and financial parameters. Business managers know that. Through Sashi and his team, Aditya would have as much, if not more, insight into the nitty-gritty of their businesses as they themselves do.

Samir narrated one incident to illustrate Aditya's policy on spending the bank's money. In 1996, when the bank was hardly a year old, Sealand Services Inc., a shipping company, invited it to Dubai for a meeting to bid for managing its cash. HDFC Bank was among those on the short list.

Cash management is nothing but collecting the cheques that a company's customers give the company, drawn on various locations. A bank needs to find ways to clear the cheques without delays.

Aditya decided to go to Dubai for the meeting and asked Goretti to book economy class tickets for the team—Aditya, Samir and Rajan. HDFC Bank tied up with the Mangalore-based Corporation Bank for the cash management service, which was then driven by a General Manager, M. Narendra, who went on to become the Chairman of Indian Overseas Bank.

On the plane, a passenger, a blue-collar Keralite employed in Dubai and seated in front of Aditya, kept pushing his seat back while Aditya was trying to have his in-flight meal. Samir called the steward and asked him to tell the person in front to be a little cooperative as a fellow passenger was being inconvenienced. The steward said such things happened during flights and asked Aditya to try the airline's business class the next time he was flying.

"Even though we've been called, I don't think we are going to get the deal. There's no point in wasting money," Aditya told Samir. "We are a start-up, let's behave like a start-up." For the record, HDFC Bank did not get the deal.

Anand Dusane, Executive Vice President & Regional Head (West 1 & 2) Wholesale Banking Operations, Western India, has another story. When the bank began its currency chest operations, it ordered chairs without handles! Its logic? When a person counts notes, he or she would have both hands on the table. When one doesn't need something, why buy it?

For the employees of HDFC Bank, the culture of cost-consciousness begins in the bank and percolates down to their families. A young owner of a ten-acre mango orchard once applied for a job with the bank. He didn't get the job but got an order for 200 dozen Alfonso mangoes from the bank's Pune branch.

The employees paid half of what they would have paid in the market because of the economics of bulk buying. Employees of the Pune branch apply the practice when buying apples, pomegranates and even rice so they can cut costs by exercising their collective bargaining power.

9

Business Before the Shop Opens

HDFC Bank's first corporate customer was the German electronics company Siemens. The bank landed the borrower even before it received its licence. Siemens issued a letter to HDFC Bank committing to induct it in its consortium of lenders. Siemens' CFO, Mahesh Priolkar, knew Aditya's team well, particularly Harish. The company had banking relationships with both Bank of America and Citibank, the two foreign banks from where the start-up bank got most of its employees. Harish, in fact, showed the Siemens letter to Samir to impress him about the bank while trying to hire him.

Getting a customer before a bank is set up is no joke. The news got around and prompted quite a few other customers to approach the bank. Pudumjee Pulp & Paper Mills Ltd. was one of them. The company wanted money. The bank grabbed the opportunity even before it formally opened its doors to customers. It could not give a loan without a banking licence; so it gave money to Pudumjee Pulp in the form of an inter-corporate deposit—a smart way of using the initial capital that was lying idle.

The entity was then registered as a company under the Companies Act and was not governed by the Banking Regulation Act. So an inter-corporate deposit was legitimate. It placed such a deposit of ₹20 million with Pudumjee Pulp, a small sum now but not in those days.

Deepak began exploring ways to get deposits for the bank. He started tapping the wealthy Indian diaspora in Singapore,

Malaysia and China. Satpal Khattar, who later became the Chairman of Khattar Holding Pte Ltd. in Singapore, was one of them. Deepak's classmate Deepak Vaidya, who was then heading Schroders Capital Partners Ltd. in India, knew Satpal well from his days with Schroders in Singapore. Vaidya arranged a meeting between Deepak and Satpal in Mumbai. At the meeting, Deepak unfolded his vision for the bank, and Satpal laid out his business plan and an interesting past.

When Partition happened, Satpal and his sister, born in the small town of Behra in Pakistan, found their way out of the country in a cargo plane to Ambala in Haryana, where their uncle stayed. Satpal's father and grandmother walked across the border and boarded a train to Ambala. Satpal did not even know whether his father had survived the traumatic Partition. Soon after the grand union of three generations, in February 1949, his father moved to Singapore to start a business.

Khattar Holding is a family investment holding company that has operations in the United Kingdom and investments in India, Europe, Vietnam and Indonesia. Satpal is a lawyer by profession and had founded KhattarWong & Partners, a law firm in Singapore.

He gave HDFC Bank a $20 million deposit for three years. Deepak also offered Satpal shares of the bank worth $4 million. A part of the public issue, around 5%, was kept for NRI investors.

"I sounded out a few banks for a loan which I could use to keep the deposits but no one was willing as HDFC Bank was not known in Singapore. I put my own money both for the equity and the loan," Satpal told me over the telephone from Singapore.

Manmohan Singh, then Finance Minister, conveyed a message to Satpal—that his investment would be approved only if it was made from Singapore and not via Mauritius. Satpal agreed. He retained his shares in a Singapore holding company right through even though opportunities did crop up later to reduce tax by transferring the money to Mauritius.

He also invested in Centurion Bank of Punjab (Centurion BoP), which later merged with HDFC Bank.

And Quiet Flowed the Money

After the first branch was opened, many companies came to HDFC Bank to keep their monies in bulk. Thakur recollects that one company wanted to keep with it a deposit of ₹330 million. But the bank would not take the deposit as the officials of the company (which Thakur declined to name) wanted a commission.

On another occasion, a broker approached Thakur with an offer to deposit ₹200 million from a clutch of companies. This time too, the bank would not accept the deposit as it entailed giving a commission.

Paying commission for deposits is not permissible by the banking regulator. "If you pay commission, the average cost of money goes up and the interest margin shrinks. If you want to maintain the margin, then you can't lend to triple-A-rated companies," Thakur said.

Besides, there was an accounting issue. How would a bank show the commissions in its books?

There are ways to skirt such hurdles. One way is for a bank to take, say, ₹100 million from one depositor and have a back-to-back arrangement with a borrower who will take the money as credit at a relatively lower interest rate, and pay a commission to the depositor. It's not an unusual practice in the Indian banking industry but it affects a bank's interest income as the borrower, who passes on the commission to the depositor on behalf of the bank, pays a smaller interest.

The only benefit a bank will get from this is that such a deal will prop up its business and build its balance sheet. The industry's obsession in those days was not profitability but a big balance sheet. For some banks, particularly the state-owned ones, it's true even now.

Towards the end of every financial year, in March, typically, a bank may get money from a company in the form of deposits and the money may, in no time, travel to the company's group firms as credit. Nobody can catch a bank for this circular trading as money is fungible. How does one prove the same fund is used for giving loans? After all, the colour of money is the same. Besides, entities at both ends may not necessarily be the same firm—they could be two separate firms from the same group.

In the first year of its operations, HDFC Bank, which was actually a mere two and a half months old, recorded a deposit base of ₹6.42 billion, advances of ₹980 million, investments of ₹2.21 billion and a profit of ₹8.02 million, after paying tax of ₹4.06 million.

There was not much business to talk about and hence its first annual report spoke about the four core values the bank stood for—operational excellence, customer focus, product leadership and professional people. The report tried to tell shareholders and investors what the bank stood for rather than what it had done, as very little had been achieved so far.

Many employees of HDFC Bank came from foreign banks. For them, the first general meeting at Birla Matoshree Sabhagriha in Mumbai was quite an experience. Shareholders asked for good tea and coffee and bonus shares.

Leave Money on the Table

HDFC Bank was the first of the private lenders to go public—even before it completed a full year. "It was a mistake," Deepak told me. The RBI required the new banks to go public within a year but all other lenders went back to the regulator and got extensions. "We didn't ask for it. We were too naïve," Deepak said. "Everybody took time as they wanted to get a premium. We sold at par, ₹10. But I have no regrets."

Deepak pushed for a par issue as the bank had nothing to show.

And the disaster of parent HDFC's listing was still haunting him, though that had happened a decade and a half ago. In 1978, India's capital market was in a different shape and mortgage was a new product, not understood by many. HDFC put the photograph of its first borrower on the cover of its balance sheet, a D. B. Remedios from Thane, who took a loan of ₹35,000 to build his house.

The public issue of HDFC bombed. In an initial public offering (IPO) of ₹100 million, the face value of one share was ₹100. ICICI, IFC (Washington) and the Aga Khan Fund took 5% stakes each in the mortgage lender and the balance 85% equity was offered to the public, but there were few takers. The stock quoted at a steep discount on listing.

For the bank, Deepak did not want to take any chance. So portions of the issue were reserved for the shareholders and employees of HDFC as well as the bank's employees. HDFC decided to own close to a 26% stake in the bank and NatWest 20%. Satpal was offered about 5% and the public 25%. The size of the public issue was ₹500 million.

"We didn't know whether it would succeed. Our experience with HDFC had been a disaster," Deepak said.

But Deepak had grossly underestimated investors' appetite for the new bank. The issue, which opened on 14 March 1995, was subscribed 55 times. The stock was listed on the Bombay Stock Exchange (now known as BSE Ltd.) on 26 May that year at ₹39.95, almost at a 300% premium. The listing process was long and arduous in those days.

Any HDFC shareholder owning between one and ten shares was offered a hundred shares of the bank. Those holding between 11–20 shares were offered 200 shares in the bank. A maximum of 500 HDFC Bank shares were offered to those owning 41 or more shares in the mortgage lender. This was to benefit small shareholders.

Investors in those days would hold shares in a physical format and not in the dematerialized form that depositories hold now on behalf of the shareholders. And the shares were held in folios. One shareholder from Ahmedabad had split his seven shares into seven folios and applied for 700 shares under seven different names. He was caught just before the share certificates were issued.

This shareholder became a regular at every annual general meeting of the bank and HDFC after that, demanding the removal of Aditya and Deepak. HDFC had to file a criminal case against him to stop that.

The track record concept didn't exist then. And, there was no road show. A public issue was more about distribution of application forms. The bank heavily focused on its strategic partner NatWest's technology, customer relationships and international reach to sell the issue.

"A lot of us asked why we weren't pricing it at a premium. We could have got a premium but Deepak said, 'leave money on the table for investors. They will appreciate this in the long term.' Today, when we have arguments with our promoters, one of the big lessons I learnt from our float is to price an IPO cheap," Luis said.

"Should we really scalp the shareholders? This is a start-up company. On what basis are we putting valuations? Today they will put a valuation even on a start-up idea," Satwalekar was blunt in his assessment.

Abhay, who heads Wealth Management and Private Banking in HDFC Bank, has a slightly different take on the IPO. "People had said ₹20, ₹30, even a ₹40 premium was fine. I asked Deepak, 'Shouldn't you quote at least ₹20 when the grey market is offering ₹30?' In those days and even today, I think our bank stock enjoys the highest multiple in Asia. By and large, everything has gone our way: 20% by default and 80% by design."

By the end of its first full year of operations, in the fiscal year 1996, the bank had 203 employees on its rolls and branches in Chennai, Delhi, Kolkata (then Calcutta), Bengaluru and Pune, besides Mumbai. It had 50 corporate clients, at least 19,000 deposit accounts, and was adding 2,500 accounts every month.

In the early days, everyone was bubbling with ideas to start new businesses and differentiate HDFC Bank from other banks. Their selling point was that public sector banks had the network of branches but not technology; foreign banks had technology but not network of branches and HDFC Bank had both. With this theme at the backdrop, they were coming up with different products across transactional banking, capital markets, etc.

Every time, an employee went to Aditya with an idea, he used to evaluate it, call the group heads and bounce the idea with them. He would invariably ask the person who came up with the idea to implement it. By doing this, Aditya tried to generate entrepreneurial spirit. He never encouraged consultants offering free advisory who don't take up the responsibility of implementation. By doing this, Aditya also got rid of those who just come up with superficial ideas without taking the onus to implement them.

Liquidity Crisis

The growth could not have been faster as the Indian banking system was struggling with a severe liquidity crisis. There was no money in the system; companies kept knocking on banks' doors but their vaults were empty, and interest rates had skyrocketed.

C. Rangarajan, then RBI Governor, and S. S. Tarapore,

Deputy Governor, jacked up the interest rates and raised the reserve requirement for banks to fight a persistently high inflation. For instance, CRR, or the portion of deposits that commercial banks need to keep with the RBI, was 15% in 1995 and SLR, or the banks' compulsory investment in government bonds, was 38%. (In December 2018, CRR was 4% and SLR 19.5%.) So, the banks were left with very little money to give loans to companies; retail loans almost didn't exist then.

Many blamed the RBI's tight money policy for the slowing economic growth that followed and the piling of bad assets at banks as many companies lost their ability to pay back. Large-scale loan restructuring followed in steel and a few other sectors by the end of the century. Despite a series of loan restructuring, quite a few banks were getting buried under heaps of bad assets and their capital was eroding fast.

Samir Arora of Helios Capital Management Pte Ltd., who was then heading Alliance Capital Asset Management (India) Pvt. Ltd., owns HDFC Bank stock from day one. It has all along been his No. 1 holding.

His investment theory was simple. In any business where the public sector competes with the private sector, the private sector will win. State-owned banks had the strength of distribution but not service; multinational banks had service but they were not allowed to open branches. So, a private company that used the working model of a foreign bank but was free of the constraints of public sector banks in terms of unionized employees and government interference would succeed, he reasoned.

HDFC Bank is a prime example of this thesis.

Alliance Capital began its India operations in February 1995, just a month before HDFC Bank's IPO. Arora used the asset management company's capital to buy HDFC Bank shares, which he was not supposed to do. When he was told that, he decided to buy back the shares himself. He even made a rule that the company's capital will not be put in stocks and will not compete with other funds run by the asset management company.

He was running a fund of ₹800 million and put around ₹100 million in the HDFC Bank IPO. Because of the oversubscription, he got much less though. "Till now we are holding the stock and have continuously been adding... ," he says. Personally, he owns a few thousand shares since 1995.

Hemendra Kothari, one of the famed three Ks of Indian investment banking—the other two being (Nimesh) Kampani and (Uday) Kotak—said investors were convinced of HDFC Bank's business plan.

"Aditya is credible. He performs what he promises. He even over-performs many a time. In difficult times, he knows how to manage the risks by staying away from risks," Hemendra-bhai (as he is addressed in the investment banking circles), said. He is liberal in his praise even though he doesn't like Aditya's hard bargaining with investment bankers to cut down their fees.

Hemendra-bhai of DSP Financial Consultants Ltd., and Ind Global Financial Trust Ltd. were the lead managers for the float. They earned a fee of 0.5% of the issue. The overall expense for the lead managers, registrar, brokers and listing fees was ₹42.5 million.

Hemendra-bhai was also present at the New York Stock Exchange (NYSE) in July 2001 when HDFC Bank's American Depositary Shares (ADS) were listed. He remembers Aditya making road shows from morning till night, covering more than a couple of cities a day, catching flights and meeting people and telling them the bank's story with a lot of passion.

By that time, the new private banks in India were six years old and had captured at least 5% of the market share, in terms of assets and deposit liabilities, but still less than the foreign banks' market share and even that of old private banks. The state-run banking industry's share dropped—close to 78% of the assets and 79% of the deposits. By 2018, their share dropped even further—less than 70%.

On 20 July 2001, HDFC Bank made its $150 million global offering, the second Indian bank to do so after India's then largest private lender, ICICI Bank, in March 2000. The bank opted for ADS to reach a wider investor base for comparatively inexpensive capital. Each ADS, representing three underlying shares, was priced at $13.83, the average trading price of HDFC Bank's underlying shares in India in the previous ten days. On the day of the ADS listing, the bank's Indian shares closed at ₹225 a piece on the BSE.

We Need Capital for Growth

Sashi, who rose to be HDFC Bank's CFO, remembers every detail of the six-month-long process that began in January 2001 with Aditya meeting a battery of lawyers. "We were growing very fast. So we needed capital. The markets were buoyant and investment bankers told us there were lots of investors in other markets who would love to buy our stock. We also wanted to diversify our shareholding," he said.

To comply with the strict regulations of the US Securities and Exchange Commission(SEC), the core group of Sashi, Vinod, Paresh and a few others had to work long hours every day with the lawyers, accountants and investment bankers. An essential prerequisite for an ADS is compliance with the Generally Accepted Accounting Principles in the United States (US GAAP).

"We were all scared. 'Will our profits be lower in the US GAAP than in the Indian GAAP?' That was kind of a conservatism that we had. In reality, however, our profits in the US GAAP were higher than those in the Indian GAAP," Sashi recollects.

In the Indian accounting system, when a borrower is unable to pay interest or principal for three months, the account is deemed to have turned bad and the bank needs to set aside money to provide for it. Was HDFC Bank making adequate provisions? In the US GAAP (Generally Accepted Accounting Principles), one needs to know a company's forecast on its expected cash flow, collateral and the present value of that. Net of that is what a bank has to provide for. There is a science behind provisioning. But the Indian norms are a bit different.

"We realized that we were slightly more conservative in the Indian accounting framework. We had to sort of write-back some of the provisions in the US framework. Our profits were slightly more in the US GAAP," Sashi said.

The SEC is a tough regulator. It goes through every document with a fine-tooth comb. Every claim in an offer document has to have supporting evidence and one cannot make a forward-looking statement. If one does, the Commission will ask the company to explain why.

This rules out loose claims such as 'We are the best Indian bank'. One needs to explain why one is the best. Also, one has to be precise when one talks about the numbers—whether for ATMs, branches or customers. An NYSE listing teaches a company to be precise and moderate in the use of language. It cannot be pompous and make aggressive, forward-looking statements without substantiating them.

HDFC Bank's ADS issue was subscribed many times over and everybody who put in money couldn't get as many shares as they wanted. Book building of an overseas issue in those days was primarily the decision of the book runners. But Aditya didn't allow Merrill Lynch and Co. and Morgan Stanley, the book runners for ADS, to decide who will get the shares and who won't. For him, public issues were not about getting money alone but about acquiring long-term loyal investors. However, unlike local shares, ADS don't give voting rights to the holders.

"I want to make it very clear. The people who supported us should be given fair amounts. I don't want you to come with your list," he told the book runners.

"There was a firmness in his tone. It's the first time I saw him outside the office. He didn't mince words," Sashi recalls. The team went through the list, name by name, and ensured adequate allocation for those who had been supporting the bank.

Along with Hemendra, Nimesh, Deepak, Aditya, Paresh, Sashi and a few others, Anil Ahuja was also present on the NYSE trading floor. He was on the bank's board representing Chase Capital Partners, a private equity company that had bought a 15% stake in HDFC Bank from NatWest when the UK bank got out.

"All of us in the room were saying, 'Show us the book. Who gave the order? Somebody must give us the book so that we can do proper distribution to everybody. We are already a listed company. We already have shareholders, long-term holders of the stock.' We didn't want hedge funds coming in. We needed some quality investors but the lead managers were interested in their own global relationships," Anil recalls.

An ex-Citibanker, Anil had worked with Aditya, Paresh, Samir, Shailendra and Abhay. He had left Citibank to join Chase Capital in early 1997.

At around 2 a.m., Morgan Stanley and Merrill Lynch executives told Aditya and his team to go to sleep and that they would finalize the list. Aditya left reluctantly but not before giving them Anil's mobile phone number (Aditya didn't carry a mobile phone and still refuses to have one). "Whenever you are ready with the list, you call us; we will come back. We will do the allotment," Aditya told the book runners.

"They were very keen to give it to whoever they wanted to rather than to the bank's key relationships, but Aditya didn't let that happen," Anil told me.

Anil and Paresh oversaw the allocation process. The pricing was already done but they wanted to close the exercise as early as possible as news started trickling down on the Central Bureau of Investigation(CBI) raids at the residence of P. S. Subramanyam, former Chairman of India's largest mutual fund UTI, and a few other top officials of the fund, for alleged corruption in private placement of funds.

Anything Can Happen over Golf

In 1997, there was a golf tournament organized by ABN AMRO at the Bombay Presidency Golf Club Ltd. in Chembur, a central suburb of Mumbai. Aditya and Anil were playing. Aditya was not his usual self. Anil knew that something was bothering him.

That was when NatWest wanted to get out of HDFC Bank after the three-year lock-in period. Aditya was worried that NatWest's 20% block could effectively get dumped into the market and push the stock price down.

Over golf, he shared his concerns with Anil. The private equity investor's reaction was atypical: Here's an opportunity to partner with one of the finest banks in the country. "Fine, why don't we do something?"

With Aditya's nod, Anil started negotiating with Christopher Fitzgerald, General Counsel for NatWest, based in London, who was looking after legal and regulatory issues —pretty much the top guy, but not the business head.

It was almost a year before the deal was struck. When the discussions started, the trigger for an open offer in India was 10%, but by the time the negotiations got closer to completion, India's capital market regulator had raised it to 15%. (The trigger was subsequently raised to 25%.) Chase Capital could buy close to 15%. Had it opted to buy more, an open offer would have been necessary.

By 2005, when Chase Capital completely exited HDFC Bank through three block deals over the previous years, the bank's market capitalization was about $3.9 billion. When Chase Capital entered, it was about $250 million. Anil had made his killing.

"As a private equity investor, I do well if the people I partner with do very well. It's a question of alignment of interest. How do you retain somebody like Aditya Puri? After many years even when I resigned from the board, his salary was ₹2.1 million; his bonus would never get approved as the RBI had some limits about how much bonus a bank's MD could get. How would you retain people?" Anil asked.

Anil was on the bank's board for six years, between 1999–2005. He was the Chairman of the Risk Management Committee of the board and a member as well as Chairman of the Compensation and the Audit and Compliance Committees in rotation.

"A team of less than half a dozen people can change the culture of the whole organization and drive the business strategy. What's important is that the core team is retained and aligned to make sure that shareholder value is created," says Anil, who went on to head the Asia operations of the London-based 3i Group.

As a shareholder, Anil's objective was to grow the bank's share price ten times so his investors could make money. All that mattered was how many dollars one put in and how many one took out. He knew the bank could only do well if the top team was retained and motivated.

Policies and stock options that were implemented in HDFC Bank, Anil believed, were by far the best in the market. "Look at the stock options that were granted. Mind-boggling numbers… This is not easy to pass through the board as a number of members come from government and quasi-government bodies."

"If you lose Aditya Puri, you lose a big chunk of the market capitalization of the bank in one day. At that time, he was 50 and there were too many takers for him."

Anil was 36 years old when he got on the board.

Aditya will turn 70 in 2020.

10

Doing Ordinary Things in Extraordinary Ways

Aditya wanted a free hand to run the bank. The others were allowed to express their views but he was clear there could be only one boss and that was him. He made that clear to Deepak as well. A gentleman to the core, Deepak kept his word. He was always there for advice and guidance, if sought, but never interfered.

Once the team was in place, Aditya explained to his colleagues how they would create a bank to match the best of global parameters. "If we can put together the products and services of foreign banks and the relationships, funding and distribution of the nationalized banks, nothing should be able to stop us," he told them.

Each member of the core team was given the freedom to hire his own staff. They would sit down as a team and define the vision—the target market, technology and products. Today HDFC Bank is predominantly a retail bank but the initial focus was on corporate banking because the cost of setting it up was lower and any loss they might incur would be smaller.

The bank decided to deal first only with triple-A-rated companies. The team had the contacts. They could develop products and services specific to companies, on the basis of their experiences at HSBC, Bank of America and Citibank. Efforts were focused on making these better than what was available in the market, across transaction banking, foreign exchange, bill discounting and supply chain management through multiple delivery channels. But funding, at least initially, had to come from retail.

So, the bank needed to open branches and then go full-fledged into retail to reflect the composition of the Indian economy—consumption, investment and government expenditure. Domestic consumption, which plays a major role in the Indian economy, was around 55% at the time. One could not afford to ignore the consumer.

As the plan was to start with the triple-A-rated companies, the bank needed to cater to their finance and cash management needs, and manage their business dealings and foreign exchange. The target companies were the so-called blue chips that were highly profitable with a good volume of business and not companies with high market capitalization, as value in the market can always be drummed up even if a company is not fundamentally strong.

HDFC Bank could meet their needs as it had the right technology—an open system that had the flexibility to introduce products faster in alignment with cheaper, centralized processing and distributed servicing.

The architecture had multiple delivery channels, such as the telephone, ATMs and the internet, besides the branches, to ensure the efficiency of the operating systems. Credit and risk were to be handled separately.

This was the broad vision Aditya had sketched in Malaysia. All members of the core team contributed their expertise and experience to flesh out the main idea. "Our aim was to focus on consumer satisfaction and have a professional, transparent and fair organization to work in and be associated with, whether one was a shareholder, investor or an employee," Aditya says.

After economic liberalization in 1991, competition just started in certain segments with the ring of protection being slowly withdrawn. Companies would take loans from Indian banks but seek letters of credit and guarantees, cash management, treasury products and foreign exchange from foreign banks. That was the mix of business for most corporate treasurers.

HDFC Bank was positioned right in the middle. It was an Indian bank—it understood the environment, was adequately capitalized and, over a period, had enough rupee funding capability. At the same time, in terms of product range, technology, quality of people and turnaround times, it could offer most of the things that a foreign bank could offer in the Indian market. And, at a lower cost too.

The CFOs of large companies could always get money by making just one phone call to banks. 'What will you give me that others don't?' they would typically ask.

So it was important for HDFC Bank, which was crawling then, to convince the CFOs that the baby in the woods too could provide them what the existing banks offered, and more efficiently, quickly, and at competitive prices.

A good brand, relationships, technology and smart marketing can open doors but after that the business has to be sustained by delivery. Many companies had their doubts about HDFC Bank's capability on that front. They liked the product roll-out, competitive pricing and advanced technology, but worried if it could deliver.

Paresh remembers how a multinational engineering company in South India shooed him out. "You have highs and lows after every call. Many a time we waited long to be told politely to come back another day. This was one occasion when it wasn't graciously done," Paresh says.

Siemens was the first corporate client. Slowly, the Ambanis (the group was undivided then), the Tatas, the Birlas, TVS and other industrial houses came forward. Given the pedigree of the team and its vision, they all promised to help the bank in its teething stages.

The bank was also choosy in picking customers. There was pressure on it as other banks were not only growing faster, as they chased relatively smaller firms who could give high rates, but also were less demanding. Aditya worked hard on marketing. When he approached B. M. Munjal, the patriarch of the Hero Group, the consortium of banks associated with the group protested. But Munjal remembered how Aditya, while at Citibank, had been the only banker to lend to him when he launched Hero Honda. He wanted to return the favour.

"They all backed me up and told me that I would not have to return empty-handed. I was assured of a place in the consortium within a couple of years," Aditya said.

The team's contacts in the corporate world were extensive. Aditya, Harish, Samir, Paresh and Rajan managed to push through quite a few deals. In their presentations, they emphasized that they did not want any privileges based on pure relationship. They would offer products better than what the companies already had. Only then should the companies sign on the bank.

Initially, they made several cold calls, informing potential customers of the birth of the bank and how they planned to proceed with its road map. After the second call, they went with a product line.

One such product was broker financing. The bank, the broker, and the stock exchanges created their own closed group to deal online.

Similarly, the bank suggested to Asian Paints Ltd. and ABB Ltd. that they could have their vendors online with the bank and it would offer them loans at a relatively cheaper rate. For Tata Motors Ltd., it drew up a complete supply chain. Each of these solutions helped HDFC Bank grow.

Ishaat Hussain, former Director on the board of Tata Capital Ltd., said that big industrial houses like the Tatas and the Birlas do not face any difficulty in accessing bank finance, but their customers and suppliers find it difficult. HDFC Bank grabbed that important niche. It became a pioneer in vendor and dealer financing.

"Tata Capital used to consider this its preserve. Being a Tata company, it felt that it should be the natural owner of this market—financing the vendors of Tata Motors, Tata Steel, Titan Industries and Tata Chemicals. But HDFC Bank got a larger share through aggression and innovation," Ishaat told me.

Conglomerates such as the Tatas look for two things from their bankers: One, the transaction should be smooth and fast; and, two, the bank should respond to their monetary requirements quickly. "There should be a bond between a banker and a borrower. I want a bank which I can rely on and which should be ready to help and give money in times of difficulty," Ishaat said.

So, if the Tata Group were to get a banking licence, would HDFC Bank be its role model?

"Yes, most definitely. You cannot be a copycat. But certainly, it would be my model," Ishaat said.

Incidentally, in 2019 when RBI opened its window for giving licences to a new set of private banks, the Tata Group did apply only to withdraw it later. HDFC Bank figured out the needs of the customer in the existing inefficient payment system: A good transactional banking facility—collection, payment—and an MIS. Citibank was offering such products but HDFC Bank wanted to upgrade the quality. In his Citibank days, Aditya had sub-contracted certain products to Corporation Bank, till recently perceived to be a smart public sector bank that was ahead of its peers in many niche areas, but HDFC Bank intended to design a better system in terms of reach, MIS and cost.

It developed a suite of products for companies to cover their receivables, products for financing vendors, advice on treasury and multi-channel banking. A meticulous product plan, the pull of the HDFC brand and aggressive marketing did the trick.

Every day the bankers would call on ten customers.

Aditya would call; Harish would call; Paresh would call; Samir would call. They would be in Mumbai in the morning, Pune in the afternoon and Chennai the next morning. Clients always wanted to deal with one of the top executives personally. A senior banker would take the local representative with him to meet the customers. After that, the local recruit could handle the delivery.

A Peaceful Night's Sleep

Harish had a reputation of delivering what he promised. Almost every customer he had worked with while at Bank of America came to HDFC Bank. As a corporate banker, Harish's philosophy is quite simple—to sleep peacefully at night. "We went for top-end corporates. We didn't get a good price but the portfolio was top-notch. The spread was low and profit marginal, but that was a defined policy. We didn't want to lose sleep over bad assets."

"Don't bullshit your customers. They will figure it out soon. Tell them what you can do and also what you cannot. So they do not have false expectations," Harish says.

"Everybody has pain. Advise them on how to alleviate pain. We didn't charge extra for that. It's free advisory. Just to convince them that we aren't taking advantage of their weakness," Harish used to tell his team.

After settling in Mumbai, the bank headed to Chennai. Harish had worked in the southern city for ten months at Bank of America. He knew almost every industrialist in Chennai, Hyderabad and Bengaluru—A. C. Muthiah and the bosses of Ashok Leyland Ltd., TVS Group and TI Group.

The next stop was Delhi. Aditya had worked there and knew a host of potential top customers. In Kolkata, Samudra Sen, a young IIM-A graduate, hired from Arthur Andersen LLP, quickly built relationships with ITC Ltd., Coal India Ltd.

and other local companies.

Partha S. Bhattacharyya, who later became the Chairman of Coal India and took it to the market, was a junior officer then. Harish called him and sought a meeting to introduce the bank. Coal India was banking with SBI at that time. Partha, then Assistant Manager for Finance, told Harish that SBI could perhaps give ₹100 million of its share to HDFC Bank out of a total exposure of ₹5 billion.

Quick research revealed that Coal India had an accumulated loss of ₹40 billion. Paresh, who was heading Risk Management, was against doing business with a loss-making company. But Harish's argument was that the Indian Government owned the company, which was also a core sector operator, and so it would not allow it to fail. It took enormous effort, including a joint meeting with the company top brass, to convince Paresh and Aditya. HDFC Bank's exposure to Coal India was ₹7 billion at its peak.

D. D. Rathi, former Director of Grasim Industries Ltd. and Ultratech Cement Ltd., Aditya Birla Group, likes the speed with which HDFC Bank operates. "I needed an extra limit of ₹1.5 billion. It was an overnight affair and I wanted complete secrecy. I called Harish in the evening after banking hours and asked for the money. It was done the next day," Rathi recalls.

Rathi's office was in the same building—Sakher Bhavan at Nariman Point, Mumbai—that Aditya, wearing a half-sleeved shirt and a tie, used to operate from while at Citibank for many days.

"Those were tough days for a new bank as the big brothers wouldn't allow anyone to enter the consortium. One day, 15 years ago, [Aditya] Puri called me and asked for a ₹25 million limit in my company. I agreed," Rathi recalls.

After that, Aditya would quietly go to Industry House, then the headquarters of the Aditya Birla Group, have lunch with the executives and get a ₹25 million limit from every group company. In those days, HDFC Bank was in the bottom 20 in the consortium for Grasim Industries; today, it's in the top tier.

HDFC Bank also opened an extension counter at the Aditya Birla Centre in Worli, the group's headquarters now, where hundreds of employees work.

Transactional Banking is No Great Science

The bank started its capital market infrastructure business a few years after it was set up. The period was seeing a determined shift in behaviour from savings to investments, and the opening up of huge potential in the investment banking and mutual fund businesses. "Since we were getting the banking business on the ground, we figured that rather than getting into businesses that will dissipate our energy and take time to build expertise and scale, there was a need for somebody to provide very reliable, efficient and low-cost banking and transactional services to all these participants in the growing capital market space," Paresh said.

What kinds of businesses were required? Collection of money and applications for IPOs and new fund offers by mutual funds. Whenever money is invested, there is an array of businesses—the entire application process, refunds, custody (as shares and bonds have to be managed), and the clearing and settlement business.

"We identified some of the inefficiencies and risks in the way these things were being done. We developed a structure and backed it with appropriate technology which substantially mitigated those risks because of the collapse of time and better information flow," Paresh told me.

There is very rapid flow of a large amount of money in the clearing and settlement business. It could be just for a day, but over time a continuous flow creates a steady stream of free money.

The transactional banking business, such as cash

management and clearing and settlement in stock exchanges, is no great science. Corporation Bank was Citibank's correspondent bank for cash management. There were a few others who had launched cash management.

New private banks, particularly HDFC Bank, could offer cash management because the basic configuration was centralized processing and distributed servicing, and all its branches were linked online in real time. They had supplemented the movement of money with MIS and integrated this with the customers' systems.

Cash management is all about managing the cash flow between a company and its suppliers.

For example, a Mumbai-based company selling its products across India gets a payment as a cheque drawn on some bank's branch in Ludhiana, Punjab. When the Mumbai company deposits the cheque in its account, the cheque goes back to Ludhiana for clearing and the money could take up to a week to be credited.

In a cash management system, the company deposits the cheque with the bank's branch or a partner bank in Ludhiana and gets the money almost immediately. The bank either charges a commission or gets to keep the money for a day or two.

The idea was to make the corporations outsource their entire receivables management to HDFC Bank. It streamlined the entire collection methodology, the fund-flow movement, the information and reconciliation and reported back to the corporations, leading to increased efficiency. This was music to the ears for the treasury department of the companies.

Today, HDFC Bank is the market leader in transactional banking services. A lot of transactional banking services involve movement of money and this is probably why it has the cheapest rate of funding among all banks. Clearing, cash managements, payment of dividends, tax collections and anything that involves processing high-volume transactions is transactional business. It was not a new business, but what HDFC Bank did was recognize transactional banking as a huge opportunity, give it the right focus, and scale it across products and geographies.

Plain vanilla cash management was developed into value-added supply chain management solutions. Wherever there were inefficiencies in the system, the bank tried to address them through its products.

In those days, most cooperative banks didn't have a licence to operate outside the state with the exception of a few. So, for the payment for a banana vendor based at Talegaon, Pune, selling banana in Delhi was by way of demand drafts. The bank charged the trader in Delhi and the vendor received the money at a later date.

HDFC Bank solved this problem by utilising the concept of 'at par' cheque. All the cooperative banks were asked to open accounts with the bank. The cooperative banks were given the limit to issue an 'at par' cheque similar to a demand draft but akin to a cheque by a cooperative bank. So the cheque issued by the trader in Delhi was encashable without any conditions and the HDFC Bank, in turn, got a free float as all these accounts were pre-funded.

Although, 'at par' cheques already existed as a concept, HDFC Bank developed its use for the cooperative banks.

In every segment, the bank took care of the supply chain to create more business.

Of NIM and CASA

The raw material for a banking business is the money customers keep with a bank in the form of deposits. The challenge before all banks is to keep the cost of deposits low and the Net Interest Margin (NIM) high.

NIM and spread are similar, but there is a subtle difference between the two. While NIM is arrived at by dividing a bank's net interest income by its average interest-earning assets, spread is the margin between the yield on assets and the cost of liabilities, or the difference between interest income and interest expense as a percentage of assets. NIM can be higher or lower than the net interest spread. NIM and spread are the two key parameters that give an indication of a bank's operational efficiency.

When a bank cuts its loan rate, its interest income declines, and if it is not able to cut its deposit rates by an identical margin, its NIM gets affected.

Normally, when interest rates rise, banks hurry to raise their loan rates but are slow in offering higher interest to depositors. Conversely, when the rates fall, banks are quick to cut their deposit rates but take time in passing on the benefit to borrowers. Floating rate deposits can solve this issue but it has not caught on as yet in India

There is a reason behind this. The impact of any hike or cut in loan rates is felt immediately as a bank's entire loan book is re-priced, but that's not the case with deposits as the new rates are applicable only when the existing deposits mature or new deposits flow in.

CASA plays an important role in lowering the cost of deposits. The 'CA' of CASA stands for 'current account', primarily meant for companies, public enterprises and entrepreneurs who perform numerous banking transactions daily. Such accounts are cheque-operated and a customer can deposit or withdraw any amount of money any number of times. Banks generally insist on a higher minimum balance to be maintained in a current account. As the balances maintained in the account are often very volatile, banks generally levy a certain service charge for operating a current account. The money kept in such accounts comes free to a bank as no interest is paid on current accounts.

A savings account, or the 'SA' of CASA, is the most common

operating account for individuals and others for non-commercial transactions. Banks generally limit the number of withdrawals an account holder can make, and also specify a minimum average balance. Till 2011, the interest on savings accounts was regulated. Even after deregulation, most banks, including HDFC Bank, are offering 4%, which was the last rate in the regulated regime. SBI is paying even less at 3.5%. Every bank wants to increase its CASA, as a higher portion of CASA in the overall deposit liability brings down its cost of money.

Among private lenders, HDFC Bank, ICICI Bank, Axis Bank, Kotak Mahindra Bank Ltd. and The Jammu and Kashmir Bank Ltd. have high CASA ratios. Among public sector banks, the CASA ratios of SBI, PNB, Allahabad Bank, United Bank of India and Bank of Maharashtra are high.

Of course, CASA alone cannot ensure the success of a bank. Quite a few banks on the list which have high CASA ratio are not in the best of health as they have piled up bad assets.

The credit for coining the acronym CASA—which every analyst now swears by—can possibly be attributed to HDFC Bank. Every internal presentation of HDFC Bank made since 1995 talks about CASA. But this is only one contributing factor to low-cost money. Even in non-CASA term deposits, one should have a higher proportion of retail than the high-cost certificate of deposits and bulk deposits. Small deposits are granular, stable and less price-sensitive.

A high NIM alone cannot make a bank profitable as operating expenses and credit costs, including provisions for bad assets and write-offs, can erode a substantial portion of NIM. Banks also need to cut their operating costs and increase efficiency. They can remain profitable even when NIM shrinks, provided they start generating more fee income.

Transactional banking was the key to HDFC Bank's business model initially because a bank typically does not get current and savings accounts on the basis of price but on the basis of other aspects that differentiate one lender from the other. This could be the strength of the brand or the distribution network or customer service or even product range.

A smart bank tries to ensure that a customer chooses the bank for his or her primary savings account. Many customers in urban India hold more than one savings account, though about half of India's adult population did not have any access to banking services till Pradhan Mantri Jan Dhan Yojana, the world's most ambitious financial inclusion programme, was launched by Indian government in August 2014. This often happens as people change jobs, and thus their salary accounts, or residences (in a city like Mumbai, a typical 'leave and licence' agreement is for 11 months; a tenant needs to move out after that time frame if the landlord is not willing to extend the agreement by another 11 months).

A smart bank also tries to make a customer have only one account for salary, dividends, making utility payments and so on. A customer will do so with a bank that offers an entire suite of products, including credit cards, car loans and home loans.

Cross-selling of products has been possible at HDFC Bank because of the establishment of a data warehouse—one of the first Indian banks to do so in 2002. The warehouse keeps a tab on all transactions irrespective of the channel that a customer is using (branch banking, telephone banking, net banking or mobile banking). The data can be used to develop a credit scoring model and marketing analytics. This helps reduce the turnaround time.

So a loan that used to take seven days earlier can be disbursed in a day or an account that used to take three days to open now can be done in a few hours. Of course, going beyond this, the bank has introduced ten-second loan, discussed in the earlier chapters. Cross-selling of products using data warehousing brings down the cost-to-income ratio.

The cost-to-income ratio is a key financial measure,

particularly important in valuing banks. It shows a company's costs in relation to its income. To get the ratio, one needs to divide the operating costs (administrative and fixed costs, such as salaries and property expenses, but not bad debts that have been written off) by the operating income. The ratio gives investors a clear view of how efficiently the company is being run—the lower it is, the more profitable the company will be.

HDFC Bank's cost-to-income ratio was 39.2% in September 2018. It has been coming down every year progressively, as digitalization gains pace. In September 2017, it was 41.5%. In March 2013, before the digital journey started, it was as high as 49.6%. Compared with a predominantly corporate bank, the cost-to-income ratio of a retail bank typically goes up because of higher customer acquisition and servicing cost.

Micro Marketing

Banks acquire customers by cross-selling products, using them as hooks to take the relationship forward. When a bank sells a car loan to a mortgage client, the borrower not only pays interest but also comes closer to the bank in the basic relationship. Such customers tend to keep their account better funded, to pay for the car loan instalments. Later, they may start paying their income tax or children's school fees from this account. The average balance swells.

Shirish Apte, former CEO and Chairman (Asia-Pacific) at Citigroup Inc., prefers to call the HDFC Bank approach 'micro marketing'. "What this involves is picking one relationship and capturing relationships with everybody who is associated with that one relationship," he says.

"Think about it—they've got a large company which has got suppliers who have other suppliers. So you keep going down the chain, knowing fully well where the risk element automatically comes in. Then, you get people who work for those companies. Micro marketing really helps you expand business both horizontally and vertically. From what I hear from people, that's what HDFC Bank does extremely well," Shirish told me.

The Big Bang Settlement Business

In the mid-1990s, there were no guaranteed settlements and both the Bombay Stock Exchange (BSE Ltd.) and the National Stock Exchange (NSE Ltd.) had one clearing bank each—Bank of India and Canara Bank, respectively.

There was always an element of uncertainty about whether a settlement would go through. In those days, a settlement was done once a week and so meant carrying the risk of an entire week, accumulating pay-ins and pay-outs.

HDFC Bank came up with a solution. With the exchanges sitting in the bank offices, it offered to build a closed user group—of exchanges, pay-in brokers and pay-out brokers and the bank—by allocating specific clearing and settlement accounts. So, before running a settlement file if an exchange ran a test, it would be able to find shortfalls in a broker's account, if any, and could ask the broker to pay up. This meant when the actual settlement was run, it would be a smooth process.

It was not about transferring the risk from the exchanges to the bank. By putting in place online real-time settlement and ensuring better information flow, the bank was essentially eliminating a system risk. Also, a broker's ability to get money from one exchange and then transfer from his bank in terms of managing his own liquidity became more efficient. A broker would have a pay-in from one exchange and a pay-out in another exchange, as most brokers were members of both exchanges.

NSE used to run a settlement fund to take care of any default. As it had no idea about a broker's balance with banks, it started to consolidate brokers' accounts at Canara Bank's capital market branch at Fort in downtown Mumbai. A floppy from the NSE system with the data of the dues from various brokers would be taken to the bank branch, which would run the disk to check whether the brokers had enough funds. The findings would then go back to NSE. This was an everyday affair.

"We studied the whole process and said, 'why don't we have them open accounts with us?' We could give them visibility on their screen. They could log into my system and find out which of the brokers didn't have funds. We created 24×7 access. We told the brokers to bank with us, 'We are a networked company and your money will be credited instantly'," Ram said.

HDFC Bank and NSE are of the same age and both were excited about the potential for the securities market. One day, in 1997, Aditya invited NSE's then Deputy Managing Director, Ravi Narain, to talk at the bank's retreat at Madh Island in Mumbai.

There were about 30 senior employees and Ravi told them the whole arena of securities transactions would explode one day, provided there was a technology-aided initiative. He envisaged a massive opportunity in the area.

Aditya grabbed the mike and told his people, "You wouldn't believe me but Ravi and I have not spoken about this at all. Clearly, this is a reconfirmation of what I have been telling you guys all along."

"I didn't know him [Aditya] at all," Ravi told me. "We tied up with a group of banks as clearing banks and HDFC Bank was one of them. From day one, they were very certain in their mind of the potential of business and their ability to manage the risks."

If a broker defaults to the exchange, it's the clearing corporation's problem. If there is a default in the lines of credit, then banks have a problem. In manufacturing or any other business, one doesn't see daily volatility but bad assets can hit a bank suddenly.

Being appointed as a clearing bank for NSE was just the entry point. This could have been leveraged to do many other businesses and the bank was shrewd enough to capture them.

The bank marketed this service to all exchange members. The service implies that any exchange member who chooses to operate through HDFC Bank has to open a clearing and settlement account with it. When a file goes by a certain stipulated hour, HDFC Bank has to bring in the pay-in money on behalf of all those brokers to the exchange. Back to back, they have to figure out their arrangements to collect the pay-in money.

Similarly, after a few hours, a clearing corporation calculates the pay-out and a reverse flow occurs for a completely different or not-so-different group of brokers and back to back for the investors.

This cycle is repeated every single day for cash equity and derivatives and all other asset classes.

What kind of risk does the bank run?

The biggest risk for a bank is the processing risk. When NSE started, it ran very tight cycles. Typically, the gap between a pay-in and a pay-out would be a couple of hours. In the early days, it didn't matter much as the volumes were small but as the volumes grew and the banks started dealing with brokers all over the country, one can imagine what can happen if they cannot meet the cycle at some point and the exchange slams the gate.

The pay-in and pay-out cycle time is sacrosanct. If there's an interruption in processing and, in turn, the flow of money, the brokers will vent their ire on the bank. This is one part of the business.

The second and bigger part is the opportunity that Aditya and his team sensed—that brokers need lines of credit, working capital and other banking services. It's entirely possible that a broker would enter into a pre-arranged understanding that he would put in 70% of the fund and the bank would have to cover the rest. That's a line of credit. This is the big opportunity and the bedrock on which all other businesses get built.

The bank gets a float and there could be fees for lines of credit. The bank may not charge for actual processing of inflows and outflows, but certainly it would charge for credit lines. If it's a daily occurrence, brokers keep balances and that becomes the float.

For all this, a bank needs to have the ability to handle very tight processing cycles every single day. It also entails understanding the credit risk of brokers and brokerages as the bank takes exposure on them. This is the hard part, given all the volatility and cycles of the market and of individual broking companies.

"It is the question of marshalling your resources—what we used to call in the early days a Germanic obsession for very tight processes with no tolerance for error and processing risk, and they [HDFC Bank] have built that in the way they operate. It was very clear very early on," Ravi said.

Bankers Flew in at Midnight for Stress Testing Brokers

Ravi recalls one incident of a very sharp market movement when many brokerages were in stress. With a market share of around 75% then, it was inevitable that HDFC Bank had a tough time. Late at night and in the wee hours of the day, the bank flew executives in various directions across India, sat with the brokerages, figured out their stress points and ensured that no accident would take place the next morning as the market is relentless.

It needn't be a default; it could just be a stress point. If not addressed, it could lead to a default. A bank that does not support its clients can cause serious financial problems. Risk magnifies for any transaction where a brokerage is involved, simply because of the nature of the business.

Just as a normal corporate entity or an individual account can become a bad asset, the brokers can also add to the bad assets if they take money but cannot pay back. The difference is that in any other business, one doesn't see the daily volatility of the capital markets and bad assets can hit one out of nowhere. If one is unprepared or has not built a risk scenario, one can be caught unawares.

Clearing bankers scarcely know what's in store for them on a given day. Typically, the day begins with assisting the brokers to pool in their funds into their respective settlement accounts by the deadline stipulated by the exchange/clearing corporation, say by 10.30 in the morning. Often it's routine, but when one is dealing with the settlement system of a dynamically volatile phenomenon like a stock exchange, there's always a very large element of risk.

18 May 2006: Markets Crashed

Chetan Shah, Co-Head of Capital and Commodity Markets Group, had been with HDFC Bank since 2005. He recalls 18 May 2006, which was not exactly a calm morning. There were some apprehensions of the trouble that was brewing but no one was prepared for what actually happened that day. The Sensex, BSE's bellwether equity index, tanked 826 points. The margin calls started mounting; brokers started making frantic calls to move their funds lying in various accounts in the bank.

A *Bloomberg* report ('India's Sensex Tumbles Most in Two Years: World's Biggest Mover') by Pooja Thakur in Mumbai that day said:

India's Sensitive index posted its biggest drop in two years, the steepest move among markets included in global benchmarks.

Reliance Industries Ltd. led [stock] declines with a 6.8 percent drop, its biggest loss, as faster-than-expected U.S. inflation fanned concern [that] rising interest rates in the U.S. may lure money out of emerging markets. Hindalco Industries Ltd. and Oil & Natural Gas Corp. led commodity stocks lower after prices of metals and oil dropped.

'Higher interest rate expectations are fueling concerns of a slowdown of flows into emerging markets,' said A. Balasubramaniam, who oversees about $3.8 billion of Indian stocks and bonds as chief investment officer at Birla Sun Life Asset Management Co. in Mumbai. 'Falling commodity prices are aggravating the decline.'

The Bombay Stock Exchange's Sensitive index plunged 826.38, or 6.8 percent, to 11,391.43 at the 3:30 p.m. local time close. That's its biggest drop since May 17, 2004. The index has lost 9.7 percent since it reached a record 12,612.38 on May 10.

The S&P/CNX Nifty Index on the National Stock Exchange lost 246.20, or 6.8 percent to 3388.90.

The rupee, the second-worst performing currency in the Asia-Pacific region, dropped after overseas investors sold almost $550 million of equities in the four days through May 16. That compares with a daily average purchase of $118.6 million earlier this month. [. . .]

'Weak Trend'

U.S. stocks fell the most since January after consumer prices, excluding food and energy, rose 0.3 percent in April, Labor Department figures showed. Economists had forecast a 0.2 percent increase.

The Fed said it would monitor incoming data to set future policy after raising the benchmark lending rate a 16th straight time last week, to 5 percent. Higher borrowing costs may leave consumers in Asia's largest export market with less to spend on goods and services.

'We are mirroring the weak trend in global markets,' said Nilesh Shah, who manages about $4.42 billion in assets as chief investment officer at Prudential ICICI Asset Management Co. in Mumbai.

Finance Minister Palaniappan Chidambaram refused to comment on the stock market's tumble, saying he doesn't speak on daily market movements, when questioned by reporters in New Delhi.

Another *Bloomberg* report ('Asian Stocks Fall Most in a Year on U.S. Inflation') by Malcolm Scott and Stuart Kelly, datelined Singapore, said:

Asian stocks fell the most in a year as faster-than-expected U.S. inflation fanned concern [that] rising interest rates will slow demand in the region's biggest export market. Sony Corp. and Samsung Electronics Co. dropped.

'Some of the falls are eye-watering,' said Donald Williams, whose fund at Platypus Asset Management in Sydney was the best performer

over three years among open-end Australian equity
growth funds tracked by Bloomberg. 'Sentiment
has been turning against stocks lately, and the
inflation report last night really pulled the trigger.'
    Japan's Nikkei 225 Stock Average slipped 1.4
percent to 16,087.18. South Korea's Kospi fell 2.6
percent, wiping out this year's gains. Benchmarks
in regional emerging markets such as India,
Indonesia and the Philippines declined the most.

The relationship managers of HDFC Bank, who were
the first to get calls, immediately swung into action, getting
the balances in the various accounts of their respective
relationships as well as keeping tabs on their overdraft limits.
Senior managers also started looking at the broker-wise data
provided to analyse the magnitude of requirement for money
vis-à-vis the expected fund flows of the brokers.

On that morning, P. V. Ananthakrishnan, then boss of the
Capital Market Division at HDFC Bank, was on a vacation
in a different time zone and Harish, Group Head, whom the
Capital Market Division used to report to, was on an official
trip abroad.

Chetan, then Assistant Vice President and seven months
old in the bank, was managing the floor. His two mobile
phones, one direct line and the intercom were ringing non-
stop. The case was the same for other relationship managers,
and regional heads, R. Balasubramanian from Delhi, Sandeep
Jhavar from Kolkata, Deven Pandit from Gujarat and C. K.
Venkatesh from the south.

Aditya's office started getting calls from the regulators,
exchanges and broker members.

On the shop floor, Chetan was fighting the fire to manage
the pay-in of the exchanges, submit margins to exchanges and
send reports to Aditya's office.

Kaizad, Head of Credit and Market Risk Management,

with his team of Deepak Maheshwari and Benjamin Frank, had taken charge of the shop floor.

By noon, the bank completed the pay-in of funds. The real-time gross settlement of the RBI was still not in place then and the cut-off time for banks for clearances of high-value cheques to the RBI was 2.30 in the afternoon. Normally, the pay-out from the exchange would have been completed by that time. But this was no ordinary day—the pay-in of the exchange was delayed and therefore the pay-out of funds was also delayed.

This was a catch-22 situation. If the pay-out of funds of the exchange didn't take place, brokers who had sold shares wouldn't receive their money. The total pay-out and high-value cheques added up to billions. The high-value cheque clearance timeline was to be met. There was no option but to let the cheques bounce, and this would have created havoc.

The brokers were requesting money from the bank against the expected pay-out of the exchange. But it was impossible for anyone in the bank to take the call. It could not give billions or the go-ahead for clearing the high-value cheques. On the other side, the pay-out from the exchange was getting delayed.

Chetan came up with a solution. He walked into Wholesale Banking Head Bhavesh's cabin. "Can we request the RBI to delay the high-value cheque clearing?" he asked.

Bhavesh called the RBI. The regulator agreed to make an exception in that hour of crisis. The delay gave HDFC Bank time to clear the pay-outs. The customers' accounts got the money to honour the cheques.

For every stock that ended higher on the BSE, eight ended in the red. The 30 stocks that constitute the Sensex all ended in the red, and 24 of them lost 5% or higher. Erosion in investors' wealth on that day was ₹2.25 trillion.

That was also the day Lakshmi N. Mittal launched his bid for Arcelor S. A.

The Lowest Touch Point

Brokers' requirements change with time. There were days in 2000 when they wanted loans against securities and bank guarantees. Later, the brokers wanted cash management service as they spawned branches across the country. They wanted internet banking.

The bank tries to go to the lowest touch point of a broker— his customers, family members—and all are captured in one loop. To manage risks, knowing a broker's balance sheet is important, but more critical than that is knowing a broker personally—his family, from where he comes and with whom he deals. Knowing these aspects comes in handy when looking for funds in times of crisis.

"There wasn't a single instance of forced selling of a share in the 2006 crisis," Chetan said. This makes it abundantly clear that there is a distinction between real risk and perceived risk. While many banks stay away from broker financing presuming it is risky, HDFC Bank's experience is different.

According to Chetan, the brokers tell him, "your MD [Aditya] is a Panju [Punjabi] but his mind-set is Gujju [Gujarati]. If he asks for a ₹200 million fixed deposit, and I give it, he would offer me 9.5% while the market rate is 9.8%." (The popular perception is that Punjabis are large-hearted whereas Gujaratis count every penny.)

This is a bank that does not know anything beyond business. Chetan told me, "When we make presentations to our MD, he says, '*Teri unchi English mere ko samajh me nahi aati hai; mere ko ye bata ki ladoo kidhar hai.*" [I can't follow your sophisticated English; simply tell me where the money is] Everybody in HDFC Bank understands what *ladoo* (a ball-shaped sweetmeat) stands for.

The presentations don't last more than four to five slides. Aditya loves talking to the point. "*Paisa kidhar hai woh dikha, mujhe aur kuch nahi samajhta hai, seedha baat pe aa.*

Mujhe tu global gyan mat de." [Show me the money; I don't understand anything else, come straight to the point. Don't give me global wisdom.]

11

The Change in Course

HDFC Bank wanted to be a corporate bank. Its business plan submitted to the banking regulator said so. The idea was to be a wholesale lender and a retail fund mobilizer as the cost of money borrowed from individuals is always less than what a bank pays to companies that keep money with it.

For a new bank, it was a struggle for survival on capital and very little borrowings. Most foreign banks were cynical and even their junior employees would fire a volley of questions at HDFC Bank's managers about the bank's credibility. Bank of America was a friend but not Citibank from where Aditya came.

Within the first couple of years, it was pretty clear that the business plan needed to be tweaked as public sector banks have more resources: They have a vast branch network and hence can lend to companies at a lower price. So, if HDFC Bank was serious about business, it had to be on both sides—retail borrowing and retail lending.

Three years after it was born, HDFC Bank decided to go the whole hog in retail, and started to look beyond the universe of triple-A-rated companies to double-A-rated ones.

It had started as a corporate bank for three reasons.

First, till it built a branch network it could not go for retail banking. In fact, any bank that starts with a limited branch network has very little choice other than corporate banking because retail customers cannot be acquired without a distribution infrastructure.

One can always argue that there are internet banks without physical distribution but this is a phenomenon restricted to sophisticated and developed markets. Indeed, the banks in India have gone beyond branches and are using many other channels in a big way to service customers, it's still a while before they can use the internet to mobilize deposits.

Second, most of HDFC Bank's senior employees, including Aditya, came from a background of wholesale and corporate business in foreign banks. By definition, most foreign banks are corporate banks. Some of them such as Citibank have large retail businesses, but the HDFC Bank recruits had worked in the wholesale side of the business.

Third, corporate business, in comparison with retail business, requires much less investment in physical infrastructure in terms of technology, branches and people. As a start-up, HDFC Bank had to earn its way before it could invest in all of those requirements.

This was the most logical way to go in the first stage because corporate business was the sort of business they understood and where they had relationships. And even if they had the expertise (which they did not) and wanted to get into retail from day one, they could not have done so because of cost factors.

The market opportunity was clear. At that point, if one were a corporate treasurer, one would be dealing with two sets of banks. Public sector banks had a large distribution network and plenty of rupee liquidity, but in the mind of a corporate treasurer they didn't have great recall in terms of service and products. The foreign banks, on the other hand, didn't have rupee-funding capability and so couldn't lend much. But they had technology and service capability.

Retail is No Half-way Affair

"Once we started growing, we realized that we couldn't be a big bank dealing with only triple-A clients. Also, if we wanted to enjoy economies of scale, we would have to fast track our retail banking franchise," Aditya says.

Now, the retail business isn't really difficult but many banks—both local and foreign—have failed simply because they take half-way measures. In retail, there can't be any half-way affair. If one puts one's money behind something, one has to see it through right till the end and be convinced about one's strategy.

For instance, if a lender gets into car and two-wheeler loans, it can make money only if it has the scale. It is not just the suite of products that matters because the lender may not want to venture into all products at the same time but the scale has to be there.

Retail banking is a volume game. A bank needs wide distribution, a lot of branches, a plethora of products and a completely different mind-set. One needs to have many products to straddle the economy of the country.

On the other hand, it is risky to embrace scale at the cost of asset quality. British bank Barclays PLC and Germany's Deutsche Bank AG, among others, had made half-hearted attempts to get into the Indian retail lending market. Both saw a huge opportunity in the burgeoning Indian middle class and its rising disposable income.

Particularly after piling over ₹10 trillion bad loans by June 2018, most Indian banks have shifted focus from corporate loans to retail loans to de-risk their balance sheets. IndusInd Bank MD and CEO, Romesh Sobti, feels some of the Indian banks may have problem with their retail assets which they have grown in the past few years after a part of their corporate loans turned sour.

As the economy grew at an average of 9.5% for three

successive fiscal years between 2005 and 2007, millions of individuals rushed to borrow money to buy homes and cars. Money was cheap and inflation, relatively low. There was a surge in personal loans and issue of credit cards—both in the category of unsecured loans.

But every bank wasn't successful in seizing the opportunity. Barclays had to pull out of the retail business and Deutsche Bank couldn't make much progress even though it was its second coming in this space in India after an unsuccessful entry earlier. Citibank, too, could not handle its retail business with care. Its non-banking finance arm, CitiFinancial Consumer Finance India Ltd., crumbled under the burden of rising bad assets, with many branches downing shutters and people retrenched. Even ICICI Bank, undisputedly a pioneer in retail banking, had to apply the brakes as bad assets grew.

The unsecured part of the retail business is particularly vulnerable. Overtly aggressive banks sold credit cards and personal loans as if there was no tomorrow. In most cases, they were sold not by the banks' staff but by the so-called direct sales agents who did not care much about the quality of the borrowers and their ability to repay. Their focus is always on the numbers as the commission comes from the number of customers and not the volume of business.

With many such customers the banks did not have any other relationship.

When customers started defaulting in a slowing economy after the 2008 collapse of iconic US investment bank Lehman Brothers Holdings Inc. and an unprecedented global credit crunch that followed as banks stopped trusting each other and stopped lending in the inter-bank market, many banks were left holding the can.

There were instances when banks' collection agents were beaten up or legal suits filed against them for alleged coercive recovery practices. Many banks abandoned the space and others slowed the business considerably. HDFC Bank quietly stepped up its presence, using the wisdom of others who had burnt their fingers in retail business.

But that's a story of this decade. In 1998, when HDFC Bank wanted to start retail, it felt it must extend its reach beyond the metros. "We wanted to go into the interiors, though then this only meant adding about 100 more branches to our existing 50," Aditya said.

In the first year, it got just 12 branch licences. By the third year when it decided to start the retail business, Vinod was made responsible for branch expansion. He was involved in setting up at least 500 branches. For every branch, he would select a location after a survey by the marketing people.

He also drafted a four-page template on why a particular location in a particular city or town was selected. "I had to justify [the location] as the licences were scarce," Vinod said. This system is still in vogue when the bank opens new branches even though the branch licence system is not there; the banks just need to keep RBI informed about it.

Indeed, the scale was different in the late 1990s but one thing was very clear—the liability side of the bank's balance sheet should be partly retail and partly wholesale. This is simply because a bank cannot totally depend on wholesale funding. Good deposits will come only if a complete range is offered to the customers. Otherwise, customers will come but not stick around. Products and a distribution network are essential ingredients for success.

Losses are Natural in the First Few Years

Again, in retail banking, losses are natural in the first three or four years. But the way HDFC Bank's shares were quoted at that time, the market was not willing to give it any concession. So, it had to grow the profitability of corporate business more than the market expectation to cover up the retail losses.

"It's not entirely wrong to say that by three years of age, when we were a toddler, we had actually become an adult in our field. We had the systems, the products, the brand. Now more success depended on the efficiency of our execution skills and God's grace," Aditya said.

Till HDFC Bank started the retail business, the boss did not know the 'R' of retail. Aditya was an out-and-out corporate banker. Some say Aditya's retail vision was influenced by that of Jerry Rao, Aditya's colleague in Citibank, who had been heading Consumer Banking when Aditya was heading Corporate Banking. He was convinced that retail gives sticky income and investors like retail. Which came first is anybody's guess.

Globally, investors give much better multiple for retail earnings than for wholesale earnings because wholesale earnings are considered risky, volatile and uncertain, while retail earnings are sticky and long term.

Creating Maximum Value

Whether or not he would admit it, at one stage, Aditya did want to maximize the valuation of HDFC Bank and he knew the retail business would do the trick. Unlike in corporate lending, the risks are well spread out in retail and a bank can never sink because of one or two bad borrowers.

At an internal meeting, Aditya, by then a complete retail convert, made this statement: "I want to make money on every transaction, every payment that happens in this country. If I am an efficient provider of transactional services of both retail and corporate side[s of the business], I can make money on every card swipe and every fund transfer. I want that."

An offshoot of Transactional Banking is the Financial Institutional Group, formed in 2002–03, under Harish.

The target was the government business. Harish kicked off the business by signing an agreement with Life Insurance Corporation of India for handling its cash management. Then he set his eyes on collection of income tax, a business done by only state-run banks till then.

Harish went to Delhi and met Ravi Kant, then Chairman of the Central Board of Direct Taxes (CBDT), and asked for a slice of the pie. Kant liked his presentation but left the decision to his accounts department—the Controller General of Accounts (CGA), the accounting authority for all departments of the CBDT.

Harish repeated the same presentation to the CGA, and was asked to make yet another presentation after three months by when CGA's new conference room would be ready.

At that time, they used to get money from nationalized banks after 15 days. "Can your bank give us the money in five days?" the CGA asked Harish. Without batting an eyelid, Harish said yes. He was very keen to get the government business.

The CGA asked him to cut it to four days. Harish agreed.

Amazed, the CGA then made the point that if HDFC Bank failed to deliver, it would be penalized. Harish agreed. "That's our USP."

By the time the CBDT agreed to issue the letter, Kant had retired. The RBI opposed the plan and it became a sort of turf war between the regulator and the tax authorities.

"Who's the CGA to take a call on which bank will collect tax?"

"Who's the RBI to tell us what to do?"

Finally, the CGA issued the letter but asked the bank to get an authorization from the RBI.

Today, HDFC Bank is the second-largest collector of direct tax after SBI. In the fiscal year 2018, it collected ₹2.61 trillion direct tax and ₹850 billion indirect tax. In addition to taxes and duties collected on behalf of several state governments, it has also collected ₹1.01 trillion goods and services tax or

GST—a nationwide consumption tax on the supply of goods and services, introduced in July 2017. The bank earns a minuscule commission but gets one-day free money or float.

People such as Neeraj, who later headed the retail business, must have played a role in influencing Aditya, but a big contributing factor to his belief in retail was definitely the fact that, from investors' perspective, retail could create maximum value.

Technology is critical for retail banking. HDFC Bank opted for the i-Flex product, which was then used by Citibank globally. The whole shift of the system, from corporate banking to retail banking, Vinod says, was done over a weekend, after Saturday closure of the bank.

Changing the Logo

Samit Ghosh, a close friend of Aditya and a former Citibanker, was hired as Executive Director to run the Retail business, but he did not last long. The first thing Samit did was to change the logo of the bank. The original logo was black–red–white, similar to that of HDFC. Samit changed it to blue–red–white. Everybody loved the new logo, but Samit could not do much beyond that as he had serious differences in terms of business strategy with his friend-turned-boss, Aditya. After a brief turbulent time, Vinod asked Samit to leave.

Samit and Aditya had been trainees together in Citibank and Samit's wife too was a Citibanker. He had left Citibank (where he was heading Retail) and was working with Standard Chartered Bank in the Middle East when he approached Aditya for a job as he wanted to come back to India.

"I told him 'we have been friends for so long and I'm not sure how it will work, I being your boss.' I was not very keen," Aditya explained.

So why did they part ways? "He had different ideas of the

way the bank should grow and I had different ideas. It was better that we parted and remained friends. The differences were on cost, on the target market segment and even on how the bank should look. He was bringing Citi [bank] here and I was setting up HDFC Bank."

Samit, Founder and Managing Director of Bengaluru-based Ujjivan Small Finance Bank Ltd., has a slightly different story to tell. "The new logo was not my only contribution to the bank. In fact, Aditya chose the colour of the logo. I set up the ATM network, telephone banking and the basic infrastructure for retail banking. We were targeting savings bank accounts aggressively to get low-cost money," he said.

Samit claims that he was doing well in Dubai as the Regional Head of South Asia and the Middle East for Retail Banking in Standard Chartered Bank but as a Citibanker and an outsider, he faced a lot of opposition within the bank and that frustrated him.

In HDFC Bank, he was the only executive director who was operating out of Bengaluru where he was building his house. Besides, his three children were studying at the Kodaikanal International School in Tamil Nadu, some 300 kilometres from Bengaluru but closer than the distance from Mumbai.

"Retail is a high-profile business... You're always in the public glare. Many of my colleagues didn't like that and I became a victim of politics. That was the worst time in my career. I left an overseas job to set up the retail business in the bank but I had to leave within two years. It was shocking," he told me.

Samit joined Bank Muscat as India CEO and remained there for six years till the bank merged with Centurion BoP and the merged entity was eventually gobbled up by HDFC Bank. Later, he set up a microfinance entity which has been transformed into a small finance bank.

Samit and Aditya are still friends, though the old warmth may have waned. HDFC Bank is one of the principal bankers for Ujjivan. "Aditya is the best corporate banker I have come across in my career," Samit says.

The Retail Push

Neeraj Swaroop gave the real push. Before Neeraj joined, J. K. Basu—an ex-Grindlays person—was heading Branch Banking. Neeraj joined as Head of Marketing, Products and Retail Business in 1999. He came from Bank of America where he was part of a team, setting up the retail business in India.

Like many retail bankers, Neeraj too had a background in the Fast-Moving Consumer Goods (FMCG) industry. He had worked with Ponds (India) Ltd., which later merged with Hindustan Unilever, for nine years. At IIM-A, he had turned down offers from banks as he found banking boring then.

"Aditya gave me a lot of space. I enjoyed setting up business after business. We started recruiting the team, giving retail loans, loans against shares, loans for cars, two-wheelers, commercial vehicles and credit cards," Neeraj recollects.

The only business in the retail space where the bank could not enter was home loans as its promoter HDFC, India's oldest mortgage company, had reservations about the bank competing with its parent, though HDFC Bank investors were keen to see it have this product in its retail portfolio, a product that its peers ICICI Bank and SBI were selling aggressively. They worked out a formula to solve the issue. The bank started sourcing housing loans for HDFC with the right to buy-back up to 70% of such loans. (More on this in the section, 'Fighting the Promoter', Chapter 17)

Selling Underwear from Bank Branches

After settling down, Neeraj wanted to set up a sales company. At that time, all foreign banks used direct sales agents for new customer acquisition. Neeraj wanted a subsidiary, a sales company that would source retail loans for the bank exclusively.

His logic for having an exclusive sales outfit ran like this: The direct sales agent outfit would never jack up the acquisition cost as, being a subsidiary, it would not get offers from competing banks. So, the bank wouldn't have the risk of distribution going out to somebody else. But creating a legal vehicle wasn't easy—it involved hiring people, managing the governance and running it.

There was stiff opposition from others. "We are a respected bank, not an FMCG company. Tomorrow, will we sell underwear from our branches?" Vinod remarked. Even the RBI was not particularly enamoured of the idea. But Aditya backed it, overruling all opposition.

This way, HBL Global Pvt. Ltd. was set up, the first by any bank in India. Aditya pushed Neeraj hard to open more HBL branches than what Neeraj was able to. At one point, the outfit had almost 30,000 people. They are 'feet on the street', not sourcing customers in the branches but going out and selling credit cards, auto loans and so on. It has been merged with the bank's wholly owned subsidiary, HDB Financial Services Ltd., a non-deposit taking non-bank finance company. (More on this in Chapter 17).

The sales company transformed the pace of growth of the retail business. "Once he is convinced that someone has a good idea, he always wants to go faster and faster. He can also withdraw very quickly if he feels you're failing," Neeraj says of Aditya.

After JK left and Times Bank merged with HDFC Bank, Neeraj was made Head of Retail. Uma Krishnan, Head of

Retail at Times Bank, was given JK's portfolio—branch banking. But Uma, also from Grindlays like JK, quit and Neeraj became the boss of the entire retail business.

In some sense, HDFC Securities Ltd. was also part of the larger retail business. Aseem Dhru built the securities outfit. The securities company has a lot of synergies with the bank as it focuses on retail business and does institutional broking to a limited extent. The bank's Retail team leverages HDFC Securities' partnership, cross-sells products and offers three-in-one accounts (savings, demat and online broking—all in one) just like ICICI Bank does.

HDFC Bank is either the leader or a close second in whatever retail products it offers. Its retail balance sheet is bigger than ICICI Bank, which had started the retail business ahead of all others. About 50% of HDFC Bank's assets are retail assets and no other bank has that. As a business philosophy, it exits any business that fails to capture any of the top three slots in a few years. Small ticket personal loan is one such business. HDFC Bank dropped it as it could not make much progress. Similarly, in 1996–97, it started investment banking but abandoned the business as it did not progress well, only to revive it much later in 2010–11.

Two-wheeler and Auto Loans

Today HDFC Bank disburses close to 675,000 car loans and at least 1 million two-wheeler loans in a year. Over 20% of this is disbursed digitally. This is backed with a customer retention strategy, by way of offering products like top-up loans and loans for upgrade.

The story for automobile financing was very different in the beginning. Ashok Khanna who heads the Vehicle Loan Financing Division, had spent the initial years of his career in the automobile industry with Firestone Tyres, Toyota Motor

Corporation in the Middle East, Kinetic Engineering Ltd. and Kinetic Honda.

He joined HDFC Bank in 2002 after a stint with Centurion Bank Ltd. with a mandate to start the two-wheeler financing business. Those days the bank was conservative, finding its feet in the retail loan space, approving only two out of ten loan proposals.

Ashok's vision centred around the fact that this business had to be processed at great speed and efficiency at the dealer counter, which would ultimately lead to scale. His first task was to change the mindset of the people internally who were cagey about customer quality.

Slowly but surely, the effort has paid off, and the two-wheeler business is now rock solid, built for scale with state-of-the-art processes and country wide distribution. Now the bank sources customers through its branches, alternate channels and to a great extent online aggregators, something unheard of previously for this segment in the industry.

In the first year after Ashok joined, HDFC Bank was disbursing about 1,000 two-wheeler loans a month in cities and major towns. Ashok's first job was to convince his seniors to come out of their cabins and feel the market. He took them to Agricultural Produce Marketing Committee (APMC) market at Vashi, Navi Mumbai, and introduced them to the mathadis—a community engaged as labourers for loading and unloading goods. Many of them love to zoom around on their bikes in evening.

Why can't the bank give them two-wheeler loans as they earn a decent income to pay the EMIs, Ashok wondered. The loan book started growing from 1,000 mopeds to 2,000–3,000 mopeds a month; in 2002, the loans were given for approximately 30,000 mopeds.

Although they had a book of 55,000 two-wheeler loans in 2003, the business was yet to break even and this continued till 2008. Many of Ashok's colleagues asked Aditya why he allowed

Ashok to burn so much money. For Aditya, it was investment in a new business which the bank did not know well.

The biggest cost for the bank was customer acquisition. There was fierce competition for market share and the dealers were typically paid 4–5% of the loan amount as incentives. Some private banks were also offering additional incentives in the form of salary to the counter staff of the dealers and their telephone bills. Some of the dealers were getting a fixed monthly commission without any business commitment only on the condition that he wouldn't have tie-ups with any other financer.

In 2006, when the head of Auto Finance Division quit, Ashok, who was involved in two-wheeler financing and small-ticket personal loans, was chosen for the position. On 31 May at 10 p.m., Aditya called him to check whether the HR Head Mandeep Maitra had spoken to him. Mandeep informed Ashok of his new position later that night before catching a flight to Paris. Aditya too left for an overseas trip that night after talking to Ashok. On 1 June, when Ashok assumed his new role, the loss from auto financing was ₹850 million and on two-wheeler and commercial vehicles loans ₹500 million and ₹270 million, respectively.

The first thing Ashok found was that the lenders were paying identical commission to dealers for auto financing as well as two-wheeler loans even though the interest rates for auto loans was almost half of two-wheeler loans (12–13% versus 24–25%). And, in both the businesses, the manufacturers were dictating the terms and pocketing hefty commission.

In 2008, after the collapse of Lehman Brothers and the global meltdown, when most banks started exiting the unprofitable businesses. Aditya sensed the opportunity. For Ashok too, it was the right moment to discipline the industry. He cut the dealers' commission to 2% and increased the interest rates. Immediately, the business turned profitable. By 2010, it generated enough profits to wipe out the losses.

Around that time, HDFC Bank was clocking loans of ₹4.5–5 billion. By 2018, its annual disbursals were to the tune of ₹400 billion. It was giving 1.2 million two-wheeler loans and about 675,000 car loans a year—the highest by any bank in India. Its market share is at least 25% in car loans and over 15% in two-wheeler loans.

In 2012, the bank entered the rural markets for auto financing. Aditya and Ashok addressed a gathering at Pimpalgaon, a village in Nashik (Maharashtra) and another half a dozen villages in and around Pimpalgaon. On the spot, there were 150 applications for car, two-wheeler, tractor and commercial vehicle loans.

Aditya handed over the vehicle keys to the successful applicants. Called 'Mahotsav', such meets, sponsored by the dealers, have been continuing. Now the rural market contributes 10% of this portfolio. At every such Mahotsav, Ashok addresses the rural masses in local language (he writes his speech in English and rehearses many times before delivering) to a round of applause from the crowd.

Credit Cards are like Lux

Parag Rao, Country Head, Card Payment Products, Merchant Acquiring Services and Marketing, cut his teeth in the FMCG sector—Crompton Greaves Ltd., Cadbury Ltd., Hindustan Lever Ltd., and PepsiCo India—before joining HDFC Bank around the same time Ashok did. According to him, the credit card business is the Lux of retail banking.

Like a soap, you need a credit card daily, and it is the only financial product where you keep flashing the brand. It is the face of the bank to the customers.

Why Lux? Well, for glamour and sex appeal. The card gives you a status in your social circle. Since this is a transactional product, a person requires it day in and day out and the more it is used, the more is the interaction with the bank.

The business, at that time, was dominated by foreign banks and Citibank was synonymous with credit cards. HDFC Bank entered the market after SBI and ICICI Bank.

While there was competition, the bank felt the need to launch this product to engage with customers and strengthen its retail presence. The challenge was identifying the target audience. The business could not be made profitable unless there was a minimum scale; at the same time, they had to keep adding value for the customers.

They started analysing the data of their customer and offering Gold Card (to premium customers) and Silver Card (to others). The team had no one with prior cards experience across sales, business and IT. Parag himself was new to the sector.

A year later, when the bank started recruiting people from the industry, the progress considerably slowed down as the new recruits were extremely conservative on whom to sell and the target market. By 2003, they were across 20 towns but the business was not yet profitable.

At a review meeting at the credit card centre of the bank in Chennai in late 2003, Aditya had too many questions: "When will you make money? Where are all my customers? Why should my customer take another bank's card when I am offering a bank card? When are we going to ramp up?"

It was a stormy meeting. The key takeaway was: "Be cautious and end up like the other players. Or, change the strategy and be aggressive." This led to a shuffle up in the management— Pralay Mondal, who was managing one of the subsidiaries of HDFC Bank which handled the direct sales channels, was made the new business leader. Incidentally, Pralay too had an FMCG background (Colgate Palmolive Ltd.).

The new team set the target for one million cards (against 2,00,000 then) in 11 months. They used posters, conducted contests, held regular meetings to track the progress. The day they hit the one-million mark, there was a grand celebration, something rare in HDFC Bank. The business, as they say, never looked back after that day.

In 2018, HDFC Bank is the largest both in terms of number of cards (almost 11 million) and the value of transactions (one-third of the total credit spends in India). Spread across 600 cities, its market share in assets was around 52% (₹370 billion out of ₹750 billion). It was the first bank to reach 10 million cards in December 2017. Incidentally, it also has the lowest delinquency levels for a business of this size and scale. So, one can be conservative yet aggressive if one focuses on the key elements which drive business scale and profitability.

Banking Made Simple

HDFC Bank does not do any complicated banking. What it does is simple transactional banking. Take, for instance, the savings bank account. Common sense says people keep more money in a savings account, which is also a conduit for dividend warrants, transactions, bill payments and so on. The bank did not do any sweep to fixed deposits—something that ICICI Bank used to offer its customers—because that would have raised costs.

"Why should we do that? And shoot ourselves in the foot?" Neeraj asked. The sweep facility ensures that when the money kept in a savings account crosses a certain level, say ₹5,000, the excess amount automatically flows into a fixed deposit and earns higher interest.

It's not a returns account but a transactional account, which makes transactions easy but doesn't offer higher interest rate. That's the underlying philosophy.

HDFC Bank also demonstrated technology as a differentiator. It would advertise only those products that are technologically superior. HDFC Bank was the first to launch mobile banking in

2000 even when it was not fully launched in the West. It was not a great offering but the bank went ahead and launched it first to demonstrate what technology could do. It's another story that now it is India's most advanced digital bank.

Even on the corporate side, there's nothing exotic that the bank does. Every product is common and simple but executed well and serves the purpose.

The Risk–Reward Trade-off

The most critical element of the bank's philosophy was never to look at growth as absolute—growth has to be seen in the context of certain margins as rewards and risks one has taken to achieve the growth.

The bank wanted to grow from day one but kept saying it would grow the balance sheet, volume and market share but the growth should not be seen as an absolute. This is as relevant today as it was in the beginning.

If one is growing faster either by taking higher risks or by accepting lower margins—as pricing can be dropped—it is better to run a hundred-metre race. But the team was building an institution, a franchise that needed a strong foundation. It was hard to achieve, but the right thing to do.

The bank has done that over a period of time. In doing so, there is probably no customer segment that it has not touched—from a customer who is part of a Self-Help Group (SHG) and borrows ₹10,000–15,000 for a small self-employment opportunity to regular retail customers, small businesses, emerging corporations, large companies, institutions and government.

When one gauges a bank, there are three key things to look at—profitability, growth, stability. There is also a critical component of trust. One associates the concept of a bank with something one can trust—'you can bank on somebody!'

Globally, banks have never failed because of lack of technology or great products or people. One can live with that. What the failed banks really missed is risk management—they did not manage the risks well. Herein comes the understanding of the risk–reward trade-off or balancing of business growth with risk taken in delivering that.

When one talks about large companies, one may give up little in margin but one takes fewer risks. That lower margin can be made good by selling letters of credit, guarantees, cash management and so on. The less received from interest income can be made up by getting the rest of the business and still retaining the advantage of lower credit costs and lower bad assets because one is managing the risks better.

It may sound a bit didactic but in banking, sometimes, it is not only what one has done but what one has not done that can make a difference between failure and success.

The 'Eat Well, Sleep Well' Dilemma

Indeed, there are risks in every business. In fact, banks typically make money by taking risks. It's the classic 'eat well, sleep well' dilemma. If one collects deposits and puts them in government bonds, one has no risks but one also doesn't have much return. On the other hand, if one puts in one's last penny in high-risk debt or equity, one may earn handsome returns (and thus get to 'eat well') but one certainly won't be able to sleep well (with the worry of the risks).

HDFC Bank did two things. When it took risks, it didn't bet the bank on anything—something, say, that Ramesh Gelli did at Global Trust Bank. He played the money in the market and lost it.

HDFC Bank normally takes moderate risks and runs a highly diversified book. It takes risks only after it sees the dimension of each risk, appreciates how much it can price that risk, and ways to mitigate it.

At one point, a major issue was HDFC Bank having gone in for broker exposure, something that could be a major risk. Early in this decade, most banks vacated the credit card and personal loan business but HDFC Bank hung in there. When everybody else got scared, this bank got careful and moderated the growth rate but did not withdraw from the business. "As long as one can manage the risks in a particular manner, it's a worthwhile thing to do," says Paresh.

It's not true that they hate taking risks; they do take risks, but in a measured manner, and manage the risks. Paresh says, "If the bank is risk averse, it shouldn't be doing credit cards or personal loans. Even in the past couple of years when the banking systems put down their shutters, the bank was doing it."

In any business, a bank would have certain portfolios in some segments and geographies where it has high delinquencies. It needs to recognize that and react to that by changing policies. One can always make mistakes, but blunders can be avoided if one is aware of what one is doing and has constant checks and controls of a diversified book with exposure to multiple segments.

HDFC Bank's Risk Management system is strong because the organizational structure provides complete independence to the risk function, with the reporting line convergence at the CEO level. Jimmy Tata, the Chief Risk Officer, used to report to Paresh who in turn was reporting to Aditya. Then, there are Neil Francisco, Head of Underwriting and Risk Intelligence and Control (who left the bank in March 2019) and Rajesh Kumar, Head of Retail Risk Policy, Collections and Analytics.

In many banks, the credit or risk management head for certain businesses reports to the concerned business head. The independent reporting line ensures that both business and risk functions can interact on an even footing with equal emphasis on growth and asset quality. Besides, the business managers in the bank share ownership for the asset quality of their businesses along with volume and profit.

K. V. Kamath, former Non-Executive Chairman of ICICI Bank, does not want to comment on the differences between the two banks but admits ICICI Bank's strategy is entirely different from that of HDFC Bank.

"You can't compare strategies in reasonable short term, particularly when there will be volatility, momentum and a whole lot of other things happening in our own country as well as the globe. The growth designs that both banks have chosen are very different: One is significantly entrepreneurial and the other is focused on steady progress. The entrepreneurial path will create turbulences as well as opportunities which can be called path-breaking. I don't think it's right to judge either strategy because each might be more relevant at different points in time. Nothing prevents any player, anyway, from changing their direction and path," Kamath, President of the New Development Bank of BRICS countries and the guru of Indian retail banking, says.

ICICI Bank, according to him, has always set an agenda in everything that it has done and has followed that religiously: "We believed what we did was right and it is for time to see whether or not our strategy has been successful. If I had to set up a bank tomorrow, I would probably do it the same way. I've always been a very entrepreneurial guy and understand the spirit of enterprise."

Entrepreneurship is the Ability to Sniff Opportunity

For Kamath, entrepreneurship is the ability to sniff opportunity. An entrepreneur has the ability to recognize a lucrative area before anything substantial happens there, tries to seize it and deliver on it, and corrects course, if necessary, but is always keen to look for a path that allows the entrepreneur to grow faster than the system.

ICICI, the parent of ICICI Bank that merged with it, was a project finance institution. The bank needed to do something different to grow as the days of long-term cheap resources were over. So, it decided to get into retail. It saw the next opportunity in going global. After that, it started looking at rural opportunities.

This, according to Kamath, is the entrepreneurial way—a path-breaking approach; looking for opportunities and taking chances that others may or may not be willing to take.

"I go back to 2000, when there were less than a hundred ATMs in the whole country and we said we wanted to set up a thousand ATMs. People laughed at us. In 1996, when we were a project finance company, we said we wanted to be a universal bank. Again, people laughed at us. A universal bank is exactly what ICICI Bank is today. Largely speaking, it has achieved what we had envisioned in 1996, in an entrepreneurial way.

But by emphasizing the entrepreneurial way, I don't mean that the path taken by HDFC Bank is an incorrect path at all. I think taking a well-measured path and executing it is a good way to go.

Interestingly, the parent HDFC is an entrepreneurial company. Its founder H. T. Parekh is probably one of the most entrepreneurial people I've ever met... I got to know Mr [H. T.] Parekh when I started my career. He always had an idea a day. And at one stage, he singled out the idea of housing finance companies and promoted that. So, at the parent level they chose to be entrepreneurial, but at the bank level they chose to remain steady, growth-wise. In case of ICICI Bank, everything was rolled into one. I think that is the key difference between the two banks," says Kamath.

According to Kamath, HDFC Bank does take risks in the areas it does business and sticks to those risks; it does not stray. "You may question whether they have taken risks in that or not—that's a question that time and the success of their business can answer. They are growing handsomely every year, have carved a niche in retail for themselves, and are doing what they have immense expertise in.

That makes them neither boring nor risk averse. It's not a question of having made any mistakes or not; it's a conscious choice of strategy that they have made. As a competitor, I had tremendous respect and admiration for them," says Kamath.

Same DNA for HDFC Bank and ICICI Bank

Kamath also says that the root culture for both the banks is the same: "We get our cultural genes from H. T. Parekh because, for almost 15–20 years, he provided us leadership. The dominant gene for both banks comes from H. T. Parekh. If you look at ICICI Bank, the predominant genes we inherited were those of Mr H. T. Parekh and Mr [S. S.] Nadkarni. In HDFC Bank's case, it is H. T. Parekh and Deepak Parekh."

H. T. Parekh joined ICICI in 1956, a year after it was formed, and was its third Chairman and Managing Director from 1972–1977 till he founded HDFC. Nadkarni was its sixth Chairman and Managing Director, appointed in 1983–84. He also headed another project finance institution, the erstwhile ICICI's younger peer, IDBI.

12

The Entire Pyramid

The shift of focus or rather expansion of credit activities from corporate to retail banking was not sudden for HDFC Bank. It was a meticulously planned move that went step by step. After dealing with the top 200 companies, the bank targeted the suppliers and dealers of those companies to grab the supply chain management business.

The next opportunity it sniffed was in financing this sector—the smaller companies involved in supply chain management who already had a credit history with the bank. "Why not give them funding on a stand-alone basis?" Aditya asked. That was the genesis of the transition in 2000 from, in the bank's parlance, 'SCM' to 'SME'—supply chain management to SMEs.

"The initial focus was on the travel portals and auto ancillary firms," says Ashima, who built the emerging corporates group for the bank. Gradually, hospitals and academic institutions crept into the list as exposure to them was considered safe: Students' fees and patients' charges can always be securitized.

By 2006, the bank decided to go one notch lower, to companies with a turnover of up to ₹1.5 billion. This was christened the Business Banking Division.

In late 2008, the bank started looking at small firms too. Its emerging enterprise group covers firms in this bracket, with a turnover of ₹50 million.

These three divisions complete the ₹400 billion SME division of HDFC Bank, spanning around 15,000 companies.

The earning from this group is pretty good as, typically, smaller firms pay higher interest than the triple-A-rated companies and, if properly managed, delinquency is not high. In 2008, in the wake of the collapse of Lehman Brothers and the credit crunch that followed, HDFC Bank stepped back; it reviewed and reduced loans to such firms. It also got rid of some of the loans that it had obtained through the acquisition of Centurion BoP as these loans did not meet the bank's norms.

Companies hate a bank that shuts the tap when they need money the most. So, a few borrowers withdrew from HDFC Bank, but the bank seems to have no regrets. "We took hard decisions which many other banks didn't. If we had a loan outstanding to any company that we considered unviable or where we were uncomfortable with the management's integrity or transparency of information, we asked it to pay back first before giving fresh money," Ashima says.

She finds promoters of small firms extremely sharp. "The kind of wealth you see in these companies is unbelievable. They would teach us a couple of things on how to invest. Unlike professional managers, they deal with their own money. Their strategies are very different," she says.

Credit Filters

HDFC Bank's ratios of bad assets to good ones have always been lower than the industry average, both gross as well as net, after setting aside money. One of the reasons why the market gave a thumbs down to its acquisition of Centurion BoP was Centurion's relatively high Non-Performing Assets (NPAs), but the impact was not severe as the size of the acquisition was relatively small.

Deepak Maheshwari, who was heading the bank's Corporate Credit Risk Management, explains why the bank doesn't have too many bad assets: "Our credit filters are high.

We also deal with companies that have the ability to face a business downturn. We limit our exposure per account." The bank also always tries to have a diversified portfolio.

Going by its internal norms, theoretically, not more than 12% of advances should be given to one industry but, in practice, the threshold is much lower—between 6–8%.

The bank had very limited exposure to airlines, power, and real estate, the troubled pockets in the Indian economy in 2012. It had reservations about NBFCs too but that is much less now. In the second half of 2018, the NBFCs faced problems. With the rise in interest rates many of them found it difficult to roll over the short-term money market instruments, leading to asset-liability mismatches. There are sectors on the caution list of HDFC Bank but that is confidential and nobody discusses it.

It has exposure to flamboyant liquor baron Vijay Mallya's breweries but not to Kingfisher Airlines Ltd., which ended the fiscal year 2013 with an accumulated loss of ₹160.23 billion and a negative net worth of ₹129.19 billion. Many banks that had lent to Kingfisher Airlines restructured ₹13.52 billion of debt into equity, at 61.6% to the market price of Kingfisher Airline stock. The airline has not returned ₹91 billion to a consortium of banks, led by SBI.

"We pick up early signals. The moment we know a company is heading towards trouble we review our exposure strategy and collaterals. We may decide to hold, cut the loan exposure or even completely exit. We give the company time to find another bank as our replacement," Maheshwari says.

A company may take three or six months or even a year to find a replacement but it obliges. It is a smart strategy—if HDFC Bank were to formally announce its exit, the company would find it difficult to get another lender. Maheshwari recalls one incident where the bank made an exit but the same account came back to it through Centurion BoP.

The Exit List

The exit list is not very long. At any given time, there are 30–40 companies on the bank's watch list, not even 1% of its universe of borrowers in terms of numbers, and roughly a third are on the exit list. Both lists are dynamic. The companies keep shifting from one to the other and some borrowers even bounce back into the healthy category, rarely though.

Maheshwari has handled very few bad accounts—those in three digits. One of them at just over ₹1 billion was the combined exposure of HDFC Bank and Centurion BoP to Subhiksha Trading Services Ltd. The banking industry sank about ₹7.5 billion and private equity investors, including ICICI Venture Funds Management Co. Ltd., the private equity arm of ICICI Bank, and PremjiInvest, the private equity arm of billionaire Azim Premji of Wipro Ltd., had to write off a hefty amount.

Trouble for Subhiksha began in late 2008 when the company ran out of cash, bringing its operations to a standstill. The cash shortage eventually resulted in Subhiksha closing its nationwide network of 1,600 supermarket stores and defaulting on loans, vendor payments and staff salaries.

Premji dubbed Subhiksha as the retail industry's Satyam (Computer Services Ltd.)—the infotech company whose promoter B. Ramalinga Raju confessed to the largest fraud in India's corporate history. Media reports suggested that Subhiksha filed a ₹5 billion defamation suit against Premji in Bombay High Court in 2012. The court dismissed it in May 2016.

From India to Bharat

The bank's increasing focus on retail was driven by its aim to diversify its assets and raise valuation. Its failure to meet priority sector lending norms forced the bank to look closer at rural India. For the financial year that ended in March 2010, HDFC Bank miserably failed to meet the sub-target of the so-called priority sector lending norms. Loosely speaking, banks in India are required to give 40% of their loans to farmers, small-scale industries and economically backward classes.

Within the overall 40% limit, 18% should go to agriculture; and within this, there is a sublimit of 8% set for lending to small and marginal farmers even as the weaker sections should get 10%, and the target for micro enterprises is 7.5%. Banks that fail to meet these targets are punished.

For instance, if a bank does not meet its priority loan target or sub-targets, it needs to invest in the Rural Infrastructure Development Fund of the National Bank for Agriculture and Rural Development (NABARD). The interest earned on this forced lending is much less than what a bank can earn from other loans and is typically locked in for a duration of five to seven years.

In 2009–10, HDFC Bank's direct agricultural lending dropped to around 6% and it had to place ₹20 billion with NABARD, earning half of what it would have otherwise made. Aditya blew his top. When things did not change even in the first half of the next financial year ending in September, at an emergency meeting of all group heads, in October 2010, Aditya asked how many of them had travelled to Bihar, Jammu & Kashmir and the north-eastern states. Not too many hands were raised. "Lift your warm little arse and go there. We'll talk after you visit these places," he told them.

The bank's executives were reluctant to go deep into rural India, since retail lending in urban India was thriving, with more and more people buying homes and cars. On the liability side, they could always get more companies for their employees' salary accounts.

After Aditya cracked the whip, a group was formed and it was decided that the heads of every business group—Corporate, Retail, Products, Branch Banking and so on—be personally responsible for any shortfall in meeting the priority loan targets. It was made an essential ingredient for their performance appraisal.

Apart from commercial vehicle and tractor loans, gold loans and two-wheeler loans are the two planks on which the rural thrust was built. Then, there are loans given to shopkeepers and small entrepreneurs. The bank found that the best—and most cost-efficient—way to make its presence felt and reach out to the rural population was through loan *mahotsavs* or festivals where its officers sanctioned loans on the spot to credit-worthy borrowers. Till March 2012, about 300 loan *mahotsavs* have been held across India.

"At Pimpalgaon, once a villager came and asked me how much loan the bank can give against gold. He wanted ₹50 million. Can you imagine how much gold there is in rural India? We can monetize that," Aditya says.

The next day, the villager turned up at the bank branch with a few kilogrammes of gold ornaments in a gunny bag as he had to offer about ₹100 million worth of ornaments to get the loan of ₹50 million! For loans against gold ornaments, a bank keeps a 20–25% margin and considers only 75% of the weight of ornaments as pure gold to allow for the copper and silver that is alloyed with the gold to make the ornaments strong.

According to the World Gold Council, the value of gold with Indian households could be as much as ₹23,000–24,000 tonnes worth ₹54.5 trillion, 50% of fixed deposits in the Indian banking system in mid-December 2018. This makes India the largest hoarder of gold in the world. The gold reserve of the country was 560.3 tonnes in the second half of 2018.

Checking whether the ornament is made of gold is relatively easy, with the right equipment. The 'acid test' is done at the branches, using a small tablet of black stone, called touchstone. The ornament is rubbed on the touchstone to create a gold mark, and a drop of nitric acid is put on the gold mark with a sort of glass cocktail stirrer. Then a drop of salt water is dropped on the mark. If nothing happens, the gold is of good quality; if it turns green, it is of low purity; and, if the mark disappears, the gold is spurious.

The next question is about the degree of purity: Is it 24 carat, 22 carat or 18 carat? That again is not a big issue and can be sorted out with help from professional valuers. The gold business has low credit risk as the value of gold is always more than the loan amount, but there are operational risks: Every bank branch needs a special vault and a valuer's expertise.

Sashi says that even in Mumbai there is huge demand for gold loans. In May 2010, the business took off with a corpus of ₹250 million. In June 2012, it rose to ₹30 billion, about 3% of the bank's total retail loans. By March 2018, loans against gold jewellery stood at ₹55 billion.

Apart from forcing the bank executives to change their mindset, the other big challenge was to decentralize the operations and servicing—which was centralized—for faster decision making on credit proposals. So, HDFC Bank linked up all its branches across 2,691 cities and small towns with real time broadband connectivity as in March 2018—about 80% of them with a 2 Mbps broadband network and others between 1 Mbps and at least 512 Kbps connection.

The managers could now zip across scanned copies of loan applications to regional credit hubs as couriers would take days. Also, more and more branches were opened in rural and semi-urban India. Of the branches opened since 2009, at least 60% are in these pockets. RBI norms stipulate that 25% of a bank's branches should be in rural and semi-urban centres. HDFC Bank has 53% of its branches in rural and semi-urban centres—2,527 branches of a network of 4,787 branches and 12, 635 ATMs as on 31 March 2018. In February 2019, it opened its five thousandth branch.

Learning the Hard Way

Reaching out to the unbanked people, a business model that HDFC Bank calls 'sustainable livelihood banking', is something that the bank learnt the hard way. The bank started a Business Division for this purpose in 2005. The ambition was to directly reach out to people who do not have access to banking facilities. But this was not possible earlier as the bank did not have enough branches at that time.

To understand the business model, it was imperative to understand the Micro Finance Institutions (MFIs) that are in the business of giving small loans to poor people. They knew how to reach out and had a sustainable business model till the industry faced a crisis in 2010. But that's a different story. Some of the MFIs wanted to work for poverty alleviation, others rushed in with growth motivation and yet others, profit motivation. That led to distortions in the rules of the game: Multiple loans were given to many borrowers who took money from different MFIs but were not in a position to repay. So, pressure mounted on them to repay loans and there were stray incidents of excesses done by a few MFIs for collection of loan instalments.

In October 2010, Andhra Pradesh, which then accounted for at least a quarter of the micro lending industry, promulgated a law to control micro lenders after a spate of reported suicides following alleged coercive recovery practices adopted by some of the MFIs. The law restricted MFIs from collecting money from borrowers on a weekly basis and made government approval mandatory for borrowers taking more than one loan.

About 9.2 million borrowers in the undivided southern state (Telangana was carved out of the northwestern part of Andhra Pradesh in June 2014)—India's fourth largest by area and fifth largest by population then—defaulted in repaying money borrowed from MFIs, the largest number of defaulters in any location in the world. As Andhra Pradesh had a population of 84.6 million, theoretically one in 11 people there was a defaulter. This, however, was not the actual case as many such borrowers had more than one account.

By industry estimates, around 4 million people of the southern state—almost all women—had turned defaulters. As the female population in Andhra Pradesh was 42.1 million in 2010, one in every ten women in this state had borrowed from MFIs but not repaid.

The impact of the crisis was felt in almost every Indian state. Bad loans piled up as borrowers refused to service their debts; some MFIs defaulted in paying bank loans and banks stopped lending to MFIs. Typically, banks give money to MFIs—who in turn give tiny loans to poor people in rural India—to fulfil their quota of priority loans to weaker sections.

Since then, the RBI has stepped in, putting in place regulations for the industry, capping the margin between the cost of the borrowing and the price at which loans are given to small borrowers, and defining loan norms.

Following the recommendations of a panel headed by eminent chartered accountant and the longest-serving board member of the RBI, Y. H. Malegam, the central bank initially capped the loan rate at 26% and the margin, or the difference between the cost of borrowing and the interest rate at which loans are given, at 12%. From April 2014, the RBI removed the 26% cap on loan rates. The current norms say the average loan rates by MFIs with a loan book of at least ₹10 billion cannot be more than 10 percentage points over the cost of funds or 2.75 times of the average base rate of five large banks – whichever is lower. For smaller MFIs, the margin is 12 percentage points.

The formation of credit bureaus, the introduction of a code of conduct, giving Self Regulatory Organisation (SRO) to industry lobby groups, diversification of the products basket and adoption of new practices to focus on customers' needs have combined to ensure governance and client protection and created an ecosystem for responsible lending.

The RBI granting eight of ten licences to MFIs for small finance banks signals that all is well now with the industry.

To come back to the HDFC Bank story, in 2003, it had about ₹750 million worth of exposure to about 25 MFIs for many of whom this was one of the first banks to give money. By 2005–6, the bank had given close to ₹6 billion to around 75 MFIs. That was 90% of its viable finance business and the rest 10% was direct loans, handled by business correspondents.

These people are the retail agents of the banks who deliver banking services in rural India for a commission. Retired bank employees, retired teachers, retired government employees and ex-servicemen, chemists' shops, fair price shops, telephone booth operators, owners of grocery stores, among others, can be business correspondents.

From 90:10 to 10:90

HDFC Bank at that time was operating in 13 states with 60% of business coming from the four southern states. There were at least 200 business correspondents and 600,000 clients spread over 35,000 SHGs. The bank's ambition was to reverse the ratio to 10:90—10% through MFIs and 90% through direct lending, which could not be done at that point because of the lack of an extensive branch network.

By 2010 when the MFI industry was hit by the crisis, HDFC Bank's exposure to the sector rose to around ₹13.5 billion and the overall size of the viable finance unit was ₹15 billion. It shrank dramatically after the sector nearly collapsed but because the loans were mostly short term, for 12–18 months, and monitoring was tight, the impact on the bank's balance sheet was not severe. As of July 2018, its exposure to the MFI sector is one-third of its total exposure to small loans and two-third is direct lending.

The intermediation through business correspondents, mostly the Non-Government Organizations (NGOs), also did not work well as the NGOs put their own interests first. "They did what we wanted them to but also did some irregularities," says Rajender Sehgal, the former Country Head of the Financial Institutions Group. "Suppose there are 300 groups one NGO caters to and only a hundred are eligible for loans, they will not disburse the full amount to the eligible groups. Instead, they will cut their money and distribute it among others who are not eligible for loans. We found out such irregularities."

The NGOs started pretending to be the loan givers to influence the SHGs, and in certain pockets there were problems of misappropriation of money too. They took the money from the borrowers when they were repaying but did not give it to the bank. It happened in Odisha, Himachal Pradesh and Maharashtra. "There are a dozen-odd cases but as a bank we don't want even one such case," Rajender says.

K. Manohara Raj, former Senior Executive Vice President-Sustainable Livelihood Initiative, the CSR initiative of the bank, and Inclusive Banking Department, insists that it was a part of the learning process and the bank always believed in directly reaching out to these people.

It's possible now as the bank has more rural and semi-urban branches and the technology is creating the so-called last-mile connectivity. Eliminating the MFIs and, in some cases even the intermediation of NGOs, the bank is directly dealing with borrowers through its field agents and forming Joint Liability Groups (JLGs), which are slightly different from SHGs. Here, loans are given to individual households but the liability is collective when it comes to repayment.

The bank is dealing with the SHGs directly as well as through creation of JLGs. Unlike the JLGs being formed by the bank, the SHGs are entities that are already in existence; they have a track record and the members of such groups do not keep money in the form of deposits with the bank. The SHGs keep their members' savings and play the role of an intermediary between the members and the bank.

Rural Banking Initiative

To understand HDFC Bank's rural banking story, one must spend time with Manohara and Rajinder Babbar, Executive Vice-President, Business Head of Retail Agriculture Division. And, of course, Aseem Dhru and Michael Andrade who had steered the initiative. Both have moved on since. Rajinder started his banking journey as a clerk with Central Bank of India in 1988. After seven years, he had no choice but to look for another job as his long-time girlfriend Inderpreet Kaur's father was not willing to welcome a bank clerk as his son-in-law; he must be an officer.

In December 2000, one-and-a-half years into his second job at Centurion Bank in Chandigarh, Rajinder got a call from Neena Singh, Regional Head of Branch Banking in HDFC Bank offering him the job of a branch manager at the Patiala branch. Around that time, HDFC Bank was an urban bank, catering to customers in cities.

Rajinder combines passion with aggression. Once in 2002, with the permission of the police, he advertised for HDFC Bank on all billboards and canopies surrounding the Sheran Wala Gate where the headquarters of State Bank of Patiala (which has since been merged with SBI) was located.

Seeing this over a weekend, an upset managing director of State Bank of Patiala asked his marketing officer how could this happen. The Marketing Division of the bank made all arrangements to paint them back for the State Bank of Patiala branding on Sunday morning but by Monday, when the managing director returned to the office, he found HDFC Bank advertisements back!

Extension Counter at Army Cantonment

Rajinder also convinced the Chief of Army Cantonment in Patiala, Brigadier C. S. Harika, to open an extension counter of the bank there with a condition attached that the bank would have to build the structure. The bank lapped up the proposal as the rent was negligible. It immediately opened 3,000 accounts.

He was made Regional Head for Retail Agriculture in 2006. Aditya was keen to explore business opportunities in the virgin market, untested by any other bank at that time. The team was disbursing maximum loans of around ₹20 million a month.

Nobody knew risk management in rural banking. The risk intelligence control unit of the bank used to check the sites before funding. Once, a potato grower asked for funds but during the field visit by the bank officials it was found the crop was in its seedling stage; there was no potato grown and hence the credit was not sanctioned.

Similarly, if the risk officers did not find the buffaloes in the stable (when they went for grazing), they would not sanction the loan. Moreover, the rural folks were not aware of the bank and hence they would not entertain the sales persons. HDFC Bank was referred to as 'sheeshe wala bank' (because its branches had glass doors).

In September 2007, Rajinder along with Neena, attended a meeting in Mumbai where the business growth was discussed threadbare. Immediately after that, Neena put in her papers and Aseem Dhru took charge of the department. At that point, HDFC Bank was competing with nationalized banks and small farmers were provided a loan of ₹200,000–300,000 against a collateral of 10–12 acres of land.

The amount was decided, based on the area and scale of finance which, in turn, was decided by the district level technical committee. The loan to be given against the collateral of each acre was ₹20,000–30,000.

Aseem set a target for the group: ₹400 million in October— ₹200 million for the north and ₹100 million each for the western and the south regions. Everyone in the northern region was shocked. They took one and a half years to reach ₹80 million a month and now they had to achieve ₹200 million a month!

Rajinder's team did a portfolio analysis and worked out a plan to meet the target. Most of them did not sleep for days. The first thing they did was visiting the head of the Potato Association in Jalandhar which, they thought, could bring in at least ₹50–70 million of business. The head of the association, Jaswinder Singh Sanga, was ready to give the business, subject to a reduction in the rate of interest.

The discussion continued from 7 p.m. to early morning next day, over a bottle of Chivas Regal. By 2 p.m., Rajinder couldn't even stand on his feet and called his wife, and said: "*Maine daru piya. Pata nahin kya bol raha hoon. Business ke liye maine daru piya*" [I drank alcohol. I don't know what I am saying. I drank for business]. It was not his wife; Aseem was on the other side! Rajinder immediately disconnected the call.

By the 29th of the month, they disbursed ₹182.5 million Aseem was requested to extend the deadline by a day or two as they started late and had not got 30 days to achieve the target. Aseem agreed. There was a ₹20 million loan proposal pending with the Credit Team Head, Kaizad Bharucha. A farmer Rakesh Bansal had 270 acres of land at Muktsar, Punjab, but the bank was not ready to sanction the amount. Rajinder convinced Aseem for a site visit. Kaizad was on a flight while Rajinder's team was ready with all documentation to complete the legal formalities at the Tehsildar's office.

The Tehsildar (an administrator of tehsils or talukas also known as Talukdar) was persuaded to wait till evening beyond his office hours; yet the go-ahead from the Credit team was not forthcoming. Aseem was finally able to reach Kaizad late evening and convinced him to sanction ₹15 million.

Finally, the file got signed at around 9 p.m.

The Celebrations Did Not Last

The celebrations did not last as the target was enhanced to ₹300 million next month.

In April 2008, Rajinder had just landed at Mumbai airport with his family, when then Business Head, P. V. Anantkrishnan, called him to say Aditya wanted him in Chandigarh.

Leaving his family behind at a friend's house at Powai, a western suburb of Mumbai, Rajinder took a flight back to Chandigarh to attend a meeting at Mountview Hotel with Aditya and other senior officers of Centurion BoP which HDFC Bank had taken over.

Rajinder was to report to Centurion BoP's Pratap Singh in Chandigarh, the new Head of Retail Agriculture. Once the meeting got over, Aditya met Rajinder. Keeping his hand over his shoulder, he told him, "Don't worry, *main hoon na*" [I am there].

That was Rajinder's second meeting with Aditya. The first time when he met Aditya at a party in Chandigarh, someone asked him to get a peg for Aditya. He went to the waiter and returned with a large Patiala peg and handed it over to Aditya. "*Kaunsa peg banaya hai ye? Tereko peg banana nahin ata kya?*" [What kind of a peg is this? Don't you know how to make a peg?] Aditya asked him.

In Mumbai, the bank started the 'Mandi group', giving loans to arthiyas—small traders. Aditya was comfortable even if the business was not making any profit as long as the priority sector lending target was met. A new departmental structure was rolled out in August 2009.

In April 2010, Aditya called a meeting of the Retail Agriculture team and asked them why the business was growing at a slow pace. Like always, he asked for a presentation. He directed the Credit team and the Retail Agriculture Business group to work together.

The Business team convinced the Credit team to raise the credit lines per acre of land but once they were out of the meeting room, Neil Francisco, Credit Head, reporting to Kaizad, told Rajinder that he was giving the credit lines the Business team wanted but "If you don't perform and disburse ₹1 billion per month within a year, I'll screw your happiness."

In May 2010, the new Business Head, Anil Nath (who replaced Aseem Dhru) at a meeting in Chandigarh, once again at the Mountview Hotel, asked the Retail Agriculture team by when they would start disbursing ₹1 billion a month.

The deadline to achieve the target was October 2010 but it was met in August. When Rajinder asked for a party, Anil asked him "*Ab do sau crore kab hoga*?" [When will it be 200 crores (2 billion)?] Rajinder was shocked; they had more than doubled disbursements and Anil wanted them to double it again with a lean workforce!

In August 2011, when the team disbursed ₹2.48 billion Anil raised the target to ₹5 billion. They started analysing the data and realised that the post-harvest period (May–June, October–December) was usually when the loan repayments took place while loans are disbursed between January–March and July–September. Further analysis showed that in February the demand for the loans was at its peak.

The group started celebrating the month as 'Fabulous February' and put in all-out efforts for maximum disbursements. For the next three years, the disbursement doubled every February: From ₹5.5 billion in February 2013 to ₹10 billion in February 2014 and ₹20 billion in February 2015.

Their annual disbursements have also been on the rise.

These are typically five-year crop loans, to be reviewed every year. Banking in rural India has a different set of challenges for loan appraisal, disbursements as well as collections. To cut cost, a bank employee has to get involved in all functions—from selling loans to completing legal formalities. The head of a particular region has to sell other products like car loans and home loans beside crop loans.

The move to go rural gathered momentum in October 2015 with a programme called 'Kisan Dhanshakti'. The team was able to disburse 10,000 loans that year.

Sons of the Soil

Like most MFIs, HDFC Bank recruits local people who have a better understanding of the geographies, its spread, customer behaviour, needs and demand of the territories. The department had around 8,000 people as on 31 March 2018, and 35% of them were outsourced. Overall, about 19,000 people are working in rural areas.

Aditya believes in focussing on the customer, not the products. This means, a customer should have access to all the products of the bank. In rural pockets, one relationship manager sells all products.

The rural vertical of the bank not only offers products that cater to agricultural production but has also built a bouquet of products which can assist the bank's existing customers to meet their requirements related to auto and two-wheeler loans, loans against property, home loans, personal loans, etc. It offers a one-stop solution for almost every financial need of the customers at the so-called bottom of pyramid.

Along with giving loans, it is also doing other things to create the right ecosystem in rural India. For instance, in 2016, it started setting up Kisan Dhan Vikas Kendra (KDVK)—farmers' training centres for soil testing, financial literacy, digital literacy, crop plantations, etc. At a few centres, the bank uses mobile applications for the training.

As part of the digital initiative, a web portal has also been set up for farmers, offering information on weather alerts and forecasts, crop prices at various mandis, farm advisory, location of godowns, livestock centres etc. This service is available in vernacular languages.

The bank has also launched Agri Smartbuy, its marketing platform (more on this in the chapter on digital initiatives), enabling the farmers online purchase of seeds, pesticides, insecticides with discounts. The farmers can track the delivery of products through Whatsapp or mobile text messages.

Going beyond loans, the bank is also building the rural liability book. Starting from 2011–12, they have been opening an average of two to three deposit accounts for one large farmer who is taking a crop loan. The deposit portfolio crossed ₹40 billion in May 2018.

The year 2017 had been a tough year for the business because of demonetization, a spate of droughts and debt waiver announcements by a few state governments. Those led to a rise in defaults. The presentation made to Aditya during the year pointed out that the bad loans which once stood at 1–2% for the retail agriculture business could go up to about 6% by the year-end.

It is the only bank which had achieved more than 100% of the crop loan target stipulated by the Maharashtra state government in 2018. The business, which was initially started to meet the priority sector lending target, has turned profitable.

It designs products keeping in mind the need of a particular state. For instance, it funds wheat production in Punjab and apples in Jammu and Kashmir. Horticulture now accounts for one-fifth of the agriculture portfolio, catered by 53% of the total number of branches. It has created 274 vegetable clusters.

Milk to Money

HDFC Bank is also active in funding the dairy business. It has digitized payments at over 1,000 milk cooperatives. This is part of the bank's Milk to Money (M2M) programme, benefiting 415,000 dairy farmers across 18 Indian states. M2M aims at bringing dairy farmers into the organized banking system by digitizing the supply chain, with specific and customized products targeted at satisfying their banking and financial needs. Under the programme, the bank works closely with dairy co-operative societies and corporate dairies to provide banking products and services to dairy farmers, leveraging technology.

Has the bank gone digital in this space? For the Agriculture Division, charity begins at home. The team has created a pan India audio bridge and all the supervisory staff of the department are connected sharp at 9.30 a.m. daily. On this platform, the business head emphasizes the key priority areas and others share the progress and problems. All employees have a mobile application to remind them about their daily, weekly and monthly tasks.

A facility known as 'KGC Turant' (KGC stands for Kissan Gold Card) has been developed to provide rural customers with loan top-up facilities in 3–5 seconds. Farmer-friendly digital modes such as ATM/ SMS/ Voice call have been used for obtaining digital confirmation.

There are challenges in rural pockets—misappropriation of land records for securing loans, false certification, customers with fake identities, stealing of cash by intermediaries and frauds. Every year, a couple of relationship managers die in motorcycle accidents (they have insurance cover). And, of course, sometimes there are communal tensions and political interference encouraging the farmers to avoid paying loan instalments.

Besides, most rural customers do not have a credit score and it is not easy to know how much loans they have already taken from other banks, MFIs and money lenders and their capacity to repay.

Although there are very few private banks present in the space, the biggest competition is from the public sector banks and the local money lenders. The money lenders charge far more than a bank but they give loans on the spot anytime of the day.

How does HDFC Bank recover bad loans? It can always sell the land given as a collateral and recover the money. But that is done in extreme situations. Usually, the 'munadi' or a person hired to make an announcement in front of the entire village, tells a gathering that a particular borrower has not paid back. This practice of shaming the loan defaulter generally works.

While these loans are backed by collaterals, HDFC Bank also gives small loans not backed by securities. Manohara who retired in 2018, used to handle this.

Sustainable Livelihood Initiative

K. Manohara Raj's banking journey started with PNB. After 16 years, he moved to Times Bank to try his luck with corporate banking. When HDFC Bank took over Times Bank, he got absorbed in HDFC Bank's Corporate Banking Division. In August 2005, at a review meeting in Chennai, Aditya mentioned that the rural segment was untapped and the bank must explore an entry and long-term sustainability in the market.

Manohara had exposure to rural lending during his PNB days. They immediately started working with MFIs to understand the business. The strategy was to learn the tricks and traits of the business. The most important learning from the MFIs is their human resource management skill; they are not only able to get a large group of people but also inculcate discipline among them.

The borrowers follow what the MFIs tell them to do—attending weekly or monthly and diligently paying back the money. Of course, the business has its own problems which time and again resurfaced in Andhra Pradesh because of giving too many loans to the same customer by different MFIs and their profitability got hit.

Conceptually, the business involved the bank forming groups of borrowers or the joint liability group and dealing with one person in the group. This helps them save time and energy they need to invest in dealing with the rest of the borrowers in the group. It also helps create peer pressure in case a borrower is not paying up. Also, since the groups are taking certain responsibilities, it helps the bank keep costs under check.

Usually, the joint liability clause comes into play when an individual defaults. If the group is certain that this is just a short-term delinquency, someone from the group pitches in to pay for the defaulter. However, if a person has been defaulting for long, due to some serious reasons such as hospitalization of a family member which disrupts their cash flow for months, then the group does not come forward. The bank does not enforce legality against the group in such a situation.

The business is largely dependent on cash transactions; here more than digitalization, the branch network comes in handy. While the MFIs collect cash at the centre meetings, for HDFC Bank, one of the borrowers collects the instalments from the entire group and deposits the amount at the nearest bank branch. Also, unlike the business model of most MFIs where the borrowers' groups meet every week, the borrowers' groups in HDFC Bank meet once a month.

Manohara recollects one incident where the reporter of a national financial daily had told the borrowers in Rajasthan that HDFC Bank made them travel to branches and they were not served at their doorsteps. He asked them, why did they still prefer HDFC Bank? One woman immediately pulled out her ATM card and told the reporter that she had access to the bank's air-conditioned branch. At the branch, both she and the village sarpanch were treated equally. They would take turns in visiting the branch so that everyone would feel nice about it.

Why did the bank opt for monthly payments unlike the MFIs, most of which go for a weekly schedule? Well, weekly payments would increase the number of footfalls in the branch and this would increase the cost of handling transactions.

Credit-plus Approach

The borrower's visit to the bank branch also leads to the marketing of other products such as small-ticket vehicle loans and home loans. The bank conducts financial literacy programmes to inculcate the habit of savings among the borrowers. It explains to the borrowers that the loan repayment and scheduled expenditures like school fees of children and new clothes during festivals might become difficult in times of emergency; it is always better to save in advance for such payments to avoid debt traps.

The bank encourages the borrowers to open recurring deposits. Manohara says his team often questions how can a poor customer save when she is actually borrowing? His answer is: By reducing small expenditures. He even advises women to cut down on their cups of tea to save.

The bank also teaches the borrowers to utilise their time effectively to make money. Instead of spending an entire day on their cattle, a borrower can spend a couple of hours in morning and evening tending to their cattle and utilise the rest of the time to learn embroidery or making jewellery that can generate revenue. They can go to the nearby towns and sell these to earn extra income.

The bank goes a step ahead in promoting the sales by allowing the borrowers to set up small stalls outside their branches, local colleges and shopping malls. It runs around 200 programmes across India where 800 trainers teach the borrowers the art of embroidery and jewellery-making. They conduct workshops for two-three days for such activities where the borrowers are served a meal and refreshments and given a small kit of materials to help them in their vocation.

HDFC Bank runs its Sustainable Livelihood Initiative (SLI) in 25 states across India. It customizes these programmes for each state. For instance, in West Bengal, the training largely focusses on zari work while in Tamil Nadu, it is artificial jewellery and cattle-related stuff (what kind of food should be provided to the cattle, how to milk the cattle, etc.). Similarly, in Gujarat, there are programmes related to dairy products and clay articles, and in Goa and Uttar Pradesh, the trainers teach embroidery. The bank offers a bouquet and asks the borrowers to select one, based on their skill and capacity.

The family members of the borrowers are encouraged to attend the financial literacy programme as HDFC Bank believes that a family cannot run on only on a woman's income and efforts have to be made to involve every member of the family.

The biggest competition comes from the money lenders who are ready to support the borrowers in times of emergency. They also give consumption loans at a hefty interest. Manohara believes that although the money lenders dominated the space during the initial years of their business, consumers have been slowly switching over to the bank because of the transparency it offers.

The money lenders have their own space in the rural

economy and cater to situations where banks cannot step in like emergencies at night and personal expenditures but HDFC Bank is working to address these situations as well with medical insurance and hospitalization programmes.

As per RBI guidelines, borrowers can borrow from more than one MFI but the limit for each borrower should not exceed ₹1,00,000. No such limit is prescribed for borrowing from banks.

Many of the bank employees are involved in financial literacy training, capacity building and other such activities to help the women borrowers make their livelihood sustainable.

Political Environment

Indeed, political environment plays a significant role in this segment of business. Post demonetization, RBI relaxed the NPA recognition norms for the lenders but that was misinterpreted by vested interest groups and borrowers were encouraged not to pay back. Then, there have been farm loan waivers by many state governments. All these affect the business and create bad loans. However, these phases generally do not last long. The credit-plus approach of HDFC Bank has probably been the biggest driver in getting the customers back to the bank's fold.

In 2015, there was a huge flood in Uttarakhand. A village near Sarangpur, where the bank had lent to about 80 families, was severely affected by the flood.

When the borrowers in the area cited concerns about paying instalments that month, the bank supported them. It also made sure that all families (including those who had not borrowed money) in the village were provided with food packets. It did not ask them to pay back the money.

Although no instalment came for the next two months, the 80 families came together one day and resumed payment of instalments. The local government had announced a waiver of loan instalments for a couple of months and the regional manager of the bank was in dilemma on whether to accept the instalment or not. The borrowers wanted to keep their record clean so that they could approach the bank for fresh loans in future.

Manohara believes that the political scenario and natural calamities will always affect the business but it all boils down to the engagement that they have had with the borrowers.

Loan Appraisal Process

How does the bank choose the borrowers? The first critical step is to identify villages where they can operate. The field officers then visit these villages and invite as many people as possible and explain to them about the SLI programme and its benefits—they were not offering loans but a sustainable livelihood.

Many villagers back out as they are not used to this; they are accustomed to take loans and pay off. The field officer then gives them time to think and visits again after two days. During the second visit, lesser number of people turn up and the officer again explains the product and the group formation process.

On his third visit, the officer explains to them the purpose of the loan and enquires whether the borrower is already engaged in some activities or has some prospective activity which the loan supports.

It takes three meetings to form the first group and once that is done, the officer goes ahead with the KYC (Know Your Customer) requirements. This process is usually digital. After that, the data is shared with credit bureaus like Equifax Credit Information Services Pvt. Ltd. and Crif High Mark Credit Information Services Pvt. Ltd. which assign a credit rating to the borrower and offer information on whether these people have other loans or not. On an average, two out of a group of 10 people turn out to be ineligible for loans; the manager then evaluates the rest of the group.

Once the manager is satisfied with the group mix, the proposal is passed on to the Credit team which then visits the village to ascertain the status of the group. Typically, the loan is given only after a villager has spent a certain number of years in a particular village.

After due diligence is done, the loan is disbursed into the group's savings account. All the borrowers are then invited to attend the induction session at the branch where it is explained why they should take the loan, what they should not do with the money, how they can open a savings account with the bank, what is the rate of interest, what are the training programmes, etc. The bank employees also explain to them the repayment schedule and how it has to be done (at the branch). After all these, the money is distributed to the group in camera.

The group meets every month to solve typical problems, like a woman getting married. If the groom is from another village, she needs to be shifted to another group in that village.

Vital Statistics

The bank gives loans to everyone who is at least 18 years old, irrespective of the marital status. The average loan size is ₹20,000. The first loan is usually ₹15,000 and the amount can go up to maximum ₹45,000, depending on the borrower's track record. For SHGs created by reputed agencies such as Pradan authorised by NABARD, the interest rate ranges between 12.5% and 14% but the groups formed by the bank pay higher interest—20–24%. The average tenure of such loans is 18 months—the maximum period being 26 months and the minimum 12 months.

The mandate of the HDFC Bank Board is to support 10 million households under this initiative. The group has so far served 8.2 million households. The figure may reach 20 million in the next four years. The initiative currently covers approximately 40,000 panchayats with 850 branches in such locations. Each branch can cover up to 100 villages within a radius of 25 km.

The bank is adding about 15,000 villages every year under the initiative. It has a portfolio of about ₹51 billion and around 8,000 employees (out of 94,000 employees of the bank) working for this business which constitutes less than 2% of its balance sheet.

Although the segment had seen a move to digitalization post demonetization, the business is back to a cash economy. Manohara expects the dependency on cash to reduce in the next couple of years.

Initially, the bank had engaged business correspondents as permitted by RBI but over a period of time realised that the branch model is better to expand the reach. However, the bank is contemplating working with some large corporate business correspondents.

Corporate Social Responsibility

HDFC Bank has a small, passionate team, headed by Nusrat Pathan, to drive its CSR efforts which kick-started under Paresh's guidance several years before CSR spending became mandatory under the Companies Act. The bank now engages with around 60 NGOs which have expertise in natural resource management, sanitation, irrigation, education, skill training, etc. under its flagship Holistic Rural Development Programme (HRDP). A particular project is usually for a period of three years and covers a mix of activities. The NGOs are responsible to undertake a needs assessment and come up with a plan and its implementation. The bank funds such projects; the CSR team works closely with the NGOs and keeps an eye on how they are run.

Usually, the SLI team supplements the CSR team's efforts and maintains an oversight on such projects; and, even after implementation, the project is under surveillance for five years. The HRDP initiative is spread across 20 states and adds approximately 250 villages every year; it acts as a supplement to the Sustainable Livelihood Initiative. The bank spends around ₹4 billion every year on CSR activities.

In some sense, HDFC Bank is everyone's bank—right from the elite to the lowest level in the pyramid under SLI. So far, it has been able to make 8 million families self-sufficient. Every employee of the HDFC Bank loves to talk about it.

Aditya says employment in India is bifurcated into three buckets—educated and skilled, uneducated and skilled and uneducated and unskilled. The second bucket includes self-employed people such as weavers, wood carvers, people rearing sheep, working on farms, etc. They will drive the next growth story in the Indian economy. The bank is helping them become self-sufficient.

For the third bucket, which includes small shopkeepers in villages and small farmers, the bank is replacing money lenders by offering loans against jewellery, loans for consumer durables, light commercial vehicles, etc.

In 1986, when Aditya, in his late thirties, became the Citibank Head, India, Sri Lanka, Nepal and Bangladesh, his *dadi* (father's mother), asked him: "*Jungle mein mor nacha, toh kisne dekha?*" [When a peacock dances in the forest, is there any one to see that?] She wasn't aware of Citibank and it didn't matter to her whether Aditya was heading it or not. Her comment has a deeper meaning—one must do something which changes others' lives.

Aditya's daughter had also once asked him whether he wanted people to remember him as someone who ran a bank or made a difference to others' lives. That is when Aditya pushed the bank board to take up SLI.

Top of the Pyramid

While the experiments to reach out to the vast masses of unbanked population and create a meaningful business proposition are on, the art of getting to the top of the pyramid and even snatching customers from competition is something this bank does with élan.

The cabin of Head, Private Banking, Abhay, at the bank's headquarters has lots of plants and resembles a tropical forest littered with books rather than the office of a wealth manager unless, of course, he follows a simple principle that money grows on trees! Possibly it does. If one listens to Gayatri Krishna Rao, who used to oversee a cluster of branches in the western suburb of Mumbai, getting top-end customers does not seem to be a big deal if one is taught the right way.

Asim Ghosh, former Managing Director and CEO of Vodafone Essar Ltd., is one such customer. Gayatri managed to get his relationship moved from HSBC to HDFC Bank. When HDFC executives were going to Asim's NCPA Apartment at Nariman Point in South Mumbai to deliver the sanction letter for his home loan, Gayatri joined them. She managed to convince Asim to open an account with HDFC Bank.

That was the first step. Later, when Asim was changing his status from that of a resident Indian to that of an NRI with an Overseas Citizenship of India (OCI) card, he wanted to know some rules from the RBI. (An NRI with an OCI card is ensured visa-free travel to India even if he or she has acquired citizenship of another country.)

HDFC Bank got him the information in a jiffy while the other bank faltered. He shifted his account from HSBC to HDFC Bank without batting an eye-lid.

Another high-net-worth customer was cheated by his personal assistant. Gayatri and her colleague went to his office at midnight and, in his presence, dug out demand drafts and physical share certificates kept by his personal assistant without his knowledge. The personal assistant was arrested by the police for defrauding him, and Gayatri even became the prime witness in the case. The customer, former Chairman and Managing Director of Shipping Corporation of India Ltd., P. K. Srivastava, wrote a letter to Aditya, saying he has seen many bright and young officers in his long career but these two young officers were among the very best. Aditya's people bought his lifelong loyalty.

13

Merger, Merger on the Wall

Akira Kurosawa's 1950 crime drama film *Rashomon* opens with a woodcutter and a priest sitting beneath the Rashomon gate at the southern end of Suzaku Avenue between the ancient Japanese cities of Heijo-kyo (Nara) and Heian-kyo (Kyoto) to stay dry in a downpour. When a commoner joins them, they begin recounting to him a disturbing story that they had witnessed.

The woodcutter claims to have found the body of a murdered samurai three days ago while looking for wood in the forest. The priest says he saw the samurai and a woman travelling the same day the murder happened. Both men are then summoned to testify in court, where they meet a captured bandit, who claims responsibility for the rape and murder.

The film narrates the bandit's story, the wife's story and the samurai's story—told through a medium. Every story lends a fresh perspective to what had happened, adding new layers of truth and dimensions to complete the picture.

The *dramatis personae* involved in Times Bank's merger with HDFC Bank in 2000 also tell us different stories. Rather, different pieces of the same story. They are no less dramatic than Kurosawa's *Rashomon*. Collectively, they present the big picture of the most fascinating merger in Indian banking history, complete with the minutest details.

Let us get to know their stories.

Deepak's Story

"Ashok Jain [then Chairman of Bennett, Coleman and Co. Ltd., the promoter of Times Bank] was known to me. We used to play bridge regularly at [former Petroleum Minister] Murli Deora's house on Breach Candy and later Peddar Road in Mumbai. Jain would come every Saturday and Sunday if he was in Bombay. He always felt that his group didn't know how to run financial companies and told me to take his bank.

I was ready to pay cash and take it but he would never sell it for cash. He wanted shares. We kept talking about this occasionally on the bridge table. When he fell ill and was admitted at AIIMS [All India Institute of Medical Sciences] in Delhi, I got a message that he wanted to see me. I took a flight and went there. Samir [Jain], Vineet [Jain] and Amit [Judge] were standing beside his bed. [Samir and Vineet are Jain's sons and Amit is his son-in-law.]

He said that he had told all three to get out of the bank and sell it to me, but only for shares. I heard him; subsequently, I spoke to Aditya about it. Both of us felt the time was right for such a deal..."

Amit's Story

"Chase Capital, headed by my friend Anil Ahuja, owned about 15% of HDFC Bank at that time. Anil called me one day and said he wanted to discuss something. He was on the HDFC Bank board. I didn't know Aditya at all but knew his wife Smiley through Satsang. [Satsang is a philanthropic organization founded by Shree Shree Thakur Anukulchandra. It has hundreds of centres in the form of *mandirs* and *viharas* spread all over India and Bangladesh.]

Anil suggested a merger. He did not actually use the word merger but said something on those lines. The next day, I hosted a lunch at my house on Malabar Hill [in Mumbai]. By that time, Nimesh Kampani had done all the numbers because we were sort of getting into an equity agreement with the Old Mutual Group of South Africa and Nimesh was our investment banker. I had with me all the numbers.

We discussed the merger over lunch. Aditya knew his numbers and proposed a ratio. I calculated my own ratio. There was a small difference. I remember after we finished lunch and were washing our hands, Aditya said, 'Look, what should we do?' I said, 'Let's go half–half.' He said, 'Fine.' I told him it would be difficult to do a formal due diligence because everybody would come to know. Aditya said, 'I trust you.'

On a Sunday, we drew up the agreement, just a two-pager. The next week we merged."

Anil's Story

"One day Amit and I were playing golf at the US Club in Colaba, just the two of us. While playing, we did discuss the bank and the opportunity for Times Bank to merge with HDFC Bank. One person who figured out something was happening while two of us were playing was Rana Kapoor [Promoter and former MD and CEO of Yes Bank Ltd.]. He, in fact, actually commented: 'You guys are cooking something.'

It was a complicated process. I remember having meetings with Nani Javeri, [the CEO of Times Bank], and there was a lot of discussion on how the board would react to such a merger. Obviously, the key issue was valuation.

The defining meeting was held at Amit's house on Malabar Hill. We went to wash our hands after our meal and that's when Amit and Aditya said this was something that they should definitely try and do.

I still remember there was a final phone call that I made—I was speaking to Deepak Parekh on one side and Amit Judge on the other, and trying to get them to agree to the merger ratio because there was a range of valuations that were floating around. No merchant banker was involved in the deal."

RBI Deputy Governor S. P. Talwar's Story

"After Times Bank was set up, the RBI observed that there were certain regulatory issues pertaining to its promoters. We were not very comfortable with them. It was informally discussed with the chairman of the bank who volunteered to step down from the board of directors. In course of time, the bank was persuaded to voluntarily merge with some other bank."

These are different parts of the same story. Let's see how the merger actually happened. But before that, a word about Times Bank. Bennett, Coleman and Co. Ltd., which runs India's largest media house, The Times Group, was the promoter of the bank. The RBI approved the bank in principle in December 1993; the company was incorporated in July 1994; it got a banking licence in April 1995, and opened its first branch on D. N. Road, Mumbai, on 8 June 1995.

For the fiscal year that ended March 1999, it had a deposit base of ₹30.12 billion, advances of ₹13.12 billion and investments of ₹10.43 billion. Its net profit for the year was ₹270.6 million.

For the same year, HDFC Bank had deposits of ₹29.15 billion, advances of ₹14.01 billion and investments of ₹19.04 billion. Its net profit for the year was ₹824 million.

Times Bank's net NPA, a key ratio to gauge a bank's health, added up to 3.01% of advances. For HDFC Bank, it was 1.25%.

In March 1999, Times Bank had 541 employees, 35 branches and 34 ATMs, whereas HDFC Bank had 827 employees, 57 branches and 77 ATMs.

HDFC Bank had its IPO in March 1995, within two months of opening shop. The issue which was subscribed 55 times, got listed at close to 300% premium. Times Bank made the public offering on 30 June 1999—four years after it opened the first branch. Its ₹350 million IPO, at par, was subscribed six times. It was listed on 20 September 1999 at a hefty premium of ₹14.70.

Merger Reconstructed

It seems that Times Bank did sound out HDFC Bank and there were preliminary discussions ahead of its IPO but they did not lead anywhere. HDFC Bank had, in fact, done due diligence when Old Mutual was talking to Times Bank for a possible equity stake.

When the issue resurfaced again, HDFC Bank's Chief Risk Manager, Paresh, led a small team for another round of due diligence, quietly and informally. Usually, deals are made with an understanding that they will be subject to due diligence. But, in this case, due diligence—however informal—was done before the deal was closed.

So far, the RBI had brokered all bank mergers in India, mainly to protect the interests of depositors. In the case of HDFC Bank and Times Bank, the RBI did not play the matchmaker. So, nobody knew how the RBI would react to such a friendly merger.

Paresh's team had Kaizad, GS, Samir and Luis.

Five of them would travel together in a car and get off somewhere near the headquarters of Bombay Municipal Corporation (now known as the Brihanmumbai Municipal Corporation or the Municipal Corporation of Greater Mumbai), and then walk down to the Times Bank office at the Times of India building, opposite Victoria Terminus on D. N. Road. After getting off the car, they would walk down separately, pretending not to know each other.

Anyway, it was hardly a couple of minutes' walk and no one would be dressed like a banker, in striped shirts and grey suits. Even the driver didn't know where they were heading.

They were coordinating with Arun Arora, then CEO of Times Music and *The Economic Times*, and President and Executive Director of India's largest media conglomerate with interests in newspapers, magazines, radio, television, internet, music, multimedia and home entertainment.

Sitting in a conference room close to Arun's cabin, they would ask for all sorts of details, and Times Bank's Executive Director, Pradip Pain, would bring the documents in sealed envelopes. There were apprehensions about the quality of assets as Times Bank had a slightly different business model, heavy on retail and SMEs.

"What are You Doing Here?"

Paresh once ran into a lady who had till recently been working with HDFC Bank before shifting to Times Bank. "Oh! Hello! What are you doing here?" she asked when Paresh was about to enter the building. He mumbled something and almost ran to come back after half an hour. Nobody got a whiff of the merger till the day both the banks gave notices to the stock exchanges saying they were meeting to consider a potential merger—26 November 1999.

The positive factor was Times Bank's insistence on a share swap deal. "We were very clear that if there were things we didn't know that the seller didn't want us to know, he wouldn't have asked for a share swap. He would have gone for cash. They were interested in continuing to be part of the bank, but didn't want to manage the bank as owners," Paresh told me.

On 25 November, a day before both the banks gave notices to the exchanges for the board meeting on the proposed

merger, Times Bank's share price closed at ₹18.30 apiece and
that of HDFC Bank at ₹90 apiece. Both banks' shares had a
face value of ₹10 each. Since there was a price discovery in
the market, both banks felt it should be fair to go by that.
That's how the swap ratio was worked out—23 shares of
Times Bank for five shares of HDFC Bank—with a very small
control premium.

"Is Paresh Okay?"

Those seven days when they were checking the books, tension
and stress were palpable on Paresh's face. He was not eating
or talking to anybody. His wife, Sangeeta, felt something was
terribly wrong with Paresh. She called up Aditya and asked,
"Is there something troubling Paresh at work?" Aditya, in his
usual way, told her to relax.

The books were checked at three places—the Times of
India building, a lawyer's office and an empty HDFC Bank
flat on Napean Sea Road. "We spent almost two weeks in the
small flat, calling for all relevant files from the bank. Had we
sat in their office for long, people would have figured out,"
Samir told me.

Relatively new in the organization, Sashi found the secrecy
of it all quite amazing. On a Sunday, at a colleague's wedding,
he got a call from his boss Vinod asking him to rush to a
lawyer's place. For the next three days, no one in the bank
knew where he was.

Sashi, Vinod and Company Secretary and Head of Legal
Affairs, Sanjay Dongre, along with Paresh and Samir, did
the desktop due diligence at the office of Wadia Ghandy &
Co., at Fort, opposite the University of Mumbai. They were
trying to figure out how the balance sheet would look after
the merger.

There weren't any nasty surprises. And, on day one, this

was an accretive merger for the bank. In other words, there was no dilution in return on equity and earnings per share for HDFC Bank after it offered a stake to the Times Bank promoters. It was beneficial for the shareholders. The Jains got a stake of around 7.7% in HDFC Bank, which they sold in stages, making pots of money.

"Even after knocking off whatever extra provisions we made on some of the loans that we felt may not be good, we came out well. It was day-zero accretive for the merged entity," Sashi says. The combined entity had higher earnings per share—something rare in the history of mergers and acquisitions in India.

No wonder then that the markets gave a thumbs up to the merger. The HDFC Bank stock started hitting the circuit breaker almost every day after the announcement. Between 26 November 1999–26 February 2000, when the merger took effect, the stock rose, from ₹98.90 to ₹227.50.

"We Weren't as Bad as Projected"

Maheshwari, who was Vice President In-Charge, Credit and Risk Management at Times Bank in 1999, and went on to head Corporate Credit Risk Management at HDFC Bank, said the popular perception that Times Bank's loan portfolio was not as good as that of HDFC Bank was true only to some extent. The NPA ratio of HDFC Bank was better simply because it used to set aside money to provide for 80–90% of bad assets, something that Times Bank did not do. But gross NPAs of both the banks were in the same range.

He also pointed out that Times Bank had long-dated government bonds in its investment portfolio, bought when interest rates peaked. By the time the merger was happening, interest rates started coming down and the bond value started appreciating. That was a huge plus for HDFC Bank. The yield or returns for investors from bonds and prices move in opposite directions.

The biggest gain was Times Bank's 39 branches, about two-thirds of HDFC Bank's own branch network then. It was adding about 20 branches a year at that time. In one stroke, the merger took the bank forward by two years. H. N. Sinor, then Managing Director of rival ICICI Bank (it was still a subsidiary of the project finance institution ICICI), had told me that they also looked at Times Bank and did not find it attractive, but they missed its branch network. This was very critical when the regulator was not liberal in giving branch licences.

Maheshwari was reporting directly to Nani, Managing Director, Times Bank. He recalls being summoned by Nani one day and being told that the promoters were trying to sell some of their stakes in the bank and HDFC was buying a 20% stake. "I knew that the 20% figure was not correct. If they were to buy the bank, they would buy entirely. The MD asked me why I was looking so nervous. In my heart, I knew that the bank was being sold," Maheshwari said.

Maheshwari was not the only person at Times Bank who did not know what was happening. Sudhir Joshi, Head of Treasury, couldn't in his wildest dream think this could happen. Just a month ago, he had accompanied Nani on a three-week road show overseas. They were looking for ways to increase lines of credit from foreign banks.

After listing, Times Bank also took up a fancy office at Kamala Mills.

"There had been talks, but my sense was that had fizzled out. The African Group also came to buy a stake but it didn't work out," Sudhir told me. After (Ashok) Jain passed away, Nani officially told some of his senior colleagues that Jain's younger son was being groomed to eventually take interest in the bank.

Ravi Duvvuru, Head, Compliance & Audit at Times Bank

and responsible for all regulatory interactions also had no inkling of it. "I was facilitating meetings for Nani with the senior management of the RBI and the news of the merger came as a complete surprise" recalls Ravi.

An SBI Den

Times Bank was a den of bankers poached from SBI. N. G. Pillai, its first Managing Director, came from SBI. So did Pradip and Sudhir and quite a few other senior executives. Nani, though, was a former Grindlays hand.

There were people from other banks as well, but the culture was predominantly that of SBI. Suranjan Ghosh and Ujwal Thakar came from Standard Chartered Bank. Suranjan was to head Corporate Banking but later was shifted to Administration, whereas Ujwal was heading the Retail Business. Ravi Duvvuru who was heading the Compliance & Audit Function, was from the RBI. Ujwal left before the merger to join BNP Paribas NV, and Suranjan within three months of the merger. Pradip took six months to resign.

Nani was the first to leave, as one bank cannot have two heads. He was followed by Rama Sridhar, Head of Direct Banking.

But not all senior employees left the bank. Quite a few stayed back with larger responsibilities. Uma was one of them. Relatively new at Times Bank—she had come from Standard Chartered Bank as a replacement for Ujwal. Uma was made the Head, Retail Branch Banking at HDFC Bank till she decided to move to Chennai. As Head of Credit Cards, she launched the credit card business at HDFC Bank.

Mandeep Maitra, Head, Human Resources at Times Bank, was another senior executive. Maheshwari came on board to head Corporate Credit. Sudhir was initially made the Head of Financial Institutions and Government Groups but a few months later when Treasury Head, Luis, moved on, Sudhir stepped into his shoes. Anil Nath, Regional Head of Corporate Banking at Times Bank, went on to head Business Banking at HDFC Bank. Suresh Prabhu, Head, Money Markets at Times Bank, continued in the same role at HDFC Bank.

This is what Luis told me: "When the merger was announced, I went straight to the dealing room of Times Bank and I told the guys—I knew the treasurer Sudhir Joshi, and had worked with him in an RBI committee—I didn't want any of them to leave. I required people. They didn't believe me.

I told them, 'Just because HDFC Bank is taking over your bank it doesn't mean that you guys will have to report to the HDFC Bank people. I'm going to be very clear that whoever is best suited for that job will be running it.' But a lot of Times Bank people didn't believe me. There were quite a few whom I wanted to retain but they left. Almost as a tribute, when I left, Sudhir took over from me. That's reflective of the fact that we wanted to build a culture of meritocracy—just because someone came from the conqueror's side doesn't mean that he will always remain on top."

Maheshwari said that the HDFC Bank employees were equally apprehensive: "An army of people from another bank—and many who were better paid and more qualified—were entering their bank. This would hurt their prospects too. The feeling was mutual on both sides; even HDFC Bank's staffers were under some stress."

The HDFC top team did complete due diligence of Times Bank management. Ravi said, "The first thing Aditya told me when I met him was I have done a reference check on you and we want you to continue in the merged entity". Ravi took over as Head of Compliance for the merged bank and continued till he joined Kotak in 2002 to help them in the transition from an NBFC to a commercial bank.

It took a few years for normalcy to return. But Aditya was on the job from day one. The first meeting on integration took place at the Times Bank boardroom at Kamala Mills. The boardroom was very impressive, equipped with the latest gadgets. The HDFC Bank boardroom wouldn't have accommodated so many people. It's another story that the bank quickly got rid of this office as it was too expensive. HDFC Bank had its office in the same compound at half the rental.

Sudhir attended the meeting, and recounts, "Aditya gave a very positive spin to the whole thing. Till the merger, HDFC Bank was primarily a corporate bank and Times Bank was evolving more as a retail bank. He explained the synergies and the first people he took on board were from the retail segment. He told us how HDFC Bank looked at business and its strategy. I do remember telling him that we also have a lot to contribute and not all our strategies are wrong." At the meeting, Aditya unveiled the business strategy for the combined bank. "Aditya was very focussed at the meeting on the business strategy of the merged entity and gave a positive assurance to the senior team of Times Bank on their roles" recalls Ravi. "Aditya specially welcomed Uma and Mandeep and said that it added diversity since HDFC Bank did not have women in the top management," said Ravi.

William M. Mercer Ltd. (now Mercer LLC), a human resource and related financial services consulting company, oversaw the human resource aspects of the integration process. It was done systematically, branch by branch, employee by employee, amid redeployment, relocation of branches and large-scale resignations.

Typically, in any merger integration of people is as important as integration of business, if not more. The smartest move was making Mandeep Chief of Human Resources in the merged entity. By doing this, HDFC Bank sent a strong signal that it believed in a fair process of evaluating people.

"Marriage of Your Vision and My Provision"

When they were discussing the merger, Amit told Aditya, "You are a bank with a vision and I am a bank with a provision. My provision with your vision will get on well." He used to look after the NBFC of the group, Times Guaranty Financials Ltd., before coming on the board of the bank. A commerce graduate from St Xavier's College in Kolkata, Amit, a serial entrepreneur, is in the business of buying and selling companies.

There were professional managers for Times Guaranty but Amit was looking after it on behalf of the shareholders. He himself did not believe in the NBFC model though. "An unnecessary appendage into the financial system, something that should have never even existed," says Amit.

He also found banking very boring. Times Bank was not going anywhere because there was not enough capital and competent employees. Amit, who many believed came to the board with a mandate to sell the bank, scrapped the plan to sell a 20% stake in the bank to the South African Group when they came very close to signing the deal. "Mere equity partnerships were not the answer... Mr [Ashok] Jain had enough money to put in. That wasn't the issue. It was to get intellectual bandwidth as well as commercial capital and relationships. I put my foot down," he told me.

Incidentally, Times Bank was not Bennett, Coleman and Co. Ltd.'s first foray into banking. The company's first Indian owner, Ramakrishna Dalmia, had a controlling stake in PNB. He sold the publishing house to his son-in-law—and business partner—Sahu Shanti Prasad Jain in 1948.

Until 1969, when 14 major Indian private banks with a deposit base of at least ₹500 million were nationalized, Shanti Prasad and his nephew, Sahu Shital Prasad Jain, had a controlling interest in PNB. Shanti Prasad served as PNB's Chairman and Managing Director between 1954–1959 and his nephew was a director on the PNB board. The Jains exited the business in 1969.

Amit joined the board of the merged entity but quit after a year as he found the board meetings 'absolutely boring'. Before every board meeting, a courier would come with so many papers and he didn't even read them. Ashok Jain's son Vineet joined the board in his place. "Vineet never interfered," Deepak said. "The board was run very professionally," says Ravi.

The merger of Times Bank with HDFC Bank was a landmark deal in the Indian banking industry in many ways. It was the first friendly merger in the banking space and the first done through the share swap route. It catapulted HDFC Bank into the big league in terms of business as well as market valuation.

That's one way of looking at it. The merger also tells us that the banking regulator often did not pick the right candidates for banking licences. The RBI withdrew the in-principle nod it had given to CRB Capital Markets Ltd. for the eleventh new bank when it came to light that its promoter Chain Roop Bhansali had defrauded at least 200,000 investors and the SBI of ₹12 billion. But this alertness was missing when it picked up the first ten candidates to issue the licences.

In fact, the Parliamentary Standing Committee on Finance, headed by former Odisha Chief Minister Biju Patnaik, was not happy with the RBI policy of giving licences to some banks. The committee wanted to know why the RBI had given a licence to Times Bank. Apparently, the promoter of the bank had a sick company Rohtas Industries Ltd. in the group. (The report of the committee is not in public domain but an RBI official told me this.)

In retrospect, three banks floated by financial institutions—HDFC Bank, ICICI Bank and Axis Bank (UTI Bank renamed)—have done well. The fourth one, IDBI Bank, with which its promoter project finance company IDBI merged, hadn't done too badly either till the merger. By 2018, almost one-third of IDBI Bank's loan book turned bad and Life Insurance Corporation of India stepped in as a White Knight, pumping in money and becoming the majority shareholder. IndusInd Bank was a laggard till a new management, led by Romesh Sobti, turned it around and put it on a firm growth path. It has even taken over a large listed microfinance company Bharat Financial Inclusion Ltd. (formerly SKS Ltd.).

Among the rest, Ramesh Gelli's Global Trust Bank crumbled under bad assets after getting too bold in stock market play and was forced to merge with public sector Oriental Bank of Commerce. Bank of Punjab couldn't get its act together and offered to merge with Centurion Bank. And, Centurion Bank, renamed Centurion Bank of Punjab after that deal, merged with HDFC Bank. That story narrated in the next chapter is no less dramatic than the one about the Times Bank merger.

14

The Anatomy of a
Big Bang Merger

The 1999 merger was an appetizer for HDFC Bank. It had to wait for eight years for the main course. In February 2008, the boards of HDFC Bank and Centurion BoP agreed to the biggest merger in Indian banking history, valued at ₹95.1 billion.

Centurion Bank, promoted as a joint venture between 20th Century Finance Corporation Ltd. and its associates and Keppel Group of Singapore, was set up around the time that HDFC Bank opened shop, but it floundered till a group of investors led by Rana Talwar's Sabre Capital Worldwide Inc. took over the reins in 2003.

Rana, a former CEO at Standard Chartered Bank, is a growth junkie and a strong believer in aggressive acquisitions, something that cost him the job at the British bank. For Centurion Bank, he pushed through three acquisitions in a row, taking over the Indian operations of Bank Muscat in 2003, acquiring the Bank of Punjab in 2005 (becoming Centurion BoP) and Lord Krishna Bank Ltd. in 2007. The latter two banks, a new one and the other an old private bank, were strong in the northern state of Punjab and the southern state of Kerala, respectively.

After the merger announcement, Aditya told the media the integration would be smooth as there was no overlap. He also said that with a 40% growth rate, there would be no lay-offs. "It should take us about the same time as we needed to integrate Times Bank. Times Bank, as a percentage of our balance sheet, was much larger; we were smaller then. It was 35–40% of our size," Aditya said. Centurion BoP added just about 20% to the balance sheet.

The market did not believe him. The stock tanked as investors rushed to sell on concerns that HDFC Bank had paid too much for Centurion BoP.

That is a summary of media reports. Now, the real story.

There were tough negotiations for this deal and quite a few breaking points—even at the board meeting that gave the nod to the merger. The meeting at Ramon House lasted for 11 hours, till almost midnight. Aditya wanted the board to take an independent view on whether or not the acquisition was required. There was intense discussion on valuation and certain tax liabilities of Centurion BoP.

PriceWaterhouseCoopers Pvt. Ltd. and Deloitte Corporate Finance Services India Pvt. Ltd., representing both the banks, made long presentations to convince the board.

Rana Gurvirendra Singh Talwar

Deepak got to know Rana when he was working with Citibank in India.

Rana Gurvirendra Singh Talwar, son of a bureaucrat and son-in-law of K. P. Singh of DLF Ltd., India's largest real-estate company, began his career in the Mumbai branch of Citibank. He became Head of Consumer Business at Citibank in the Asia-Pacific region and the Middle East before he left for Standard Chartered Bank where he was Group CEO till a bitter boardroom battle led to his ouster in 2001. In his consumer banking days, Rana used to pick up tips from Deepak on mortgage business. "We weren't friends. I knew him as a banker and we used to meet at some parties," Deepak said.

One fine morning, out of the blue, Rana called Deepak and

offered to merge. The discussion didn't move much. Months later, Rana called again. This time, there was urgency in his voice. He wanted to do something very soon.

Deepak called him over for lunch at his house on a Sunday. Over Heineken beer and lunch, Centurion BoP's Managing Director, Shailendra, Rana, Aditya and Deepak discussed a possible merger and swore to keep it confidential. "They were in a hurry and for some reasons Rana was saying that either we do it today or he will go across the road," Deepak told me. Rana possibly meant that if Deepak was not interested, he would approach another bank.

Too many retail loans were going bad and they had to set aside a fat sum to take care of bad loans. This would have affected Centurion BoP's earnings and stock price. Rana wanted to seal the deal to cover up the March earnings.

A few days later when they finally shook hands, Deepak called Venu (Yaga Venugopal Reddy, then RBI Governor). Not too many in the Indian financial sector address Reddy as Venu and that shows Deepak's relationship with him, which goes back to the early 1990s when Reddy was with the Finance Ministry.

"I want to see you."

"What for?"

"Something very urgent and important... We had a talk with Rana. We want to take over Centurion Bank of Punjab."

"No need to see me. We are happy. Leeladhar [Deputy Governor V. Leeladhar] will call you."

It was around 6 p.m. and Leeladhar had just left his office on Mint Road in Mumbai and was on his way home on Napean Sea Road. Once he heard from his boss, Leeladhar called Deepak and returned to his office. He was heading the critical department of Banking Operations and Development at the RBI.

Other deputy governors called Deepak and said he had solved their problem.

Reddy's reaction was instant not because he knew Deepak well but because it fitted well into the RBI's consolidation strategy in the Indian banking sector. Centurion BoP was one of the relatively small and weak banks that the RBI was closely monitoring. The banking regulator was not hunting for any suitor but when Deepak appeared on the scene with the proposal, Reddy felt hugely relieved.

The Original Suitor

HDFC Bank was not the original suitor. Rana had first spoken to Deepak about merging his bank with Infrastructure Development Finance Co. Ltd. (IDFC), of which Deepak was Chairman. (IDFC became a universal bank in 2015 and three years later got merged with NBFC Capital First Ltd. and was rechristened to IDFC Capital First Ltd.)

IDFC's Managing Director Rajeev Lall had always felt the need for a banking licence to get access to the cheap funds desperately needed for infrastructure financing, but could not take the idea forward because the then Finance Minister P. Chidambaram, I am told, was not inclined to say 'yes' to it. Creation of IDFC was Chidambaram's idea to address the infrastructure financing concerns in a growing economy. It was part of his 1997 dream budget.

"How about merging with HDFC Bank?" Deepak suggested. At this stage, Aditya got involved. Till then, V. S. Rangan, then Financial Controller of HDFC, was the other person in the know of things. Rangan is now Executive Director at HDFC.

Shailendra remembers the lunch and beer at Deepak's home. "Deepak suggested a swap ratio to which Rana said 'no'. He wanted to improve it," Shailendra told me.

Rana wanted one share of HDFC Bank for every 23 shares of Centurion BoP. He was basically trying to squeeze the last drop but Deepak was not playing ball; they walked away from the meeting. After months of negotiations the deal was struck—but at a different ratio.

Rana insisted that HDFC Bank must agree to absorb all the people from Centurion BoP. Aditya agreed.

"Leave Off-site; I Want You in Mumbai"

Paresh was not in Mumbai. He was attending an off-site on credit at Jaipur, Rajasthan when he got Aditya's call: "Can you come back? There's work for you here."

Paresh sensed something. "I am required in Mumbai; something has come up. You guys continue with the rest of the agenda," he told his colleagues and took the next flight to Mumbai. It was a long drive to the airport.

Aditya wasn't in Mumbai either. He was on an all-India tour to review performance of all local offices of the bank. His colleagues call this the '*Bharat Yatra* [India Voyage]'. Aditya was in Hyderabad. After talking to Paresh, he called Sashi and asked him to look at all information on Centurion BoP available in the public domain.

Sashi picked up his laptop and headed straight to the conference room on the sixth floor at the bank's headquarters with his colleague Deepak Majithia. The security locked the conference room from outside. By midnight, a two-page fact sheet on Centurion BoP was ready.

Paresh was back in office the next day. Both Paresh and Sashi had apprehensions about the quality of Centurion BoP's assets. They were also concerned about the price at which the bank's stock was trading. Its price-to-book ratio was '4', equivalent to that of HDFC Bank. The bank was not cheap by any means.

Price-to-book is a ratio that compares a stock's market value with its book value. It is calculated by dividing the current closing price of a stock by the latest quarter's book value per share. A lower price-to-book ratio could mean the stock is undervalued. It could also mean that something is fundamentally wrong with the company. On the other hand, a higher ratio doesn't necessarily mean it's a great stock; it could also mean investors are paying too much.

Aditya wasn't yet back in Mumbai. Over telephone, he told Paresh and Sashi to meet Keki, HDFC's Vice Chairman and Managing Director then. Keki, Deepak's trusted lieutenant, was also on the board of HDFC Bank. On a Saturday, at Ramon House, they told Keki, "It's not attractive and it doesn't make any economic sense to take over this bank at this point." After the meeting, Paresh went to the Hanuman temple near St Xavier's High School at Dhobi Talao, his Saturday afternoon ritual in Mumbai.

Aditya returned over the weekend and joined Shailendra and Rana at Deepak's house for the Sunday lunch. Neither he nor Deepak were fully convinced but said, "Let's try and explore."

They were given just three days to perform due diligence. A team of a dozen officers with heads of audit, credit, legal and operations trooped into the Centurion BoP headquarters at Mahalaxmi in Mumbai to check facts and figures. They also appointed Deloitte to scan the tax liabilities.

On the other side, Anil Jaggia, Chief Operating Officer of Centurion BoP, and Amit Khanna, Head of Strategic Planning, were assisting Shailendra.

HDFC Bank's core team had two members—Paresh and Sashi. The duo met Sanjay Sakhuja, CEO of Ambit Corporate Finance Pvt. Ltd., and Ashok Wadhwa, the boss of the investment bank, at Ambit House, literally next door to the bank's headquarters at Lower Parel. Even then, they were cautious. Neither Paresh nor Sashi would give their names at the reception desk at Ambit.

For Times Bank, most checks were done at the lawyer's

office because on-site due diligence had been done earlier. In this case, they needed to check every minute detail in 72 hours. So, 12 of them would pretend to go on calls. They would be in separate cars; land at the same place but at different times in the evening after office hours when most people had left. Each day the exercise would last till 4 a.m.

50:50

The findings were 50:50. The numbers weren't great but Centurion BoP's network of 404 branches across India was a big positive. "If I were to superimpose Centurion BoP on HDFC Bank after cleaning it up, would the earnings per share in three years be more than what we would have done in organic basis? The answer was 'yes'. It made sense," Sashi said.

Paresh had a certain level of comfort with Shailendra being a former colleague from Citibank and HDFC Bank, but nonetheless he decided to go through the entire exercise meticulously. When negotiations reached almost the last stage, he switched off for a few hours. "I am willing to drop it," Paresh told Aditya as he felt they were asking for a little too much.

There was hard bargaining. Ashok of Ambit was at his persuasive best. Centurion BoP, according to him, was a right fit for HDFC Bank. Rana's objective was not only to maximize the profit but also to make sure that the bank's employees had a career. But Paresh was a hard nut to crack.

Both banks being listed entities, there was price discovery in the market but Paresh still insisted on a discount to the market price. Only when everybody accepted that—one share of HDFC Bank for every 29 shares of Centurion BoP—was the stock market announcement made.

Paresh's reasoning is quite simple: In a stock swap, had there been something drastically wrong, the other side would also suffer as they would hold HDFC Bank's shares. It's the same philosophy that clinched the Times Bank deal.

There were a few nasty surprises, minor though. The holes in the credit portfolio weren't deep but there were business-related issues. "Our impression was that they hadn't run the shop tightly. It's more related to processes and integrity at lower levels. Some branch managers were taking deposits but not putting the money into the system," Paresh said. Centurion BoP had done three acquisitions in quick succession but hadn't integrated all the portions fully. The issues surfaced from lack of control and loose supervision.

Four-Banks-in-One

The integration process this time was not as smooth as it was in the case of the merger with Times Bank as the size of the merger was larger. And Centurion BoP was four-banks-in-one. On day zero, HDFC Bank ensured that all incremental underwriting of credits was being done in accordance with its established norms.

Then came the integration of people. It wasn't easy as there were 7,500 employees, about a third of the number of employees of HDFC Bank. The solution, they thought, was to create new positions for both teams. No one would know whether he or she has gone down or up the ladder. Every belly button of Centurion BoP and HDFC Bank was evaluated to ascertain who was doing what and the actual work involved. Again, Mercer was appointed as a consultant for the integration of human resources.

"I was given the offer to join the board as an Executive Director. I told Aditya I would think it over. I was there till they formally did the merger. Frankly, after having left once, to come back again and do the same thing didn't make sense to me. My role was to get the thing done, not the subsequent thing which can go on for years—the closure," Shailendra told me. Formally, the merger happened in May 2008. Shailendra left in August.

Jaggia became Head of Technology at HDFC Bank after Ram left in March 2008. Insiders say Jaggia's package, including stock options, was so hefty at Centurion BoP that at least for a year his salary was frozen and HDFC Bank had to be liberal in giving options to its senior executives to maintain parity. Centurion BoP Treasurer, Tarini Vaidya, stayed back but left later for personal reasons. She didn't want to continue with a full-time job. Vivek Vig, Head of Retail, left as there was no defined role for him in the merged entity. Neeraj Dhawan, Head of Retail Risk Management, was made Head of Collections.

It took about a year to integrate Wholesale Banking, Treasury and Retail Systems and many employees of Centurion BoP left. Integration of two banks is very different from integration of two manufacturing outfits. Here, beyond business models and employees, millions of customers have to be integrated. Cheques, debit and credit cards, ATM cards, demand drafts—every single instrument needs to be uniform. If one messes up, one will lose customers. Centurion BoP had 2.5 million customers.

Technology was indeed an issue but there was no disruption as many might have feared. Both banks had centralized processing but with different vendors—Finacle for Centurion BoP and i-Flex for HDFC Bank. Finacle was superior to i-Flex's retail solution but HDFC Bank stuck to its vendor.

At the end of the day, apart from purely technical aspects, such decisions are driven by facts such as the number of people who need to be trained, the number of branches that need to be converted and the costs involved. HDFC Bank had almost doubled the branch network and three times the people.

The Markets Give a Thumbs Down

On the day the share swap ratio was announced, Centurion BoP shares, which had run up in anticipation of the merger, fell by 14.5% to ₹48.25. HDFC Bank shares fell by 3.5% to close at ₹1,422.70 a share.

Investors felt HDFC Bank had paid too much for the branches. "You've to realize that people were paying that for Centurion BoP as it existed. Its share price was reflective of the market perception about its business potential, branch network and the overall franchise as it existed. We paid less than what the market was paying. It might have still been high but we knew that when we would push it to our level of profitability, huge value would be created," Paresh said.

Times Bank was quoting at 1 or 1.2 times the book and HDFC Bank was quoting 3 or 4 times the book in 1999. So, just the arithmetic of the deal created value. In this case, underlying valuations weren't very different though the underlying franchises were of different quality. HDFC Bank's defence for the high price was that it wasn't paying for what was only there; it was looking at the merger as what it could make of the deal.

Centurion BoP was about 20% of HDFC Bank's size in terms of the balance sheet (₹1.31 trillion versus ₹254.04 billion as of the third quarter of 2007–08) and even less than 20% in terms of profits, but was 55% in terms of branches.

Region-wise, Centurion BoP had about 170 branches in the north and around 140 branches in the south. Most of these branches were located in Punjab, Haryana, upper Rajasthan, Maharashtra, Goa, Kerala and Tamil Nadu where economic growth is higher than in other Indian states. After the merger, HDFC Bank became No. 2 in Mumbai and Delhi in terms of branch presence, second to India's largest lender, SBI.

All for Branches

At an internal meeting, Aditya told his colleagues, "Don't go by the fact that they have low businesses. They have only two products, savings and insurance. We have all the products. With our product range and execution, we can build the business. You're getting the infrastructure."

Deepak admits they paid on the higher side but defends it saying it was for the branches: "To get a branch licence from the RBI takes time and here we were getting readymade branches." That was the case those days. The RBI since has liberalised the branch licensing norms for Indian banks.

On day one, on almost every parameter, including the three most critical ones, Centurion BoP was inferior to HDFC Bank.

HDFC Bank's CASA was about 47% of overall deposits, whereas Centurion BoP's CASA was 26%. For the merged entity, it came down to 43%.

HDFC Bank's cost-to-income ratio was 48–49% before the merger against Centurion BoP's 69%. On merger, it became 55%.

HDFC Bank's gross NPAs were about 1.3% of advances against a little over 3% at Centurion BoP.

The challenge before HDFC Bank was to get back to where it was on all these parameters and create value after the integration was completed. It set a deadline of 30–36 months for the completion but managed to get it done in 24 months. In two years, HDFC Bank got back to the pre-merger CASA and cost-to-earnings ratio level, and in three years, it covered the ground on bad assets.

This was done in a very difficult environment. Four months after the merger, US investment bank Lehman Brothers collapsed, leading to an unprecedented credit crunch across the globe. Economic growth in India halted while the outside world plunged into recession even as the government and the banking regulator joined hands for fiscal stimulus and liquidity to pump prime the economy.

For HDFC Bank, it was difficult but doable as it was a stronger brand, had a wider product range and had systems in control. As business flowed into the under-leveraged, under-utilized distribution network of Centurion BoP, the gap across segments was bridged.

The big difference between the Times Bank merger and the Centurion BoP merger was that the former was an accretive merger from day zero but the latter took three years to become an accretive merger. The stock market initially gave it a cold shoulder but that's the risk Deepak and Aditya took consciously—the biggest gamble that the normally risk-averse bank has ever taken.

There are critics of the merger even within the bank. Abhay is one of them. He thinks it was a very expensive branch acquisition. "What have you got from the bank? The clients were a question mark, the quality of the portfolio was not the best, not more than 10% of the talent stayed back...What does it boil down to? I didn't celebrate the merger. People gave me dirty looks," says Abhay. Of course, he admits that the merger hasn't panned out as badly as he had thought but he still doesn't approve of it.

After the collapse of Lehman Brothers in September 2008, one of Aditya's colleagues apparently said they could have bought Lehman Brothers for $1 instead of paying so much for Centurion BoP!

In hindsight, it was possibly a risk worth taking, to close up with ICICI Bank, the largest private lender then, and power the retail business. HDFC Bank has a much bigger retail portfolio than ICICI Bank though the latter had spotted the opportunity ahead of it and went headlong into the field.

15

Warts and All

*We are recognizing our obligation for accounting
purposes; however, it is clear that the company should never
have been put in a position like this as we relied on Bankers
Trust to advise us on these transactions. We have taken
measures to ensure this will not happen again.*

These are the words of Benjamin J. Sottile, Chairman,
President and CEO of Cincinnati, Ohio-based Gibson
Greetings Inc., the third-largest greetings card manufacturer
in the USA. Benjamin's comment came in 1994, in a filing
with the US Securities and Exchange Commission, after his
company discovered that it had made $20 million losses
for the quarter that ended in March 1994 on interest rate
derivatives transactions with Bankers Trust.

William L. Flaherty, Gibson's CFO, clarified that the loss
being recognized for accounting purposes was the current
market value of the derivatives transactions, as determined by
a Bankers Trust valuation model, based on the projected value
of the transactions at maturity.

Hundreds of companies in India—mostly small and
medium and a few large—faced a similar situation in late 2007
and early 2008. With the greenback depreciating fast against
some global currencies such as the euro and the Japanese yen,
their losses mounted every day. Many moved court against

banks. There have been a few out-of-court settlements and a few cases are still on.

In April 2011, the RBI penalized 19 banks for their role in the so-called derivatives scam. HDFC Bank was one of them.

The banks were penalized for their failure to carry out due diligence with regard to the suitability of the products they had offered their customers. The regulator said the banks sold derivatives to companies that did not have risk management policies. The banks explained their positions but the RBI was not happy with their explanations. The regulator was convinced that, indeed, the norms had been violated—and hence the penalty.

Before we start dissecting the derivatives saga, let's get a feel of the global perspective. Gibson announced the loss on an interest rate swap with Bankers Trust in April 1994. Under the arrangement, which covered a notional amount of $30 million, if the interest rates dropped Gibson would benefit. But if the interest rates rose, Bankers Trust would have made large profits and Gibson large losses.

Gibson made profits initially but was saddled with losses later. For financial sector observers in the USA, this did not come as a shock. As early as January 1992, Edward Gerald Corrigan, then President of the Federal Reserve Bank of New York and also Chairman of the Basel Committee on Banking Supervision, had warned of the danger of derivatives transactions. He did this in a speech delivered at the New York State Bankers Association.

Susan Philips, another member of the Federal Reserve Board, too, had warned the US Congress of the risks from over-the-counter derivatives. But not too many people paid attention to such warnings till Gibson announced its derivatives loss.

Procter and Gamble Co. followed Gibson and announced huge losses before filing a complaint against Bankers Trust, claiming a loss of more than $100 million due to alleged fraud.

The government of Orange County, California, declared bankruptcy after losing $2 billion in speculative transactions. It had invested its entire tax collection in structured notes and 'exotic' instruments. Its elected Treasurer, Robert Citron, who was heading Orange County's Trading Desk, was dealing with several brokerages, including Merrill Lynch.

Other municipalities and educational institutions also lost hugely in derivatives trading in the mid-1990s when structured instruments such as death-backed bonds, worthless warrants, heaven and hell bonds, exploding options, sushis, down-unders and kiwis flooded the USA market. The profit-to-loss ratio enjoyed by the derivatives dealers in the USA in early 1990 was 2,000:1, but that dramatically changed after the Gibson disclosure.

First Derivatives Loss in India

In India, the first time the media reported derivatives loss of a company was in 2006 when the Food Corporation of India—which lends price support to safeguard the interest of farmers, distributes food grains and is responsible for ensuring national food security—suffered a loss in its swap transaction with a British bank. Being a state-run company, it did not hide its losses, but hundreds of small and medium companies that bought such products from banks were tight-lipped about their transactions till such time the potential loss was enough to wipe out their entire net worth. That was in early 2008.

Lawyers and risk management experts hired by the companies that burnt their fingers in 2007–8 started accusing banks of 'mis-selling' and enticing companies to 'speculate' instead of hand-holding them to genuine hedging. The banks, in turn, called these lawyers 'ambulance chasers'—a derogatory phrase that typically refers to attorneys in the USA who solicit business from accident victims or their families.

In March 2008, P. Chidambaram, as Finance Minister, made a statement in India's Parliament that banks operating in India had ₹127.86 trillion of derivatives on their books as on 31 December 2007. The 'outstanding notional principal amount' of derivatives, according to him, was 291% higher than the corresponding number on 31 December 2005.

By itself, the amount was not important as it was the notional amount of all derivatives transacted such as overnight indexed swap or dollar/rupee forwards. This number included two legs of transactions that could actually be reversing or closing out any risk that a bank had. Typical products that were permitted by the RBI till that time were forwards, currency swaps, interest rate swaps and foreign currency options.

Banks in India carry a market risk on their foreign exchange contracts but that is largely controlled by the net open position limit that the RBI prescribes for each bank. The larger risk that the banks carry is the credit risk. Since they are not allowed to keep a cross-currency book, they always need to enter into a mirror contract with an overseas bank when they sell cross-currency options to their customers. So, a customer can back out from the second leg of the contract but a bank cannot. Here lay the main problem.

Hundreds of Indian companies that had bought these complex cross-currency options and structured products to seemingly protect themselves from foreign exchange risk started crying foul when significant losses started staring at them. Banks that sold such products geared up for legal battles with clients-turned-adversaries, predominantly small and medium Indian companies, many with unsophisticated internal risk management practices, who were questioning the very legality of such products.

On one side of this battle were new-generation private banks such as HDFC Bank, Yes Bank, Kotak Mahindra Bank Ltd., Axis Bank and ICICI Bank; quite a few foreign banks operating in India such as Barclays, Deutsche Bank, J. P. Morgan, HSBC, BNP Paribas, Crédit Agricole S. A., Citibank, Standard Chartered Bank, Bank of America, Royal Bank of Scotland; and a few public sector banks, including SBI, backed by powerful law firms such as Amarchand & Mangaldas, Suresh A. Shroff & Co. and AZB & Partners.

On the other, was a growing list of small companies, some publicly traded, as well as the well-reputed law firm of J. Sagar Associates, a crack team of investigators at auditor KPMG and independent consultants such as the late A. V. Rajwade, a leading expert in derivatives.

At that time, India's accounting laws did not require companies to report notional losses arising out of derivatives contracts and hence none had an exact idea of the losses. The numbers floated in media reports could be hugely exaggerated.

The banks and their lawyers claimed the derivatives—a financial term used to describe an instrument whose value is a function of an underlying commodity, bond, stock or currency (also simply called underlying)—were legal. They are used as a risk management and mitigation tool. But the lawyers and consultants advising the affected companies said the products that were sold violated the country's Foreign Exchange Management Act, which regulates all foreign currency transactions, and the RBI guidelines.

Hedging or Speculation?

At the core of the battle was a debate over whether these were sold for hedging or speculation.

The issue first came to light in late November 2007 when software company Hexaware Technology Ltd. set aside $20–$25 million (about ₹800 million to 1 billion at the prevailing exchange rate) to cover exposure from unauthorized deals entered into by an employee which involved derivatives. The company later reported a net loss of ₹810 million for the quarter that ended in December 2007, after the actual damage on account of these transactions ended up being ₹1.03 billion.

Sundaram Brake Linings Ltd., Rajshree Sugars and Chemicals Ltd. and Sundaram Multi Pap Ltd., among others, hired law firms to fight it out with the banks.

According to Berjis Desai, Managing Director of J. Sagar Associates, whose firm advised around a dozen affected companies, such transactions are worse than betting on horse races or playing slot machines in Las Vegas. "Banks can say that the contracts are fine but, under the Indian Contract Act, wagering is not permitted. Nobody can punt on any currency under RBI norms," Berjis told me at that time. But Cyril Shroff, Managing Partner of Amarchand & Mangaldas & Suresh A. Shroff & Co., claimed there is enough jurisprudence on derivatives contracts all over the world and they are not wagering contracts.

Deepankar Sanwalka, then Head, Forensic Wing of audit and consultancy company KPMG India, too, said some of these transactions were in violation of the RBI's derivatives guidelines. "The issue is not as simple as some of the banks are projecting. The documentation of such contracts is not always watertight and if the firms decide to go to court, the contracts can be null and void," Deepankar told me while I was writing a report for *Mint* in 2008.

The derivatives involved include swaps and options—a sort of insurance that companies with exposure to dollars or other currencies buy as a protection against any adverse movement in these currencies that can hurt their income (for exporters) or increase their liabilities (for companies that have borrowed overseas).

Theoretically, a swap is a financial transaction in which two counter parties agree to exchange a stream of payments over time at an agreed price. An option is an agreement between two parties in which one grants to the other the right to buy or sell an asset under specified conditions.

Thus, in case of a currency swap, both parties have the right and obligation to exchange currencies. In case of options, the buyer has the right but no obligation, and the seller, the obligation but not the right to exchange currencies.

A Black Swan Phenomenon

Bankers claim there was nothing wrong in such transactions. Both the buyer and the seller understood the products well, but who would have anticipated that the dollar would touch 100 yen? It's a 'black swan phenomenon', they say. A black swan is a large-impact, hard-to-predict and an extremely rare event beyond the realm of normal expectations.

Till then there were two sets of RBI guidelines that banks, consultants and lawyers used to swear by—comprehensive guidelines for derivatives, a 30-page document, dated 20 April 2007, and a 53-page master circular of risk management and inter-bank dealings, released on 2 July 2007. Subsequently, the Financial Markets Regulations Department of RBI released a 97-page master circular on risk management and inter-bank dealings, updating all relevant directives with regard to foreign exchange derivatives contracts, overseas commodities and freight hedging, interbank foreign exchange dealings, among others, updated till 8 October 2015. Yet another 94-page master circular on risk management updated these directives till 2 April 2018.

The RBI insists that such transactions must be 'suitable' and 'appropriate' for the end users. Besides, every derivatives contract must have an underlying transaction. RBI norms also say that when companies enter into such derivatives contracts to reduce their costs, such transactions must not increase 'risk in any manner' and should not 'result in net receipt of premium by the customer'.

In private, some bankers admit that there could be a few companies that used the same 'underlying' for many derivatives transactions that they have entered into with different banks without their (the banks') knowledge but they vehemently contest allegations of mis-selling.

All phone calls made from banks' treasury are normally recorded and one can hear the tape and decide who enticed whom. They also claim all derivatives contracts follow the guidelines of the International Swap Dealer Association; and they proceed only after getting the board resolution from a company and a confirmation that their risk management policy is in place.

Bankers blame the dollar's weakness against global currencies for the turn of events. Between April 2007–March 2008 when the lit fuse on the derivatives time bomb got shorter, the euro had appreciated 17.8% against the dollar, the yen more than 16% and the Swiss franc some 21%, making most of the bets against currency movement go horribly wrong. Thus, a company that transformed its dollar liability into a yen or Swiss franc liability through complex derivatives faced significant losses.

Typically, these have 'knock-out' and 'knock-in' clauses. While these options protect a company's yen or Swiss franc exposure against dollar depreciation, this is only till a certain level; once the dollar's weakness crosses this, the knock-out clause is triggered, leading to losses.

Similarly, if the dollar rises and touches the knock-in level, the customer makes money. If the dollar continues to depreciate and losses increase, the companies can either terminate the deals midway or wait till they are mature, hoping that by that time the currency movement would have been reversed.

After 2008, most banks have stopped selling such products as companies' appetite for such products has gone down. But risk management consultants say the demand was never there and banks led the companies up the garden path. A few banks settled their disputes with companies by sharing the losses whereas others advised their clients to get into new contracts by shifting currencies or close the contracts to cut losses. Yet a few others fought court cases challenging the contention of companies. HDFC Bank is one of them.

Reputation Risk

HDFC Bank was penalized ₹1.5 million by the RBI. By no means is this big money but such regulatory actions tarnish the image of a bank. In the financial world, they call it reputation risk. HDFC Bank couldn't escape this despite its hatred for risks. What went wrong?

Is selling derivatives compatible with the bank? "Yes, it is, as it meets customers' need to hedge risks," Paresh replies. Financial markets offer a range of products and no bank can sit in judgment on whether or not products add value to a customer. They can only have policies on which product is appropriate for which type of customer.

Could it have been a little more measured in its approach? Did it avoid some of the most over-leveraged, most complex structures? The bank claims that from a pure risk point of view, it never ran the book. When it comes to non-rupee-related derivatives, Indian banks are allowed to do this only on a back-to-back basis. So, HDFC Bank, like many others, didn't take any market risk on the product; it was taking only credit risk.

None of the customers actually lost big money but they were afraid that they would lose. The rates moved and there was high volatility in cross-currency markets. So, while an actual crystallized loss might have been very little or a modest amount, the companies had a much bigger potential loss staring at them as they were extrapolating volatility. Risk management socialites and lawyers saw an opportunity in this. Once they rushed to seize it, a fear psychosis gripped the companies and that did the banks in.

"We didn't flirt with the worst of the lot, and not even ten out of over a hundred derivatives customers accounting for less than 5% of such deals challenged their contracts or sued the bank," Paresh told me. There have been about eight cases, and a couple of them came as a legacy from Centurion BoP.

At least some of the companies that moved the court did a flip-flop. The Bengaluru-based home textile manufacturer, retailer and distributor Himatsingka Seide Ltd. first filed a case against HDFC Bank for alleged mis-selling. But when the market moved back in its favour, the company asked for the transaction to be unwound and paid off its dues. (I did not reach out to the company for its comments.)

No Out-of-Court Settlements

GS, Country Head for Internal Controls and Compliance Risk Management, said the bank has not gone for any compromise settlement: "We steadfastly refused to do any out-of-court settlement because we believe we didn't do anything wrong." HDFC Bank has won an arbitration award in a case filed against Centurion BoP by apparels and garments maker Sportking Group of Ludhiana. The company had challenged the award in the Bombay High Court, which was dismissed by the court.

The RBI has taken quite a few steps to ensure that the market doesn't indulge in complex derivatives trades anymore. The change in regulations, which came in 2011, allows transactions in only plain vanilla derivatives and combinations of vanilla derivatives. The banking regulator has also made it necessary for corporate governance in companies to be at a certain level if they want to transact in structured derivatives—a tacit acceptance that such trades were indeed allowed earlier.

GS cites an instance where a customer filed a case against the bank after making a loss but the company had earlier gained. He wouldn't name the customer though. "They were so happy that after a few months they came and said that they wanted to do one more transaction. They repeated the transaction and when they lost money they sued the bank. While the case was being filed, currency again moved and when they came back 'in the money' they wanted to withdraw the case," he told me. 'In the money' simply means one's derivatives contract is worth money and not in losses. His point is that a company understands the transaction as long as it is making money but professes not to when it loses.

GS claims the bank has improved its risk monitoring systems and reworked on its derivatives offerings. Has there been a tightening of the internal norms? "Yes." Is there any room for improvement? Here too his answer is in the affirmative.

That's typical of HDFC Bank. No admission of guilt; no aggression; a measured response to everything related to risks.

The IPO Scam

The derivatives scam is not the only episode where HDFC Bank was tarred with the same brush as many other banks. It got involved in another scam, in which a few unscrupulous market intermediaries cornered a sizeable portion of shares kept for retail investors by opening 'fictitious' demat accounts with banks.

The RBI penalized it for not displaying prudence in the opening and operations of certain deposit accounts and failure to comply with the KYC norms in certain accounts. It was also reprimanded for not exercising due diligence while opening such accounts. The demat or dematerialized accounts are for individual Indian citizens to trade in listed stocks or debentures in electronic form.

The IPO scam, unearthed in April 2006, involved depositories, depositary participants and many market operators who allegedly used or abetted certain entities in creating 59,000 fictitious demat accounts to corner shares of many IPOs meant for small investors. Apparently, in 105 IPOs between 2003–2005, scamsters cornered shares meant for retail investors by creating multiple identities.

Typically, 35% of any share issue is kept for retail investors. A retail investor is an individual who applies for securities valued up to ₹2,00,000. In a booming market, companies rush to raise money through public floats and most shares are listed at a hefty premium. For instance, in 2005, there were 63 IPOs and 54 of them were listed at a premium. In that year, the bellwether equity index Sensex rose by 46.7%. In 2004, there were 32 IPOs and 27 of them offered handsome gains on the listing day. The Sensex rose by 13.08%. In 2003, eight out of ten IPOs witnessed listing day gains and the Sensex rose by close to 73%.

Investigations by India's capital market regulator, the Securities and Exchange Board of India (SEBI), revealed that certain entities had illegally obtained IPO shares reserved for retail applicants through fictitious demat accounts. They then transferred the shares to financiers, who sold the shares on the first day of listing.

Roopalben Panchal

Roopalben Panchal of Ahmedabad, allegedly the linchpin of the operation, had opened hundreds of fake demat accounts and raised finances on the shares allotted to her through branches of an old private bank. Media reports suggest she advertised free photo shoots in local newspapers and used those pictures to create fake demat accounts to trade in the shares.

SEBI found that the National Securities Depository Ltd. as well as the Central Depository Services (India) Ltd. 'failed to exercise oversight over the depository participants' and directed them to take 'all appropriate actions, including revamping of management'.

It also found HDFC Bank's due diligence lacking. Its interim order on the IPO scam in 2006 said, "It emerged that HDFC Bank had failed to exercise due diligence and has opened demat accounts in the name of fictitious/*benami* entities."

SEBI's 252-page interim order was quite castigating. The regulator had said that during the verification, HDFC Bank had confirmed that it has complied with the KYC norms with respect to its demat account clients. "In the light of the findings of the inspections, the confirmation by HDFC Bank appears to be totally divorced from reality as established," SEBI said in its order in 2006.

According to SEBI, "286 savings bank accounts opened by the key operator (Purshottam Budhwani) with HDFC Bank is clearly proof enough for the plan of action to open multiple dematerialised accounts and channelise the funds in the manner they would bury the audit trail." Budhwani had these accounts under different names with joint account holders in various HDFC Bank branches in Mumbai.

Budhwani, SEBI's investigation found, is one of the key operators who cornered the retail portion of IPOs from companies such as Suzlon Energy Ltd. "The role of HDFC Bank raises serious concerns on its compliance, while suggesting it had truck with Purshottam Budhwani in so far as it had actively lent its system to be misused by wily operators," it said.

SEBI banned HDFC Bank from opening fresh demat accounts but later revoked the ban. In 2009, HDFC Bank settled with the markets regulator through the so-called consent process by paying ₹100,000. A settlement through the consent process means neither admission nor denial of the charges.

An internal SEBI note, to which I had access, said, "KYC norms have been followed but not in the true sense of what it stands for as per SEBI regulations so we would like to put in as 'KYC norms followed but not followed'." This sounds like either a puzzle or a poem.

The RBI slapped a penalty on HDFC Bank in two phases—₹500,000 first and ₹2.5 million later. Many other banks too were fined 'for violation of regulations on KYC norms, for breach of prudent banking practices and for not adhering to its directives/guidelines relating to loans against shares/IPOs'.

As the issue is sensitive and the regulators are involved, HDFC Bank does not talk about this. I don't blame them. Purely from a process point of view, if one were to look at what KYC requirements are—the 'ticking-the-box' that one needs to do in terms of ensuring that the people actually exist, they have ration cards and photographs, and so on—the bank met the process. Where the bank slipped up and didn't do what it should have done is to go beyond the obvious. 'This customer does exist but given this profile, should he or she be investing in an IPO?' The bank didn't ask this question.

"The Bank is No Investigative Agency"

GS said that a bank deals with documents and it's not an investigative agency. That's fine. But there were 215 savings accounts opened by XYZ and the second holder in all these accounts was the same. Shouldn't HDFC Bank have been more careful? Incidentally, these 215 accounts were opened over six years, on 32 occasions, and in various branches. Budhwani was the common name appearing in all 215 accounts.

Technically, they were not *benami* accounts because the bank had the documents and the people involved actually existed. This was a case of name lending. The individual account holders existed but they were used by somebody else. A smart Budhwani ensured every original election ID, address and ration card was produced but the people who sold their identities to him for little money didn't know that the shares allotted to them fetched much more than what they were given.

HDFC Bank should perhaps have gone beyond the documents and checked where these people actually stayed and if they had the means to invest in the stock market. In the end, probably the bank was as much a victim as the market and the gullible people who lent their identities.

The 2002 RBI circular said banks had to comply with the KYC norms but they also needed to ensure that their procedures weren't so straightjacketed as to deny a person the normal banking facilities that he or she was entitled to. A few rogue investors took advantage of the system.

Although a settlement through consent doesn't mean admission of guilt, HDFC Bank has introduced additional checks and balances, one more layer of document verification, to plug the loopholes.

The IPO scam also speeded up the process of converting branches into sales outlets and pushing all processing into back offices. This system has got a significant advantage because, when a customer walks in, if the branch manager knows the person well, he or she can get influenced and accept the documents even if they are not up to the mark. As volume grows, the branch manager may find it difficult to meet all the customers and may start delegating responsibility to junior colleagues. Under pressure to bring in more and more accounts, a branch can be flexible in checking the documents and verifying the originals. But when these documents come to a back office, the process is much more streamlined. And the back-office employees can actually go and check if they find anything suspicious.

The bank had also shown the door to a dozen employees in Ahmedabad and Mumbai. Budhwani was issued 1,000 cheque leaves and that helped him apply for so many IPOs. The bank's system did not catch this, but it should have as HDFC Bank has a process whereby if the number of cheque leaves exceeds a threshold, the issue is flagged to a senior person. The senior person in this case did not find anything wrong in issuing so many cheque leaves. He had to go.

"Those were very painful days," Rajan told me.

Paresh said, "The fact that we tightened the processes and took some action means that there was some room for improvement. However, in the light of the events as they unfolded, was there a major failure of the processes? A complicity in helping the fellow to do this? No, certainly not. There wasn't a scent of any moral turpitude or collusion."

But had the senior person noticed the red flag that the system raised, it would have been a different story.

Operation Red Spider

There is always room for improvement.

On 14 March 2013, Neeraj Jha, Communications Head of the bank, barged into the boardroom while an important meeting was on. He informed everyone about what TV channels were flashing. A sting operation, named Operation Red Spider, was conducted by Cobrapost, a media outfit which specializes in investigative journalism. Operation Red Spider alleged that some banks in India, including HDFC Bank, were involved in money laundering, using false accounts to convert black money into white.

In the undercover operation, Cobrapost disclosed several secret tapes with branch employees of several banks and insurance firms, showing how these institutions were laundering money. The operation was carried out by an associate editor, assuming an alias of Syed Masoor Hasan, masquerading himself as a trustworthy lieutenant of a politician, and making cold calls to banks and insurance firms, stating how his objective was to launder his black money into white.

According to a Cobrapost press release, the reporter was never disappointed as "Almost every banker and insurer was willing to help launder huge amounts of unaccounted cash." The so-called expose alleged that various methods, including forged PAN Cards and multiple accounts were employed to launder money.

Deepak Parekh was the first person to call Aditya. Then Finance Minister, P. Chidambaram, also called Aditya to get a brief on the issue. Aditya and Bharat spoke to Shardul Shroff, Executive Chairman of law firm Shardul Amarchand Mangaldas & Co, and requested him to rush to Bank House.

V. Chakrapani (Chaks for his colleagues), Country Head-Internal Audit and Chief of Internal Vigilance, and Sashi huddled into one room. On the advice of the law firm, it was decided that the bank must issue a press statement immediately. The job of drafting it was given to Paresh, the gatekeeper of risks.

Initially a deputy governor of RBI issued a statement that there was nothing wrong with the anti-money laundering system in India and that no scam had taken place but later the Indian central bank launched an investigation against three private sector banks—HDFC Bank, ICICI Bank and Axis Bank—to probe their KYC procedures and anti-money laundering measures.

An RBI release in June 2013 stated that the scrutiny of these three banks revealed violation of certain regulations and instructions in respect of (i) arrangement of 'at par' payment of cheques drawn by cooperative banks; (ii) KYC norms and Anti-Money Laundering (AML) guidelines like risk categorisation and periodic review of risk profiling of account holders; (iii) omission in filing of Cash Transaction Reports (CTRs) in respect of some cash transactions, sale of gold coins for cash beyond ₹50,000; (iv) source of funds credited to a few Non-Resident Ordinary (NRO) accounts; and (v) non-submission of proper information stipulated by the RBI.

HDFC Bank was penalized ₹45 million, ICICI Bank ₹10 million and Axis Bank ₹50 million. There was no evidence for money-laundering by any of the three banks.

HDFC Bank appointed one of the 'Big Four' accounting firms Deloitte Touche Tohmastu for a forensic audit even as a team of lawyers examined if any of its employees violated the bank's code of conduct and ethical standards. In the meanwhile, the employees involved in the alleged scam were suspended.

A statement issued by the bank at that time said:

> "The matter is being investigated on top priority. The bank has a well-defined Know Your Customer (KYC) and Anti-Money Laundering (AML) policy which contains procedures and controls to identify and prevent the types of transactions mentioned in the Cobrapost press release.
>
> Segregation of frontline sales activities and back office operations and post-transaction monitoring processes are in place to ensure independent checks and balances and adherence to all the laid-down policies and procedures of the bank. Any deviation is viewed very seriously and stringent action is taken both at an organisational and employee level.
>
> We would like to assure our customers and other stakeholders that the bank has always adhered to the highest standards of compliance and corporate governance and will continue to do so."

HDFC Bank's 2013–14 Annual Report acknowledged the findings of the RBI and the penalty imposed on it and outlined the steps taken to strengthen its controls and processes, including the discontinuation of sale of third-party products and gold to non-customers apart from tightening the process with respect to arrangement with co-operative banks and risk profiling of customers.

All the employees purportedly involved were immediately suspended.

The initial findings indicated that some staff spoke irresponsibly while others were interviewed in a particular fashion. While the popular perception is immense pressures on the bank staff to meet their targets had led to this, Sashi claims that the number of such cases was minuscule (not even 0.001%). There were only 20 such transactions—of non-reporting of PAN, insurance policies bought in cash—over a period of three years.

The cooperative banks come under the purview of RBI; if they don't take KYC of the customers to whom they issue cheques, how can HDFC Bank be held responsible for them? He also says the insurance companies ideally do the KYC and not the banks. There were 298 cases of gold sold against cash and, in one instance, it was sold against credit card but no regulation bars a bank from doing that.

Apart from sacking 20 employees, HDFC Bank also introduced the concept of mystery shopping after the Cobrapost episode—the scope of the Audit team was extended to go incognito, pose as a customer and conduct surprise checks at branches.

In 2014–15, the Financial Intelligence Unit (FIU) also imposed a penalty of ₹2.6 million, based on the cases reported by Cobrapost.com, stating that there was a failure in the bank's internal mechanism for detecting and reporting attempted suspicious transactions. HDFC Bank filed an appeal before the Appellate Tribunal, Prevention of Money Laundering Act, in New Delhi against the impugned order, stating that there were only roving enquiries made by the reporters and there were no instances of any attempted suspicious transactions.

The Tribunal in the judgment passed on 28 June 2017 ruled in favour of the bank and squashed the penalty imposed by FIU. However, on 27 March 2018, the bank was informed of an appeal filed by the FIU-IND, against the judgment before the Delhi High Court. The matter has not come up for hearing at the High Court while I write this.

Yet Another Scam, Another Penalty

Sometime in October 2014, HDFC Bank was caught in another scam related to trade transactions.

Popularly known as 'advance remittance against imports', this channel was used by a few scrupulous importers to send money abroad. Advance against remittance is a facility whereby an importer pays an advance to the exporter and, within six months, the importer is required to submit the proof of the transaction in the form of 'bill of entry'. A non-receipt of the bill by banks implies that the goods have not been received. In other words, the transactions are fake.

Although the transactions involved Bank of Baroda, HDFC Bank's employee Kamal Kalra colluded with the senior employees of the public sector bank. Initially, the importers opened an account with HDFC Bank and made an advance against imports. After six months, when they could not produce the bill of entry and HDFC Bank stopped any further transactions, they approached Bank of Baroda and continued business.

The scam involved ₹60 billion in illegal remittances that have suspected to be flown out from Bank of Baroda's Ashok Vihar branch in New Delhi to Hong Kong and Dubai.

Although the regulations permit a remittance of $ 100,000 without insisting on a bill of entry, HDFC Bank, Sashi claims, insisted for a bill of entry. When the importer could not provide it within six months, they were given another three months but all the transactions from the account were stopped. After nine months, the bank filed the transaction in Suspicious Transaction Report. However, by that time the damage was already done and the news report was out.

In October 2015, the Central Bureau of Investigation (CBI) conducted raids across bank branches, including those of Bank of Baroda and HDFC Bank, as part of the foreign exchange scam, where bank employees had allegedly liaised with certain people to illegally transfer funds to various accounts in Hong Kong and the UAE, flouting foreign exchange norms set by the central bank.

While CBI arrested Suresh Kumar Garg, the Assistant General Manager of Ashok Vihar branch and Jainis Dubey, the Foreign Exchange Head, the persons arrested by the Enforcement Directorate(ED) include Kamal Kalra (HDFC Bank's Forex Sales Manager), Chandan Bhatia, Gurucharan Singh and Sanjay Aggarwal, who were allegedly involved in the transaction of 15 accounts.

Bhatia, Singh and Aggarwal are said to be owners of companies based in Hong Kong and Dubai towards which the money was being transferred through 59 accounts at the bank's Ashok Vihar branch. ED had said that the HDFC Bank employee Kalra was allegedly helping Bhatia and Aggarwal in remitting the amount through Bank of Baroda against a commission of 30–50 paise per dollar remitted abroad.

At that time, a HDFC Bank release said:

> The bank has a zero-tolerance policy for any misconduct on the part of its staff and any deviation from its clearly defined processes is viewed very seriously. Swift action is taken both at an organizational and employee level, and as per process the employee in question has been suspended pending the outcome of the investigation.

In July 2016, RBI penalized HDFC Bank ₹20 million. Bank of Baroda was penalized ₹50 million and PNB ₹30 million. In a stock exchange filing, HDFC Bank said that the RBI had issued a show-cause notice to banks, seeking more information regarding a foreign exchange scam that was reported in the media. "After considering the bank's (HDFC Bank's) submissions, the RBI has imposed a penalty of ₹20 million on the bank on account of pendency in receipt of bills of entry relating to advance import remittances made and lapses in adhering to KYC/AML guidelines in this respect."

Chaks says that RBI found the bank filing the report late but the FEMA regulations give them a six-month window. "Probably, we should have been more diligent but we did not violate any norm," he says.

From the first day, HDFC Bank's level of tolerance for negligence by its employees is zero. Srikrishnan recalls an incident. In the second month of operations in 1995, the bank faced a hefty potential loss, exposing the gaps in operational controls. It was a clearing error (a big chunk of money flew out of the system) on account of negligence in due diligence on the part of clearing member group.

Aditya kept his cool and did everything to fix the damage. At that time, he made it clear that accountability had to be fixed to make sure that such a mishap doesn't happen in the future. No one was sacked but it was a wake-up call for everyone.

III

The Puri Legacy

16

The Common Sense Banker

One morning in February 2016, when Aditya got up from his bed, he felt an acute backache. He told his wife Smiley to rub a cream on his back while he lay down but when she found him sweating profusely and turning pale, Smiley insisted on seeing a doctor immediately. Usually, the driver does not turn up before 8.30 a.m. when Aditya leaves for office. She went out, hailed a cab and rushed to Hinduja Hospital at Mahim. On her way to the hospital, she called one of her doctor friends in the hospital.

Aditya didn't have a blockage in his heart but it was something more serious—a clot at the cross section of the main artery, called a widow maker's clot.

Aditya came out of the angiography room, smiling, unaware of the gravity of the attack. He shouted at others that they unnecessarily frightened him; the doctors didn't even put a stent. When someone told him that his son and his family were coming from Singapore, that's when he realised that something was seriously wrong.

Aditya's grandson was upset and said "Why did you do this dadu, I will shoot you." He wanted to shoot him because with Aditya lying on his hospital bed, whom could he play with?

Dr Sudhanshu Bhattacharya and his second-in-command, Dr Laxman Khyade, operated on Aditya at Breach Candy Hospital—a bypass surgery. Whenever anyone from office visited to ask him about his health, Aditya would smile and then ask how the business was going.

After the stitches were removed, Aditya saw the doctors' bill. He was surprised—not at the amount but how his bank had missed out this segment of customers. From the hospital, he called Sashi and asked a branch manager to speak to Dr Bhattacharya. The doctor had his primary account with Standard Chartered Bank but after this incident he moved it to HDFC Bank.

Aditya did not come to office for about a month or so but regularly kept updates of the work that he had delegated. Initially, he would come to the bank for half a day and over a period of time he was back in form.

Aditya realised that the bank never focussed on doctors and asked the bank staff to work out a plan to woo them. He himself converted his dentist into the bank's customer by responding to her queries and solving them to make sure she was happy with the bank. The dentist had the problem of parking her car at the bank branch and was not able to register bill payments. He immediately shifted her account to HDFC Bank's Breach Candy branch where there was valet parking and also helped her with her bill payment.

Two years down the line, in February 2018, when they were holding a meeting in the boardroom at the Bank House, suddenly Aditya asked all the eight people present there to follow him. He walked down on the streets of Parel (in the vicinity of HDFC Bank's headquarters) and asked them to choose any shop where he would go and try to sell his products. When none of them could figure out where to go, he himself walked down to a lane off Senapati Bapat Marg.

Aditya went into the first shop —a garment shop. He asked the shop keeper whether he wanted anything. The shopkeeper said that he had everything by God's grace and didn't want anything else. "*Bhaiya main MD hoon HDFC Bank ka. MD aya hai kuch toh de sakenge na*"[Brother, I am the MD of HDFC Bank. The MD has come, surely we could give something]. Aditya explained to him all the offers of HDFC

Bank and the shopkeeper immediately shifted his account to the bank. He also checked with the shopkeeper regarding formalisation of payments with the advent of GST. Someone was video recording the conversation and it went viral.

Then, he went to another hardware shop and repeated the same thing. At yet another shop, he asked "*Aap kya karte hai? Kiske sath business karte hai? Kiske sath banking karte hai? Main apko acchhi facilities du toh mere sath karenge?*" [What do you do? Whom do you do business with? Whom do you bank with? If I provide good facilities, will you bank with me?]

There is a background to this. Aditya had a vision of getting organised merchants on the banking platform. Although approximately 2 million such customers were already into the fold of banks, the market was too large. He asked his employees to capture the market by experimenting with the customers. The feedback of the employees on this was that they tried but even if they were out in the market some of these merchants did not have proper documentation or couldn't fulfil eligibility criteria for loans.

He wanted them to go out in the market instead of sitting in the office and see it themselves. These merchants have enough appetite for banking products. One day, at the morning meeting he lost his cool, stood up in anger and said, "I have had enough of you. Only one of us can be right." He left the meeting room, took the lift and walked down the road; others followed.

Flashback to 1994.

On 15 July 1994, a gentleman in corduroy trousers and a T-shirt, wearing leather sandals, entered Ramon House. He definitely did not look like a banker, even in his Friday casuals.

"I am Aditya Puri," he introduced himself to Goretti, then Vinod's secretary, and gave his tickets to her for flight confirmation. He was scheduled to fly back to Kuala Lumpur that night. Goretti knew who he was. She had just sent an application to the Foreign Investment Promotion Board for the government's nod on the NatWest stake in HDFC Bank. The application form named Aditya as the Managing Director of the bank.

He joined on 12 September 1994, at Sandoz House.

If you go out with Aditya for lunch, make sure you have a wallet on you. He does not carry one. Nobody in the bank laughs at this anymore. Aditya's work–life balance (read: Eating lunch at home and leaving the office at 5.30 in the evening) is always tilted in favour of life and yet he ends up doing the right thing at the right time. His refusal to carry a mobile phone, to check e-mails, and his habit of wearing a tie with a half-sleeved shirt, or of eating *roti* and *dal makhani* at roadside *dhabas* or eateries in a suit, make Aditya different from his peers.

How much of this is put on and how much genuine?

People who know him well find all this natural. He is a Punjabi who does what his heart tells him and does not bother about what others say. Which is why, instead of heading to Europe for a holiday in the summer, he prefers to spend time at his farmhouse at Lonavala, a hill station near Pune, to unwind.

He grows strawberries, mulberries, guavas and Italian lemons there, and plays with his favourite dog, Bushka, a mix of a Great Dane and a Doberman. This is one place he loves to show off to his close colleagues and friends. Every few months he rearranges the furniture to make the house look different.

It's his love for a good life—not for banking—that made him a banker. At his first job as Executive Assistant to the Finance Director of automobile company Mahindra & Mahindra, Aditya was jealous of his cousin Vikram Kochar, a Citibank trainee, who used to live in an air-conditioned and carpeted apartment with his batchmates on posh Carmichael

Road in Mumbai. There was a cook and a butler on call. On top of that, the young men were to be trained in Beirut.

"What the hell am I doing—living as a paying guest in Colaba, surviving on a toast and half a cup of tea in the morning, and catching a train to Kandivali [a western suburb in Mumbai where Mahindra & Mahindra's factory is located] every day?" Aditya wondered.

He asked Vikram to get him an interview with Citibank. After all, how different can banking be from accounting? Both are driven by common sense. He got the job, the comforts and a hefty pay hike.

Aditya nearly lost it once, though. Seeing him leaving office rather early almost every day, his boss at Citibank asked him whether everything was all right with him. Aditya was then working in Kolkata. "Yes, of course, I am working very hard. I am in office until dark," Aditya told him. That was in December when evening descends around 5 p.m. in Kolkata. His boss advised him to look at his watch before leaving.

Aditya does not wear a watch. And normally does not stay in office beyond 5.30 in the evening even when he is the boss.

He has always been a straight talker. In the early 1980s when Victor Menezes, then Head of Citibank in India, asked him to go to New York, Aditya opted for Saudi Arabia instead, where he could save more money. There was a 60% hardship allowance for Saudi Arabia.

A Banker by Accident?

Those who know Aditya's lineage find it hard to believe that he is a banker by accident. After all, how many can claim to have two family members who were central bankers? His grandfather, Shambhu Lal Puri, was on the board of the Reserve Bank in British India and Shambhu Lal's brother K. R. Puri was the twelfth governor of the RBI between

August 1975–May 1977. Before this, he was Chairman and Managing Director of Life Insurance Corporation of India. His family was also one of the early shareholders of PNB and the Sunlight of India Insurance Co. in Lahore.

Originally from Sargodha, an agricultural trade centre in the northwest of Pakistan, Aditya's great-grandfather Rai Bahadur Lala Brij Lal Puri shifted to Chandigarh, Sector IV, after Partition. They used to have a summer house in Shimla, which is now a hotel called Bridge View.

Aditya's father, Tapishwar Puri, the spoilt son of a rich family, joined the British Air Force and was the aide-de-camp to the first Indian to head the Air Force, Subroto Mukherjee.

An Air Force kid, Aditya's schooling was all over India. He led a cushy life. Wherever he went, there were clubs and friends and if he had nobody to play with, orderlies could always make a cricket team for him. Chandigarh was a very organized city then and more than three cars on the road meant a traffic jam. Aditya did his Bachelors of Commerce from Panjab University, Chandigarh, and his chartered accountancy from the Institute of Chartered Accountants of India, New Delhi, before joining Mahindra & Mahindra.

His rather casual approach to work camouflages Aditya's appetite for challenge. Today HDFC Bank's strongest point is its retail business, but its managing director's core competence was never retail. Aditya was an institutional banker throughout his career. He could change his area quickly in sync with the organizational demand because, banking, according to him—whether corporate or retail or investment—is all about common sense, something he has in abundance.

It may sound very simple but is definitely not an easy task. If one is successful, one tends to stick to one's comfort zone. The biggest reason for the downfall of any bank is success itself because it tends to go the same way it has been historically successful in.

One can go off the beaten track only if one has one's ears

to the ground, has common sense and is street smart. Aditya has the big picture but he's not an economist or someone who thrives on complicated theories.

According to Satwalekar, former Head of HDFC Standard Life Insurance Co. Ltd., who was on the bank's board for eight years, the biggest thing about leadership is asking questions and not necessarily providing the answers. "That makes your people think. Look at the retail portfolio of all banks and NBFCs in 2008—whoever was aggressive got decimated. The exception is HDFC Bank as they were always very clear in their mind on what could and could not be done. Aditya would ask the right questions and make his people see what was required. The top line was not a target for him. Value creation through profitability was the objective," says Satwalekar.

In one aspect though, Satwalekar does not find Aditya fully transparent. "He gives the impression of being an extremely aggressive guy; but if you look closely, his banking is as conservative as can be. He is an extremely conservative banker. You see his risk management strategy. Who is his most senior guy there? Paresh Sukthankar. Paresh by nature is risk averse. Aditya has got a bunch of aggressive people to go out and get business. But the gatekeeper is someone who dislikes risk as much as himself and in whom he has complete trust," Satwalekar told me.

Common Sense Banker

Common sense and curiosity are far more important than anything else in banking which has been on a roller-coaster ride in India since the birth of the first set of new-generation private banks in 1994. Early this century, a couple of new private banks set up shop, and after more than a decade, in 2015, two more private banks were born. Around the same time, the RBI also gave licences to ten small finance banks and 11 payments banks (a few of them have surrendered their licences as they could not find the right business model). Technology, products and profile of competition have been changing and, to understand the change, one has to be like a school kid or a teenager while heading an institution.

Aditya has done that remarkably well, and very differently. Nobody knows this difference better than Arun Maira, member of the now defunct Planning Commission, Aditya's neighbour in Samudra Mahal on Worli Sea Face in Mumbai in the 1980s. Arun was an Executive Director of Tata Engineering and Locomotive Co. Ltd. (TELCO) now Tata Motors Ltd., and Aditya was with Citibank, looking after corporate banking. Arun's responsibility was getting TELCO into new markets.

At that time, he was working on a proposed joint venture with General Motors Co. to develop a pickup truck suitable for southern regions of the USA and the Middle East. General Motors would assemble the truck at one of its factories and distribute it. Arun had earlier worked on a similar project in Malaysia in the 1970s, but it did not do well.

General Motors was pushing for a very stiff price formula as it believed that the rupee would depreciate and, therefore, TELCO would gain a lot even though they would not have to pay much in dollars. Arun asked for Aditya's view on the rupee.

Aditya's projection was quite different from what every other person in the financial services business was saying. "He was just talking from common sense. He wasn't a fancy financier," Arun told me.

Aditya, according to him, is a bit of a rebel and, like a Punjabi peasant, he is proud of himself. "He likes to have his simple but certain opinions about things, a good earthy Punjabi trait, if I may say so. People like me who went to St Stephen's [College, Delhi], Doon School [in Dehradun] or Oxford [University] may not always appreciate his views but that's him. Rebel may not be the right word. He's different," says Arun.

After an overseas stint when Arun came back as the Chairman of The Boston Consulting Group in 2000, HDFC Bank was six years old and India was in a frenzy of work. People in the finance and corporate sectors in India were working much harder and longer than people in the United States from where Arun had just come.

Amid all these, he observed that Aditya would wake up in the morning, have a cup of tea with his wife, and then go to the golf course. He would come home, go to the office, come home again at 1 p.m. for lunch, go back to work and was back home after 5 p.m. to be with his wife and children. "One would feel tempted to say that Aditya was not taking his job seriously but results of the bank were there to show what he was doing," Arun admits.

Arun also knows Deepak well. In fact, one of HDFC's first big projects was with TELCO in Pune. The Tata Group company didn't have enough money to build a big colony like it had done in Jamshedpur, though it had land. Hasmukh-bhai came up with a proposal that HDFC could lend money to the TELCO workers to build houses.

HDFC lent to the TELCO employees and the company took the responsibility of repaying by deducting money from their salaries every month—a unique arrangement in those days. Deepak had just come back from the USA and Arun was a young general manager, in charge of the Pune factories.

Deepak asked Arun to join his board but expressed helplessness in not being able to offer much money as RBI rules did not allow the bank to pay commission to its directors. Aditya advised him not to jump at the offer unless he was convinced that money was not important. Arun listened to him.

"Deepak is someone very sound and conservative in his approach who wants to do the right thing. Aditya has the same approach but he is different from others," observes

Arun. For instance, Deepak's business habits are similar to common business habits such as playing bridge with friends, but Aditya spends time only with his family. Deepak spends long hours in office, Aditya does not. Even if his chairman calls, he may say he does not have the time.

"If you are calling because you are the boss and it's something about work, Aditya would say, 'Let's talk tomorrow.' Deepak would say, 'Your friend is quite a character.' Deepak could have initially been irritated because he has a style of how he gets his work done and he suddenly finds a character with whom he can't work like that. Aditya is a character," Arun told me.

Aditya is a Character

He is indeed a character. Samir recollects this story:

One day, Aditya said, "*Chalo, main sabko khana khilata hoon. Aa jao, gaadi mein baith jao, acchi jagah lekar jaata hoon.*" [Let's go, I'll take everyone out for a meal. Come, sit in the car, I'll take you to a nice place.] He promised to take them to a place where the food would be something they would have never eaten before. He had a Maruti Esteem at that time. Since the others did not know which place he was talking about, he told those who weren't in his car to meet him near the Siddhi Vinayak Temple at Worli.

They all drove and got off near the temple, wondering where to go. There was this small *dhaba* with the typical benches and tables. Aditya sat and said, "Let's eat here." The place was full of taxi drivers and others had to wait to get a seat.

"We had *naan*, *paratha* and other Punjabi dishes. The food was great. We had a great time even though I didn't like the glare—all of them were looking at us in our suits and ties," Samir says.

Aditya once went to an awards function in a Hyundai Getz, packing his entire family in it, something no CEO would do even if he was not winning an award. He was footloose. Now, of course, Aditya has changed—his preferred vehicles are a white Jaguar and an E-Class Blue Mercedes Benz.

Aditya loves his whisky and food but not the five-star types. Mughlai food and *kheema* at Olympia in Colaba and Malvani food at Sindhudurg in Dadar are his favourites. He likes Madras Café at Matunga a lot—*dosa* and coffee on Sunday mornings. And *batata vada* and *pav* on his way to Lonavala, 96 kilometres away from Mumbai.

But the simplicity vanishes when it comes to business. And, he can be really uncanny. I am told he often asks his office boy Suryakant to do rounds on the fifth floor of Bank House, Mumbai, where most group heads sit, at 9.30 a.m. to see who has arrived on time. At times, he himself does it.

A few years ago, a register was kept at the foyer for latecomers to sign. Rumours have it that most big guys used to scribble their names in such a way that nobody could make out who had come late.

Aditya can be ruthless. Samir recalls another incident, which also reveals Aditya's business philosophy. One day, a cheque came for clearing from a gentleman who was often seen in Aditya's cabin at Sandoz House. Samir was aware that the boss knew him well. The gentleman did not have the required balance in his account. He was a current account holder and people like Samir who were on the front desk could always take the call of sanctioning a temporary overdraft, depending on whether the person was financially solvent.

Samir cleared his cheque and then triumphantly walked into Aditya's room and said, "*Boss, aapke dost ka cheque maine clear kia.*"[Boss, I've cleared your friend's cheque.]

Aditya looked at Samir and said, "*Mera koi dost nahi hai. Main yahaan bank chala raha hoon, bas* [I don't have any friends. I am running a bank here]. Now go and get the money yourself from him. If you don't get the money, I'm going to debit your account for it. There are no friends in business."

Samir was sweating when he came out. The quick word went around the bank: "*Boss ka koi dost nahi hai, yaad rakhna.*" [Remember, the boss has no friends.]

To get a loan a little cheaper or to get a little more interest on deposits, if a corporate customer ever told Samir "*Main Aditya se baat karta hoon,*" [I will talk to Aditya] Aditya in turn would tell the unfortunate fellow, "*Tu mere logon se baat kar, main yeh sab nahi dekhta hoon.*"[Go and talk to my people, I don't deal with such matters.]

Aditya would tell them all decisions are made in the bank by a set of people who are empowered. "You are my friend, but please talk to my people if you need anything."

During the initial days, the bank had exposure to a company of a large group. HDFC Bank was part of a consortium which had given loan to this entity. The loan was declared as an NPA; the promoter was arrogant and reluctant to pay the bankers and was trying to route their cash flows through a group company. Luckily, the group company's account was with HDFC Bank too. The bank immediately froze the account and seized the money which the company did not like and moved to court against the bank. The court case is still on.

In February 2015, the bank had an exposure to a large steel company. By that time, the RBI had come up with the concept of Joint Lenders' Forum (JLF) to speed up the decisions in relation to stressed assets. The decision by the JLF, taken by the majority, was to be followed by all the members of the forum.

In this case, although the JLF thought that the projections given by the steel company were feasible to lend fresh money, Aditya was not convinced with mere desktop projections.

When he told the promoter that he would not give a new loan, the promoter threatened Aditya that he would pay up to other lenders but not HDFC Bank. Aditya just said, "No problem; go ahead and do that. I know how to extract the money." Within the next 8 hours, Aditya sold the bank's exposure to an asset reconstruction company, before even the JLF could take a decision.

There are No Friends in Business

The promoter of a now defunct airline and Aditya were good friends. While the airline was at the height of glory, he approached the bank for credit lines. Although denied, the gentleman, known for his flamboyance, wanted to meet Aditya to leverage on his relations with him. Aditya told him that they were good friends but the bank didn't want to go ahead with the project as they were professionally not comfortable with it. The airline boss got upset and said, "Aditya, I thought you were a good banker but I am convinced that you need to learn some more banking". A calm Aditya retorted that time would tell who knew banking and who did not.

Aditya has the guts to say no to many such high profile promoters. A fugitive diamond merchant had approached him twice for a credit line in 2017, a year before he left India after PNB complained to the Central Bureau of Investigation of being defrauded by his company around $2 billion.

Sashi was with Aditya when the gentleman approached them for the second time. A sweet talker, the diamond merchant said that two reputed organisations like his and that of Aditya's should come together and do business. Aditya was very clear that if there were opportunities and synergies then they surely would, but at that moment the bank did not understand the diamond business and was not willing to get into it.

Satwalekar was at the receiving end of Aditya's 'nobody is a friend in business' philosophy when he was heading the group's Life Insurance Company. HDFC Bank was one of its key distributors. "Every year, we had to go and re-negotiate because [Aditya] Puri's team would come back to us and say, 'Hey listen, MetLife is offering us this thing, Bajaj Allianz is offering us this much. How much are you giving us? Don't tell us about the HDFC brand and HDFC Group. All that doesn't matter. We have to make money for our shareholders. Tell us what you are going to give us.'"

Satwalekar is pretty sure that ICICI Prudential Life Insurance Co. Ltd. did not have similar issues with its parent ICICI Bank. "When I met him [Aditya] he would be very nice, but when it came to putting pressure to extract a few pennies more, he would be relentless."

Building Relationships

Aditya is shrewd both in strategy and in building relationships. In corporate banking, he would make it a point to meet the small guys who give the business. Before getting into any meeting with a company, he would invariably ask his colleagues, "*Dhanda kaun deta hai?*" [Who is giving business (the money)?]

Typically, in an organization, the letter of credit is issued by a junior guy. For Aditya, he is as important as the CEO of the company. He would walk up to him and say, "Hello, I'm Aditya Puri, I'm the MD of HDFC Bank; thank you very much for giving us the business."

That's one of his main principles—no matter how high one may climb the ladder, one must be sure to acknowledge whoever is giving business.

Aditya would wait for hours for a petty officer in a company who is supposed to be dealing with the bank. Others would get impatient but he would say, "No, sit, nothing doing—he is giving us business, right? So wait."

He does not waste time being friendly with those who do not give business, however big the company. Piyush, who heads DBS in Singapore, recalls his Citibank days in Mumbai in the 1980s when he used to report to Aditya.

Citibank was probably the only bank that did not have dealings with one of the large industrial groups in India in those days. "Piyush, if I get into a relationship with this group, it would be a one-sided relationship. All the banks run around them. It would be an unequal relationship where they would call the shots. We should run business on equal relationships," Aditya told Piyush.

Many bankers equate maintaining good relationships with maintaining a good credit portfolio. They lend money to maintain relationships. While giving money, the banker becomes the company's best friend but if it does not do well, the bank turns into its worst enemy. The most important ability for a banker is how to say 'no' without damaging a relationship.

Shirish swears by Aditya's ability to do this with ease. Shirish had worked with him in India in the 1980s. He was the Chief Risk Management Officer and Aditya was the Head of Corporate Business, both at the same office, in Sakher Bhavan at Nariman Point. "He can tell a client that he can't lend because it doesn't make sense and then they have a drink and the guy goes away baffled, trying to figure out what happened!" says Shirish about Aditya.

Eye for Detail

As a banker, the most remarkable thing about Aditya is probably his eye for detail. Sashi told me an incident that illustrates this. Once in 2007, they were in New York for the bank's third ADS offering. On a Manhattan street, there was a Chase Manhattan ATM with a sign saying it's the fastest ATM.

"Can you just click that?" Aditya asked him. Sashi clicked a picture of it with his mobile phone camera. "We need to understand about this fastest ATM," Aditya said.

Sashi sent a message and the photograph to Rahul Bhagat, then Head of Retail Liabilities, Marketing and Direct Banking Channels at HDFC Bank, asking him to check it out. Rahul checked with ATM-maker NCR Corporation and got back to Sashi and Aditya saying it could be just a marketing gimmick. Aditya did not agree.

"When you go to Singapore, I want you to meet NCR there. Chase Manhattan won't make that statement without genuinely having it faster. Go ahead and talk."

In Singapore, Sashi got to know of a software called the Customer Power that has the ability to reduce the number of clicks a customer uses to transact at an ATM. It has intelligence and saves 40% time. This means more customers can use it and the bank needs fewer ATMs.

"There is cost savings; and the time saved can be used to cross-sell other products," Sashi told Aditya.

"Even though it is expensive, go ahead and do it from the strategic perspective," Aditya told him.

"Frankly, that has yielded fantastic results. The investment is large but we're saving on operating expense on an annual basis," Sashi had told me in 2012. Of course, since then the scene has changed. Shift in the customers' choice from physical channels such as branches and ATMs to digital has impacted the use of ATMs. This is why the bank has stopped adding new ATMs in past three years.

Aditya has this simple logic—to understand technology, one does not need to be a techie. As Ram explains, Aditya is one guy who, without knowing the technology, knows what technology has to deliver. He would say, "A car is a car and one just needs to know how to drive."

Crosses and Arrows

Samir recalls how HDFC Bank discovered the big business of supply chain management. "We used to dread the small notes that used to come from the MD's office. Aditya would spend more than half the day reading magazines, business reviews and would pick out one or two essential things. We would regularly get these small notes from his office. One day, I got a piece of paper with some supplier/dealer information written on it. There were crosses and arrows going all over. I couldn't understand anything."

"Do you know you are missing the biggest opportunity of financing?" Aditya asked Samir.

"What's that?" asked Samir.

Aditya spoke about how the bank should link all the suppliers and dealers of large companies and set up this massive financing opportunity. HDFC Bank went to Tata Motors, the first to link up. Within three years, it built a business worth ₹50 billion and was the only bank that had effectively done the entire financing linkage for a large number of companies.

All of that just came on a piece of paper in 1997. "We all read, but the ability to read between the lines is what sets him apart," says Samir.

Every month, Aditya meticulously reads every branch report—their business plans, the scope, and competition. If one customer's accounts balance drops, he would say, "The customer must have opened an account with another bank and it must be checked out. What's the other bank offering?"

He reads all reports and at least 500 mails a day. There is no computer on his table; Goretti (till she retired in 2018) and Govind hand over the printouts to him. About a dozen sharp pencils are always on his table. Aditya uses them to scrawl his remarks on the reports and mails.

By 5.30 p.m. when he leaves the office, there's not a single piece of paper on his table. When he is on leave, all papers and e-mail printouts are sent home and they come back by the end of the day.

The people in the bank believe that Aditya knows everything. You might prepare for hours and hours on how to discuss with him a particular problem. But when you go to him, he identifies the problem in a jiffy and within next couple of minutes you are out of his cabin with a solution. Chaks often feels that somebody has already told Aditya about the problem and he is prepared for it when one meets him, looking for a solution. He has the ability to strip away all the superficial issues and concentrate on the core problem. He demystifies things and solves them using clarity of thought and common sense.

Piyush used to report to Aditya in the late 1980s in Mumbai. They developed a very close working relationship—Aditya ran the business and left the middle and the back-office work to Piyush.

The first thing that strikes Piyush is Aditya's ability to simplify the most complicated things. He'll take the most complex situation and distil it down to a couple of things.

The second is his ability to prioritize. Once he focuses on what he sees as important, he does not let extraneous items cloud the agenda. Other things can wait or be taken care of by others, but he will focus on those couple of things that matter.

"Unlike a lot of other people who have 20 balls in the air and end up dropping some balls or killing themselves trying to keep all 20 in the air, Aditya knows which three balls matter as he can prioritize. He doesn't focus on the balance 17. I don't know anybody else in my working experience who has that ability to just focus on the crucial things, prioritize and deliver," says Piyush, the highest-paid banker in Asia.

Work–Life Balance

The key to his work–life balance is that Aditya just does not let his life get complicated by the things that are not important.

Initially, Piyush used to come to work at 8.30 a.m. and spend time with Aditya to figure out what he needed to do. After a few months, Aditya refused to see him before 9 a.m. Even though he would be in office, he would say the first half an hour of the day is for him. He would use the time to do the big-picture thinking.

Piyush worked for him for three years from 1988 to 1991 in Citibank, Mumbai, when Aditya was heading Institutional Banking. 'When you run into trouble, come to me. If you don't come to me, I assume you're doing your job,' was Aditya's style of work.

He used to leave office by 5.30 in the evening and tell Piyush's wife Ruchira, "Your husband is inefficient. He is in office till 8.30–9. I am out at 5.30."

"The reason for that is you make me do all the dirty work; you do all the good work and go away," Piyush would retort.

"I do what I am good at, what I'm supposed to do."

Amit of Times Bank is well aware of this side of Aditya's personality. "He is a man who does extraordinary things in an ordinary way. He doesn't try to do complex transactions in a complex way. He never delegates. He empowers," Amit gushes about Aditya.

There is a big difference between delegation and empowerment. Aditya empowers people. He doesn't keep checking "*Iska kya hua? Uska kya hua?*" [What happened to this? What happened to that?] with his colleagues. Only in empowerment, there's trust and that gives confidence to the empowered person. In delegation, this doesn't happen.

Aditya is one of the most phenomenal operational managers that Shirish knows: "He picks up a lot of information, which is natural when you go to cocktails and dinners. This guy has the ability to analyse the information very quickly and figure out some trends around it."

Shirish says, "He would tell me, 'You know yesterday, I was at this cocktail party and there was one guy who was asking questions about such and such topic. I think you should take a look at this. Something didn't sound right to me.'

Then, we'd start reading into it and a year down the line, it would be clear that there was a problem that Aditya could read into and make the connections ahead of all of us.

You can't fool him. He had no consumer experience. So he hired people to do consumer banking. Initially, it didn't go very well; he got rid of those people. I was chatting with him one day and he told me that he has figured out this business and it's not very complicated. These guys make it too complicated. What you really need to have is a lot of common sense about how to run it. Then you pick the right people and leave it to them.

That's his style. He'll pick the right people and once he agrees to hire a person, he trusts him implicitly. If he is not the right person for the job, Aditya will get rid of the recruit very quickly but in a nice way. He'd say, 'I think you should try your hand at something different.'

The most valuable lesson I have learnt from him is that you can't be doing someone else's job," Shirish told me.

Of course, despite all the balancing act, everyone in the bank believes that Aditya drinks, eats, sleeps and dreams HDFC Bank. Even on a Saturday, he will be sitting at home and his mind is working. Quickly something would come in his mind, he would call Sashi and tell him what are the things he wants to get done by Monday and have a discussion.

Giving a Long Rope

Aditya's style is to give people a long rope. If he trusts, he trusts completely. Neeraj was trusted by him. When he left, Aditya didn't replace him. He had two people under him but neither of them got Neeraj's job and nobody was brought from outside. He didn't want to lose either by promoting one; if he had brought in an outsider he ran the risk of losing both. He himself took over the Retail portfolio.

Aditya loved to be flanked by these two people—Rahul Bhagat, former Head of Retail Liabilities, and Pralay Mondal, Head of Retail Assets till June 2012 when he left to join Yes Bank, another new-generation private bank, set up ten years after HDFC Bank.

Rahul, every inch a *sahib*, speaks with a clipped accent and likes golf. An alumnus of Doon School and with a major in history from St Stephen's College, Rahul was very bullish on mobile banking. An art aficionado and a regular at book launches, he acted in Satyajit Ray's *Seemabaddha* when he was eight.

An IIT-ian, Pralay had a fleet of cars but used a battered WagonR on the days he drove. He had a fantastic collection of colourful ties and Aditya always had him around when he met foreign delegates.

Another *pucca sahib* and a colourful character is Navin Puri, recently retired Head of Branch Banking. Navin, known as the 'other Puri' in the bank, and Rahul, always lunched together before Rahul left the bank. Their cabins on the fifth floor at Bank House were adjacent to each other. Aditya calls them remnants of the Raj. Tall Rahul and bulky Navin were Laurel and Hardy in the bank. Navin has light blue eyes and is often seen in blue shirts. He would lend his secretary Joyce to Aditya when Govind was on leave.

They are great pals but their two divisions—Retail Products and Branch Banking—do not necessarily collaborate always. They compete and want to outdo each other. Aditya also has his own contribution through creation of what others call 'constructive tension' between different business groups. Sashi thinks Aditya does that to shatter complacency.

Once, things came to such a pass that the middle-level executives of both the business groups virtually stopped talking to each other. The Retail Liabilities Products group devises products and the branches sell them—it is absolutely critical for the two to work in close coordination but they were two silos.

To break the ice, Aditya called them for an informal outing at Lonavala over a weekend. In the evening, three groups were formed led by Sashi, Arvind Kapil of the Direct Sales group and Ravi Narayan of Branch Banking. The three walked Aditya's dogs—Scooby, a highly energetic Mudhol hound, was given to Sashi; Arvind led Pogo, a mix of a Doberman and an Alsatian; and Ravi, Bushka.

There were 30-odd people and none of them really knew how to walk a dog. So, they had to share tips and help each other manage the three unruly pets. By the time they came back to Aditya's house after the walk, everybody was talking to each other. The party started in right earnest and by 9 p.m. Aditya ran out of the stock of booze. It was business as usual in the office next week.

Keeping Politics Out of Work

Aditya has a unique way of keeping politics out of work. If anyone ever comes to him and complains about a colleague, he simply picks up the telephone and calls the colleague, "Come here, your friend is saying this about you. Let's discuss."

So, either the person has to have the guts to openly speak his cause of complaint or he will die over there and never go back to the boss with false complaints! Everyone knows that if one goes and tells the boss anything about a colleague, one has to substantiate, one has to have the guts to face that person.

Ram says Aditya made sure that he got the right people and gave them complete freedom. "Whenever I used to say, 'Why don't you meet this big chief coming from IBM or HP?' he would say, 'Why should I meet him? You are the MD of IT. You meet him.' That is the kind of confidence he had in us and in empowerment. But, he had his eyes on the ball."

Abhay finds him a fantastic reader of the human mind who understands colleagues' motives and behaviour very well. He thinks the key to Aditya's leadership is being able to deal with different people differently. "If there was a book telling you how to be a perfect manager, everyone would have been a great manager just by mugging it up. You can't have one fixed rule; you have to be flexible. Aditya does that. If I and X colleague of mine were handled the same way, either I would have left by now or my colleague."

Abhay's field is not really related to banking. It has more to do with capital markets. "The only reason why I haven't left or even tried looking for another job in the past so many years is personal rapport. Aditya is very flexible, though it doesn't come across like that. If you ask anyone, they'll tell you he's a hard taskmaster; Aditya is very disciplined but he isn't dogmatic, he's open to dissent," says Abhay.

Anything Negative?

Is there anything negative about him? Yes, there is.

Vinod says if anyone upsets Aditya that is the end of the relationship. Aditya won't do any harm but he will give the cold shoulder and make the person feel unwanted.

Samir says in the early years he always thought that HDFC Bank was a little behind in doing highly innovative stuff. It wasn't a risk-taker at all. When its peers were launching something or the other all the time, Aditya would always say he wants to be the best, not necessarily the first. "Let somebody do something, let us learn from that, let us see how everything happens," was his refrain.

If he wants to, Aditya can be really abrasive too. In a meeting, if you haven't prepared something despite him telling you to do it or you have missed something right under your nose, he can be brutal and cut you to pieces. He would say, "You haven't done your job; I think you are useless, you should just be out of this place. What crap is this? I'll sack you if you don't work!".

And every time he would do that, it would be for such a valid reason that one would want to hang oneself. "How could I have missed that?" one would wonder.

He just means business. If he does not want someone to continue with the bank, he does not ask the person to go directly. He always says "I am not the kind of guy who will tell you to go; if you have your own humility and self-respect, you will go on your own."

Is there anything he can do differently? He does have some idiosyncrasies but that's what makes him brilliant. He will not stop until and unless he gets the level of perfection that he expects. Often business heads think they have done a good job but then he rips them apart because it doesn't have the level of precision that he expects.

Aditya always does his homework for every meeting and presentation. He spends extensive time on numbers and has a grasp of detail. In a flash, he knows the mistakes that need rectification.

"By design or by default," Abhay says, "Aditya sometimes just does not call a spade a spade. He'll get someone else to do that. This is the only thing that has puzzled me in all these 15 years. In an open meeting once, I told him if he had something to say, he should tell me directly, not lean on someone else's shoulder to fire the gun.

The general perception in the bank is that he doesn't tolerate dissent but I don't think so. I believe that if your point makes sense and if you back it up with logic and rationale, he will buy it. There have been times when he has said, 'I buy your point but I'm the MD,' and I think that's fair enough. There are rare occasions when he has used that argument.

There have also been times when he has said, 'I agree, but what to do, such is life,' hinting at constraints in implementing a plan even if it makes sense. This speaks volumes about his leadership."

Harish says, "At times, Aditya exudes a lot of aggressiveness towards customers who tend to believe in him. He promises something but later when he realizes it can't be done, he finds it difficult to go back and say so."

Anil of 3i finds Aditya very decisive, which is good and bad. "He takes a decision very quickly, which is why his table is always clear, which is why he can go home at five. He takes a lot of decisions and in a very short period of time too. The decision making is centralized and is very quick, which makes it a one-man organization."

Anil doesn't know how well the bank treats its people below a certain level. "There is a core top management team that is very well taken care of. But outside it's a factory," he says.

Neeraj finds Aditya a bit impatient at times. "He's a people's guy—he can motivate but he doesn't have time for softer things. For him, it's about action, business and, if not business, golf or some activity. He won't stop and talk to people about the small things of life—that is left to us."

Aditya has no patience for non-performance or slow decision-making. When all are killing themselves for 12–14 hours a day, he will take critical decisions in ten minutes. If he doesn't give a decision within ten minutes, even if he does not say a 'no', it's 'no'. If he says he will get back, it generally means 'no'.

Aditya would rather take a decision, even if it is wrong, than not take a decision at all. If he is surrounded by good people then it works. If he takes a decision without understanding all the risks involved, he needs somebody around him with courage to tell him that.

Importantly, Aditya is also willing to reverse the decision if it's not right. He can say he has made a mistake. "So what? Let's change it."

He has become successful and therefore a little larger than life; so people who work for him challenge him less and may be scared to tell him he is not right. That's a danger in Aditya's style of functioning. Many in the bank feel that one of the very few who could do that was Paresh. But after he left there is probably no one who would be willing to put up a contrarian view. After all, Aditya is India's most successful banker.

Shirish finds Aditya is willing to admit his mistakes. As a risk manager, once Shirish shared his apprehensions about a company, which made Aditya upset. The next morning, as Shirish entered his room, he found Aditya waiting for him. "He said I was right and he was wrong and offered an apology for what he had said. Sometimes Aditya makes decisions and says things very quickly but he reflects on it and if he thinks he has made a mistake, he's not shy to walk up to anybody and admit to it," Shirish told me.

Why Do People Leave HDFC Bank?

From the original team—the lucky 13—Shailendra was the first to leave. Rajan left to come back. Samir, Luis and Ram left for good. Neeraj, not part of the original team, left after a few years. Shailendra, Samir and Neeraj left for bigger roles as they knew that as long as Aditya was around, none of them had any chance to be the boss. Luis and Ram left for different kinds of assignments. Paresh was the last senior executive to leave in November 2018.

How does Aditya react when his dear colleagues leave?

Samir Left for Barclays

In 2006, Samir got a call from a headhunter for the top job of British bank Barclays. He asked Aditya, "*Milke aaoon kya?*" [Should I go and meet them?]

After he met the people at Barclays, he confessed to Aditya that the offer of Managing Director was up his alley and he was tempted because he had never headed an organization.

"*MD bana rahein hain kya?*" [Are they making you the MD?] Aditya asked him.

Samir replied in the affirmative.

"I'm around for a lot many years; if you've the ambition of becoming an MD and are getting a good opportunity and decent pay package, then go and have that experience because you won't have that experience here for a long time."

Samir went back to Barclays, negotiated, and showed Aditya the offer letter. Aditya recommended some changes such as the inclusion of a severance package in case they shut shop. Aditya's foresight was immensely valuable. Indeed, Barclays shut its retail shop.

Abhay did look for a job once, but just once. It was a large corporate house and a very prestigious offer. Before saying 'yes', he wanted to talk to his boss. They were in Barbados, watching the cricket World Cup.

Over Banks Beer, Abhay explained the offer and the money. Aditya heard everything and asked, "How many times have I called you outside working hours?" The answer was twice. And those times were when Aditya needed Abhay for something really important. He told Abhay that this group would call him on Sunday afternoons to make presentations. "I want you to first think about whether you're ready to face that. If you're willing to do that, then we'll discuss how good your offer is."

That got Abhay thinking. He knew he wouldn't be able to do that. "I didn't go any further after that. For a long time, they kept coming back to me, asking what the problem was. I couldn't tell them the real reason because that sounded very stupid.

Aditya hadn't really talked to me from the finance or economics point of view. He just made one simple statement and that disarmed me completely. He knew the sort of person I was and didn't even make any counter offer."

Srikrishnan Left for Yes Bank

In 2003, one of Srikrishnan's ex-colleagues from Bank of America, Rana Kapoor, was in the process of starting a bank with Ashok Kapur and Harkirat Singh. They had the inprinciple licence from the RBI but Harkirat Singh was on his way out of the trio for personal reasons and they were looking for a suitable replacement. When Rana approached Srikrishnan, he evaluated the opportunity from multiple angles. It was a board position (executive director) and he would have been the initial subscriber to the equity of the bank.

He also knew that Aditya was not retiring any time soon. So, between being the country head in a 10-year-old, well-capitalized private sector bank, floated by HDFC, and a board position in a new bank started by professionals with backing of Rabobank, a Dutch multinational banking and financial services company, Srikrishnan chose the latter.

Of course, Aditya was reluctant to let him go but when he was convinced, he helped Srikrishnan with the terms of negotiations to get the maximum from the opportunity. He joined Yes Bank in April 2004.

Neeraj Left for Standard Chartered Bank

Neeraj raised the subject while on a road show in Paris. Standard Chartered Bank had approached him in February–March 2005. A foreign search company from the United Kingdom was talking to Neeraj.

"Are they serious?" Aditya asked Neeraj.

"They could be."

"Find out whether they are serious."

After meeting half a dozen times, Neeraj got some understanding about the offer and went back to Aditya. Aditya tried to talk him out of it without directly saying 'no'. "It's useless as in the matrix structure in a foreign bank, nobody would report to you," he told Neeraj. He even spoke to Ashok Sud, then Head of Corporate Banking in Standard Chartered Bank in India, in front of Neeraj on a speakerphone. Ashok had worked with Aditya in Mahindra & Mahindra.

Ashok's voice was loud and clear; he was not reporting to the CEO.

Christopher Low was CEO of Standard Chartered Bank in India at that time.

"What are they offering you?"

Neeraj explained. "It's too little. You should get a better deal."

Neeraj did some negotiations and improved the package, slightly. It was significantly better in terms of cash but poorer in terms of stock. As the package was not improved much, Neeraj stopped answering their calls.

Then he got a call from London. Mervyn Davies was on the line.

"Hello, my people have been calling you. I am told you aren't finding it attractive. I want to meet you."

Mervyn was the Group CEO. He would be in Singapore for a board meeting and called Neeraj there.

When Neeraj informed Aditya of this, Aditya told him they

had not improved his package and asked what was the point in meeting again.

But Neeraj found it difficult to say 'no', especially because Mervyn had called him personally.

Mervyn, a charmer, had arranged an exclusive lunch for Neeraj. He called the human resources director to the meeting with Neeraj, made some changes in the offer letter, and signed it off.

When Neeraj showed it to Aditya—his colleague, well-wisher and boss rolled into one—he was in a fix.

The next day, Aditya told Neeraj he'd had a long chat with his wife Smiley and she advised him to let Neeraj go. "You are not fair to him," she told Aditya.

The Last High Profile Exit

The last high profile exit from HDFC Bank was that of Paresh. In August 2018, Paresh—considered by many as Aditya's heir apparent, resigned from the bank for 'personal reasons'. Nobody knows the real reasons for his exit except Paresh himself. Some speculate that though he was a contender for the CEO role, the uncertainty and ambiguity in this regard might have led him to take this decision.

He was made the Deputy Managing Director in June 2014 after Harish retired. Both Harish and Paresh were executive directors. Around the same time, Kaizad was also inducted into the board as an executive director. A year later, Aditya's tenure was extended beyond 65 (with RBI raising the retirement age for the CEOs of private banks from 65 to 70).

Paresh left the bank in November 2018. After Paresh quit, the post of deputy managing director has been abolished. I am told when he was made Deputy Managing Director, it was communicated to him that while he would be in contention for the top job in the future, he should not consider himself as an automatic choice for Aditya's successor.

Aditya has always insisted that the board will take the call in appointing his successor even though he will have his inputs. He has also been saying that as part of the process, both internal and external candidates would be considered, and there is no certainty that an insider would succeed him.

Some say a perception was sought to be created in certain quarters both inside the bank and outside that Paresh had been a great No. 2 but may not have been an ideal No. 1 as he had not handled business in the bank.

That may not be exactly true. Given his functional responsibilities, Paresh worked closely with the business heads who talk about his understanding of the nuances of their businesses and grasp on financials. He had been involved in and led the bank's capital-raising programmes all along and enjoyed great relationships with the investors. Since he was heading Credit and Risk Management, there was a perceived conflict of interest and it's only natural that he would stay away from direct involvement with the business side of the bank.

Gentle, soft spoken and extremely competent Paresh, who had been with the bank since its inception, says he "feels blessed to have been part of the bank journey for so long" and insists that the reasons behind his leaving are 'personal'. Someone who knows him well said that while both Deepak and Aditya have been on record that Paresh was a contender for the top job, the race (for the corner room) has not even begun and hence it would be unfair to speculate on whether Paresh would have been ahead or behind in the race.

"Paresh is someone who believes in the 25-25-25 theory," he says. What's this? The first 25 years of one's life is for learning, the next 25 years for earning and the last 25 years are for returning or giving back to the society.

Paresh, 56, spent more than 33 years in the banking industry out of which 24 years were in HDFC Bank. "He has

already invested more than 25 years in earning. He will do things now which he wants to do," this person says.

When I asked Paresh the reason for his leaving, he did not say much except quashing rumours of his taking up the top post at some other bank (he has had quite a few such offers in the past). He said if he had wanted to do a full-time banking job, he would rather have continued with HDFC Bank. He does not want to take up any one role which would not allow him to do quite a few interesting things that he plans to do.

Beyond that, he did not want to reveal anything when I asked him in the last week of August 2018.

Ahead of the Curve

Aditya has always been ahead of the curve. What he tries to do is set objectives and change what is necessary for the future. Initially, no one in HDFC Bank wanted to approach rural and semi-urban markets. His reaction was: "If you don't want to take priority sector, bear the cost of it."

He had foreseen the digital banking revolution and knew a convergence would happen and people would want everything on phone. Netflix hadn't come to India by then but Aditya used to say that when he goes to Singapore or US, he uses Netflix and watches his stuff. Nitin remembers Aditya quoting that he wants to be the Netflix of banking. That was the level of convenience he wanted to give the bank's customers.

Ashok says that a person needs to learn the art of cross-selling from him. Aditya believes in the concept of once a customer always a customer; the customer should not use one product of the bank but have access to all products.

Rajinder looks up to Aditya as the God of Indian banking and believes that whatever Aditya says is bound to happen. While drawing the business projections for 2017, his assessment of next year's liability growth was around

20% while his boss wanted it to grow at 22%. This two percentage-point difference led to an hour-long discussion and eventually Rajinder was able to convince his boss to stick to 20% projection. When the team presented the projection statistics to Aditya, he simply said, "*Rajinder is projection me kuch maza nahin aya; ek kaam kar is ko 30% kar do.*" [Rajinder, there is no fun in this projection; do one thing, make this 30%.] Rajinder nodded his head, and by the year end, achieved it. The same story was repeated the next year.

"What can I do? I can't say no to MD. Whatever he says, that happens!" Rajinder says.

Never under Stress

Goretti, Aditya's secretary till early 2018, has never seen her boss under stress. Even if he is, he does not show it. He always says there is a solution to every problem. "I have never seen him flinging his hands or scratching his head. He walks the same way as he used to 24 years ago. I have never seen him rushing or pushing around or screaming in the corridors," Goretti says. Even in the worst of times, like during the derivatives and IPO scam and the fall of Lehman Brothers, Aditya laughs loudly. Even under stress, he smiles and there's a dimple on his cheeks!

And, he is also mischievous and loves to play all sorts of pranks. Once one of his close friends playfully asked Aditya what he would be sending him on his birthday. "Flowers," said Aditya.

Goretti was asked to get the biggest cauliflower from the Dadar market, one that could feed two dozen people. It was sent in a nice box with a birthday card.

The next year, Aditya decided to gift his friend a rooster. The rooster was kept in a huge basket, covered by a nicely decorated net so that it could breathe. The bird was terrified and didn't make any noise. When his friend, a Marwari and a strict vegetarian, opened his gift, that rooster ran all over the house.

That's Aditya, at his best and worst. He knows how to humour people and get the best out of his colleagues and corporate contacts and ensure fabulous returns to investors.

17

Whose Bank is It Anyway?

The 2011 sequel to Jim Collins' 2001 bestseller *Good to Great, Great by Choice: Uncertainty, Chaos, and Luck—Why Some Thrive Despite Them All*, identifies seven characteristics that make companies truly great over an extended period. Through painstaking research over nine years, Jim and his co-author, Morten T. Hansen, a management professor at the University of California, Berkeley, tried to find out how a company achieves lasting success in an environment of change, uncertainty and chaos.

Jim began his research and teaching career on the faculty at Stanford Graduate School of Business, where he received the Distinguished Teaching Award in 1992. In 1995, he founded a management laboratory in Boulder, Colorado, where he conducts research and consults with executives from the corporate and social sectors.

In an article in *Fortune* ('How to Manage through Chaos', 17 October 2011), the duo said that from an initial list of 20,400 companies only seven could make it to the final list through 11 layers of cuts. The project started in 2002, the year the bull market crashed and a year after the attack on the Twin Towers of the World Trade Centre in New York that shook the United States' false sense of security. Ahead of that, the internet bubble burst.

"Why do some companies thrive in uncertainty, even chaos, and others do not?" the duo asks.

What are their findings? The successful leaders aren't the

most 'visionary' or the biggest risk-takers; instead, they tend to be more empirical and disciplined. They rely on evidence over gut instinct and prefer consistent gains to blowout winners. Successful companies are definitely not more innovative than others. They don't always adopt internal changes as a response to a changing environment.

Jim and Morten call them '10Xers' for beating their industry indices by ten times or more in terms of shareholders' returns.

The entire theory is built around the stories of the great Norwegian explorer Roald Amundsen and British naval officer Robert Falcon Scott—two men who set out separately, in October 1911, to become the first explorers to reach the South Pole.

Roald won the race by setting goals for each day's progress and by being careful not to overshoot on good days or undershoot on bad ones—a disciplined approach shared by the 10Xers. Robert, in contrast, overreached on good days and fell apart on bad days.

Roald and Robert were 39 and 43 years old, respectively, and with comparable experience. They started their respective journeys for the Pole within days of each other, both facing a round trip of at least 1,400 miles into an uncertain and unforgiving environment, where temperatures could drop twenty degrees below zero even in the summer.

In October 1911, the two teams made their final preparations in their quest to be the first in history to reach the South Pole. For one team, it was a race to victory and a safe return home, and, for the other, a devastating defeat that ended in the death of all five members. Roald reached the destination 34 days ahead of his rival.

What separated these two men?

Roald and Robert had exactly the same ratio—56% of good days to bad days of weather. As they faced the same environment in the same year with the same goal, environment couldn't be the cause of one's success and the other's failure.

The outcomes were different because they displayed very different behaviours.

In an interview with *Forbes* in 2011, Jim said, "The 10X winners didn't generally out-innovate everyone else; they combined creativity with discipline so that the discipline amplified the creativity rather than destroying it... Hand in hand with this is that the leaders who led successfully in the face of turbulent disruption and rapid change were not generally more visionary, more risk-taking, or more blessed by luck than their direct comparisons."

According to him, one should not place big bets without empirical validation. Firing an uncalibrated cannonball before firing bullets to validate a concept is taking excessive and unnecessary risks. Fire the bullets first to gain empirical validation and then fire a cannonball. This allows one to get the exponential results of concentrated bets, while also limiting one's risk. When one engages in inherently risk-oriented activities, such as entrepreneurship, the key is in managing the risks, to achieve 'big hairy audacious goals' and to stay above the 'death line'. Never forget, the only mistakes one can learn from are the ones one survives.

Market Hates Volatility

Jim's book reminds Helios Capital's Samir Arora of the HDFC Bank story. "Market doesn't like volatility. It always rewards steady, predictable growth. Aditya Puri controls himself in good times and doesn't lose control in bad times. Since 1994 there have been quite a few crises but in none of them has HDFC Bank been exposed," says Arora. He owns HDFC Bank stock from day one.

Arora isn't the only one who hates volatility. Satwalekar believes that in the financial sector, the biggest strength of an entity is the steadiness, the lack of volatility. "I do respect a lot of the things ICICI Bank has done but it has been too volatile for a financial sector stock. HDFC Bank is different," he says.

Performance of some of the foreign banks in India is also volatile. Typically, the CEO, an expat, comes in for a three-year term. He cleans up the balance sheet in the first year, grows it in the second and repeats in the third year what his predecessor had done. Then he gets a promotion and moves on. This was the story till recently.

The experience of some of the state-run banks where the chairman's tenure has not been long is similar. The incoming chairman typically invests the first year in cleaning up the balance sheet—undoing the incumbent's doing—but he leaves behind the same legacy, like his predecessor, in striving for growth: Rising bad assets that eat into the bank's profitability. And the cycle continues.

Aditya has been at the helm since the inception of the bank for 25 years. This makes him the longest serving CEO of a bank of this size globally. He will step down in 2020 when he turns 70. Of course, if the RBI raises the retirement age to 75, it will be a different story.

"For HDFC Bank, there has been no volatility in the earnings or growth and, therefore, no volatility in the market price. It's never worried about the market share. You'd need to create value over a long term. Buying a market share today is the easiest thing one can do but later it becomes extremely expensive. HDFC Bank hasn't bought the market share. It has bought solidity," Satwalekar told me. He was on the bank's board for the first eight years till 2002.

Even Kamath, former Non-Executive Chairman of ICICI Bank, which competes with HDFC Bank, admits that. "For the last so many years, HDFC Bank has shown steady growth—unrelentingly so. They have been performing well, in a very measured way. By measured, I mean predictable; they do things which are tried and tested and they do them exceptionally well.

When you record this sort of growth, a few things strike you. One is, clearly, the leadership. It's always a function of two components—how the board looks at growth and momentum in an enterprise and the level of executive management. As you move further down, it percolates to how well you have built your team. In all these respects, HDFC Bank has done very well. The HDFC Bank story is a very good one for anybody looking at banking—a mini tutorial for building a business in a developing country.

They have followed a measured growth trajectory where growth is substantially high and yet the path is well defined. Its valuation is basically a reflection of the belief that this growth is sustainable," says Kamath.

After Aditya, Who?

After Aditya, who?

In one of the analysts meets in September 2017, for the first time, Aditya spoke about his retirement in October 2020 but it was not reported in media. He repeated it in 2018 and the media caught on in a big way. This has been the most talked-about succession plan after the Tata Group Chairman, Ratan Tata, retired in December 2012.

Who will take over the mantle from Aditya? Will the person be an insider or an external candidate? Will an international banker be chosen to head HDFC Bank? Has Aditya groomed someone as a successor? If not, why hasn't he groomed one? Is he insecure? These are the questions everyone is asking.

Aditya says that he hasn't developed one but many successors who are directly under him and each one is capable of running the bank. About 95% of those who directly report to him are in their 40s and running businesses independently. He might be consulted for the appointment of his successor but the final call rests with the board of the bank.

One of the reasons he hasn't groomed a successor is that this is against the spirit of corporate governance. The next CEO must not be his choice—the person will be chosen by the board. There will be enough time to groom the successor as he will handhold the person for at least six months before he steps down. Once he leaves the corner room, he does not want to be associated with the bank in any capacity.

Incidentally, he is on the board of the bank's NBFC subsidiary HDB Finance Ltd. as its Chairman. Since the RBI norm on the age limit of the chairman of a bank does not apply to an NBFC, many hope that Aditya would continue with this.

Aditya believes that the organization should not be dependent on one person, and the young talent pool should always be prepared to take the place of senior executives when they quit. At the same time, Aditya also believes in getting fresh blood from outside. This is why he brought in Rakesh Singh to set up the Investment Banking Division and Rahul Shukla from Citibank to head the corporate bank.

The Puri Legacy

The Puri legacy is all about creating the next batch of lucky 13 who can take the organisation to the next level. This is an institution which will continue to grow even when he is not there. His passion is to leave the organisation in such a state where none can say that after Aditya left, the drive, the hunger, the value, the ethos, the culture, the growth consistency— everything has just vanished

In the past, Neeraj Swaroop left HDFC Bank to head Standard Chartered Bank in India, Samir to head Barclays, Srikrishnan first joined Yes Bank and now is heading Jio Payments Bank Ltd., Pralay is Executive Director with Yes Bank and is now with Axis Bank. More recently, Aseem Dhru left to head a private equity-funded NBFC. Will the bank import the CEO or an insider will fill in Aditya's shoes?

There is enough talent within the bank and also the HDFC Group but none will be surprised even if an outsider succeeds Aditya. In August 2018, exactly 24 years after joining the bank, Paresh quit, citing personal reasons. A few weeks before that the bank raised ₹240 billion capital, out of which ₹85 billion came from HDFC, and Paresh supervised the process. None of the investment bankers of the 12 banks that handled the issue and closely interacted with Paresh for over three weeks had any inkling that he might leave so soon; Paresh's engagement with them was total.

The decision to quit appears to have been sudden and caught everyone by surprise. HDFC Bank, in its filing with the stock exchanges, said "The board of the bank places on record its sincere appreciation for the contribution made by Mr. Sukthankar in his long association with the bank and wishes him the very best in his future endeavors."

Posted on the bank's website, at an audio recording of a conference call of Aditya with the investors a few days after Paresh's exit, he is heard saying, "This (Paresh's exit) has got nothing to do with who will be the successor. He has his personal reasons. I tried to ask him but he requested to leave it at that and I left it at that. He has given his life for the bank—please do not demean that.

We are very sorry to see him go and we wish him the best. It has been the most graceful exit; there is no acrimony, no differences of opinion, so please stop speculating. In fact, he offered to join the call. Of course, I am sad personally—he spent 25 years with me. However, at the same time, life goes on.

The process (of identifying Aditya's successor) would start in 18 months and Paresh was a contender. It was put out that we will look out 18 months before and a replacement will be in place 12 months before my retirement (in 2020). That process doesn't need to change... I am not going to choose my successor. I will have an important role but so will the other four directors in the committee. We haven't even started looking... When the committee is appointed before the end of the year or the middle of next year, then they will have their terms of reference, which will be put out," Aditya told the investors on a Monday morning (14 August), before trading started on stock exchanges three days after Paresh resigned (10 August, Friday).

He also pointed out that the bank has enough talent within its ranks.

On 14 August, the bank's stock recovered from the day's low of ₹2,075 to end at ₹2091, 1.15% down from Friday's close of ₹2,114 on BSE. Its ADR on the New York Stock Exchange dropped close to 3.82% over two trading days after Paresh resigned.

Deepak, Chairman of HDFC, told media that Paresh was not leaving for competition. "He said he has not applied anywhere and I believe him." Deepak told *DNA Money*, "When Mr Puri retires, he would have been one of the most able contenders, but not the only one. We cannot give the post to one person, we would have to look at others also and make the best choice."

"Paresh has worked very hard for the bank for 24 years and he has done immense work for the bank," Deepak said. When asked why he did not persuade Paresh to stay back, he said, "Of course, I did. But then it is the individual's choice. Even one of our board members and former RBI Deputy Governor Shyamala Gopinath asked him to stay, but he said he is leaving for personal reasons." Shyamala is the bank's Non-Executive Chairperson.

Keki, another board member of HDFC Bank and Vice Chairman and CEO of HDFC, said that Paresh "had a good chance of being the managing director and chief executive officer, but the bank was planning to look for candidates for the top post, both externally and also internally."

"He is a sober, down-to-earth, non-political professional, who was always straight-forward and got things done," Keki told *BloombergQuint*.

Growth Outliers

It's for the same reason that HDFC Bank as well as Infosys (Kamath was also the Non-Executive Chairman of Infosys) figure in an elite group of ten companies identified by *Harvard Business Review* (*HBR*) which have consistently performed better than others around the world over a decade. Calling this group as growth outliers among 4,793 listed companies with market capitalization of at least $1 billion, *HBR* in its January–February 2012 issue said that some of the things these companies do 'don't match up well with some conventional ideas about growth'.

In an *HBR* article titled 'How the Growth Outliers Do It', in the same issue, Rita Gunther McGrath said they searched for listed companies that have grown by at least 5% each year over a ten-year period ending 2009. The results showed that only ten companies—three from the USA, two each from India and Spain, and one each from Japan, China and Slovenia—grew their net profit by at least 5% during this period. And only five grew both revenues and net profit every year.

Rita, a professor at Columbia Business School, wrote in the article:

> *Data suggest a need to rethink our assumptions about corporate performance. Steady, consistent growth is difficult to achieve even at modest rates, never mind the double digits that corporate leaders are fond of promising.*

Her analysis challenges some of the conventional beliefs. It was found that a company's growth rate is not determined by the industry it is in, that the larger a company gets, sustaining growth doesn't get harder, that consistently higher growth rates need not happen only in fast-growing markets or single geographic regions, or that growth doesn't necessarily slow down as companies age.

Rita wrote:

> Our outliers are in wildly different industries, including pharmaceuticals, beer, construction, and banking. All outperformed their industry. Moreover, most of them are in very competitive industries, without the protections that patents or trade secrets provide. [. . .]
>
> No single geographic region dominates the outlier group, which represents both high-growth emerging economies and mature economies. Nor did the degree to which the companies had globalized seem to be a factor. Although Infosys and ACS both planned from the beginning to focus on overseas opportunities, Yahoo Japan conducts business almost entirely in Japan, HDFC Bank operates only in India, and Atmos Energy focuses on the U.S. market. Tsingtao Brewery earns 50% of its revenue from exports, but it didn't venture outside China to manufacture until 2007. Krka Group [headquarters in Novo Mesto, Slovenia] is mainly a regional player, manufacturing generic pharmaceuticals throughout Eastern Europe.

HDFC Bank has been growing at a Compounded Annual Growth Rate (CAGR) of at least 25% every year in deposits, advances, net interest income and net profit from the start of the millennium. This is more than the industry average. Its growth rate is almost double that of the industry leader, SBI, which is more than three times bigger than HDFC Bank in terms of assets (₹34.86 trillion vs. ₹11.7 trillion in September 2018). Going by the figures of Capitaline, a digital corporate database of over 35,000 Indian listed, unlisted and subsidiary companies, HDFC Bank has consistently outperformed the industry with 29.5% credit growth, 28.34% net profit growth and around 27.4% net interest income since 2005. The industry's average credit growth has been 17.8% and net interest income 14.7%. In 2018, the Indian banking industry recorded a loss In 2018, the Indian banking industry recorded a loss.

The 16-year average return from the stock is 32%, higher than the 22% shown by India's bellwether equity index, the Sensex, and the 29% shown by BSE Ltd.'s banking index, Bankex. (I am talking about 16 years and, not beyond that, since Bankex data is available since 2003.)

Since December 2008, after the collapse of Lehman Brothers which changed the banking scenario globally, in the last 39 quarters till 30 June 2018, while the net profit growth rate for the banking sector has been extremely erratic and many of them have been in the red for successive quarters since December 2015 after the RBI introduced the first-of-its-kind asset-quality review and forced the banks to come clean, HDFC Bank's earnings growth rate has been between 15.15% (December 2016)–33.92% (June 2010). During this period, its gross NPAs ranged between 2.05% (June 2009)–0.91% (December 2009) and net NPAs between 0.6%–0.2%.

Though the stock is not the most expensive in terms of price to book ratio, it is the most valued bank in India ₹5.6 trillion (August 2018). At that time, the stock was trading at 3.44 times price to fiscal year 2020 book value.

A Classic Compounding Story

It is a classic compounding story, which has never got rerated or derated by the analysts. A ₹10 share in 1995 is worth ₹10,350 in August (after the split, the face value of the stock is ₹2 now)—more than 1000 times in 24 years (excluding dividends). Very few companies globally have offered such a return to their investors.

According to Bloomberg data, since 2000, till August 2018, the HDFC Bank has given an annual return of 22.89% compared with 13.34 return offered by Sensex, and 13.31, that of Nifty. It is the highest return offered by any Indian bank (ICICI Bank: 12.94%; SBI 17.77%) but lower than 23.32% return that the investors have received from technology bellwether stock TCS Ltd.

HDFC Bank hit the capital market with its maiden equity issue in May 1995, after SBI but before ICICI Bank. TCS entered the market much later—in August 2004.

Why is the HDFC Bank stock so dear to every investor's heart? Why does it command so much value? Till a few years back, CASA or the low-cost current and savings account was one of the key strengths of the bank. The higher the CASA, lower the cost of money for a bank. After the RBI deregulated the savings bank interest rate in October 2011, many banks now have as much CASA as HDFC Bank (they might be offering higher interest rate though while HDFC Bank has stuck to 4% interest, the last regulated rate).

Indeed, the bouquet of products differentiates HDFC Bank from others and so does its stride in digitalization. But banks such as ICICI Bank, Axis Bank, Kotak Mahindra Bank and a few others, including India's largest lender SBI, too are going digital but the pace of transformation for them is not as radical as in HDFC Bank.

The key differentiating factor between HDFC Bank and others still remains its quality of assets. No bank in India probably knows risk management and credit appraisal and monitoring better than HDFC Bank. Saying no to an exposure to a particular company, a group, or even a sector is critical. HDFC Bank does this with the finesse of a trapeze artiste—an extremely delicate balancing act.

Similarly, in the retail loan portfolio, managing credit quality, underwriting and fraud control, and using technology and analytics to balance growth and asset quality have made HDFC Bank different from others in the pack.

Two Hidden Gems

The bank also derives its valuation from its two wholly-owned subsidiaries. The triple A-rated non-banking subsidiary HDB Financial Services Ltd. (HDBFSL) gives secured and unsecured loans and also offers Business Process Outsourcing (BPO) services, including form processing, document verification, finance and accounting and collection, among others.

HDBFSL is a non-deposit taking non-bank finance company that started operations in 2007. It caters to the growing needs of an aspirational India, serving both retail and commercial clients through a network of 1,165 branches across 831 cities and towns in 22 states and three Union Territories, through at least 80,000 employees.On one hand, it offers business loans of up to ₹150 million to retailers, traders and manufacturers and, on the other, provides consumer and personal loans, starting as low as ₹15,000 to individuals.

The bank owns about 95.9% stake in HDBFSL. Aditya is its Non-Executive Chairman. The assets under management for HDBFSL has risen to a little over ₹440 billion with a CAGR of about 60% since 2010. Its net NPA level in fiscal year 2018 was about 1%.

The bank's 18-year-old stockbroking subsidiary, HDFC Securities Ltd., caters to both retail and institutional investors.

A Goldman Sachs report in June 2017 has said HDFC Bank may cross the $100 billion market capitalisation-mark by fiscal 2019–20, expecting the bank's earnings to grow at 21% CAGR in the next three financial years to 2019–20. "HDFC Bank leverages the market share shift from state-owned banks; the retail under-penetration using its large distribution network, highest efficiency among retail peers, and low cost of funds; and a shift of financial savings from deposits to other products. Under our bull case, we see potential for market cap rising to around $137 billion, assuming valuations re-rate closer to one standard deviation above median on potentially higher growth and best-in-class profitability," the Goldman Sachs note said.

Globally, ten banks are in the $100 billion market cap club. The list includes JP Morgan Chase, Wells Fargo, Bank of America, HSBC, Citibank and three Chinese banks.

Can the bank grow faster? Sashi says it can grow faster but not at the cost of diluting risk or margins and also subject to availability of core liquidity in the form of deposits, refinance and capital. The bank raised ₹240 billion in July 2018 after ₹100 billion in 2015 for investing in the next growth phase and this can see it through for next four years. It intends to raise capital every three to four years.

Bouts of Stress

It isn't an easy task to be consistent and record a rather monotonous 25% growth rate quarter after quarter. There have been bouts of stress, particularly in the beginning, as certain senior employees of HDFC Bank didn't get along well with each other. Then, there have been issues on which the bank and its promoter didn't see eye to eye.

The tension between Harish and Samir, two of Aditya's key men in corporate banking, is well known among their colleagues. Neither of them would talk about this but it got to such a level that Harish, the Corporate Banking boss, volunteered to give up his role. Aditya was worried that Harish might leave the bank.

"Tu kya karega?" [What will you do?] he asked Harish when he confided in Aditya his desire to get out of corporate banking.

"I won't leave the bank. I will do something new," he assured Aditya.

Harish started the Financial Institutional group in 2002–03 to focus on mobilizing money from government business. He gave up chasing assets (advances) and started dealing with only liabilities (deposits).

The tension between Vinod, Deepak's man Friday, and others in the initial years is the stuff legends are made of. It started with Aditya snatching his secretary, Goretti Soares. Vinod had brought her from Mather & Platt. Aditya joined the bank in September 1994 at Sandoz House, whereas Vinod, Goretti and a few others still remained at the Ramon House office. One day when Aditya called Goretti to take charge of his office as his secretary was making a mess of things, she politely told her managing director to get Vinod's okay. "I don't take permission from people; I instruct them what to do," Aditya told her.

Vinod was a tough and stingy person who would count every penny. Many even considered him Deepak's spy. "The feeling with some of the bank people was that I had planted Vinod to oversee them. He was a finance guy, a conscientious book-keeper. He had to be strict. He wasn't liked by some people but at no stage did they ask for him to be taken away," Deepak told me.

Aditya describes Vinod as 'the original Brit'.

Clash of Cultures

Vinod's first impression about Aditya is 'a typical Citibanker, a roaring lion'.

Vinod saw two different cultures in the bank—of Citibank and Bank of America, the two US banks from where most employees came. They were poles apart. The Bank of America people were modest, down to earth and friendly; the Citibank boys were aggressive, demanding and arrogant. Vinod formed the third culture, a strict disciplinarian who would need to know how a penny is spent, prefer to hire furniture on rent for senior employees instead of buying it, and be happy if they took flats in suburbs where he himself lived, instead of fancy localities where the rent is very high.

"I am not in the right place. Let me quit," Vinod once told Deepak.

"You better get used to the Citibankers. I am also doing the same," Deepak replied.

Vinod listened to his friend's advice. Initially, there was confrontation between Vinod and Aditya, eight years his junior, but after about 18 months they got to know each other well and started liking each other.

Vinod would always sit to Aditya's left at every meeting and kick him under the table whenever Aditya would shout. Occasionally, Aditya has shown his bad temper. Vinod used to tell him to check his blood pressure. Aditya didn't let Vinod go when he turned 60 in 2001. He was given three extensions for three years each, rare in the bank.

Fighting the Promoter

The tension between HDFC and the bank has primarily been on two counts: One, compensation for the bankers and two, sale of home loans by the bank.

"Senior team compensation was a key issue and the subject of many meetings. My sole objective was for the bank's value to go up. This would not have been possible without Deepak Parekh's support," Anil Ahuja told me. He was on the HDFC Bank Board for six years between 1999–2005 as Director from Chase Capital Partners, which had bought the bulk of NatWest's stake in the bank.

"I never got into the HDFC compensation structure; never tried to compare it. If you go down that path, you are asking for trouble. This is a banking company and the compensation package will be different here. If you don't pay, people will walk out of your door," Anil says.

In a bank, the top team of half a dozen people drives the business strategy and the core team has to be retained. To do that, HDFC Bank worked out one of the best stock option programmes in the market. This wasn't easy to pass through the board. In fact, this is one of the key reasons behind the bank's success. In some sense the senior executives of the bank are entrepreneurs and they own the bank.

The first bank to give stock options to its employees, HDFC Bank uses this route to create a balance between short-term rewards and long-term sustainable value creation. The options play a key role in attraction and retention of talent. Currently, only employees in a certain band with a specific performance rating are eligible for stock options.

Since inception, around 424 million shares given to senior employees as stock options have been vested. This is after taking into consideration a stock split. In July 2011, the bank split its ₹10 face value stock into five shares of a face value of ₹2 each. The options are not granted at a discount but at the prevailing market price of the shares at the time of each grant. So, the gains for individual employees are a function of the future performance of the bank and its shares.

The 2018 Annual Report of the bank says, during the year, Aditya got 701,600 options, Paresh 319,000, Kaizad 232,000 and at least six group heads 180,000 each. Since the options would vest over the next four years, Paresh would not be able to exercise them as he has quit. Aditya and his family held 3.56 million shares of the bank as on 31 March 2018, according to the report.

Duplication of Business

The bank's investors were keen that it must sell home loans to complete the suite of retail products but HDFC had reservations on this 'duplication of business' which, it felt, would create confusion in the market. Besides, banks don't make money on housing loans as they are cheaper than other retail loans, it argued.

"If the bank started giving home loans and HDFC started giving car loans, consumer loans and personal loans, it would have caused tremendous confusion in the market," Keki says.

In fact, well before it promoted the bank, HDFC did make a foray into the consumer loans business in the early 1990s, partnering with GE Countrywide Consumer Financial Services Ltd., a unit of General Electric Co. of the USA. It used to finance white goods, office equipment, two-wheelers, used cars, furniture, jewellery and travel. Later, it withdrew from this space by selling its stake to GE.

The solution was found in 2002–03. HDFC Bank got into the mortgage business but not directly; it was decided that the bank would source home loans for HDFC and buy them back partially.

Keki claims that housing loans are the least profitable among retail products as they are relatively cheaper. And, it's a specialized business. "It isn't credit alone. There are other technical and legal aspects with regard to property and, therefore, home loans [require] an expertise which many banks don't have," says Keki.

The bank had a two-fold interest in home loans—firstly, it wanted to complete its product range so that it could meet its customers' need for mortgages, and secondly, it wanted on its books home loans that qualified for priority sector lending.

Both Keki and Renu, the Managing Director of HDFC, worked hard to find the solution. After rounds of discussions and tough negotiations, it was decided that the bank would source housing loans for HDFC as it has a strong distribution network. It would also have the right to buy back up to 70% of the loans. Simply put, if the bank arranges a loan of ₹100 for HDFC, it can buy back ₹70.

So both HDFC and HDFC Bank sell the same (HDFC's) home loan product and there is no confusion with the branding of home loans or with customers. All loans originated at HDFC Bank are first processed and booked by HDFC on its books and the bank earns a selling commission. After that, the bank has the option (not the obligation) to buy up to 70% of the loans originated by it.

Both HDFC and the bank say it's a 'win-win' arrangement, leveraging their respective strengths—the former's expertise in mortgages and its economies of scale and the latter's distribution and customer base.

The pricing was also decided upfront. The bank would buy it at 1.25 percentage points lower than what the home loan taker was paying to HDFC. This payment is for the processing and collection services. In effect, if the interest rate on the loan was 11%, the bank would buy it at 9.75% even though the customer would continue to pay 11%. This used to be the practice till 2014 but due to regulatory changes, now the entire interest is passed on to the bank which pays a 0.75% processing fee to HDFC.

What does the bank gain from this arrangement? Under RBI norms, Indian banks need to give 40% of loans to the priority sector consisting of agriculture and small businesses. Relatively smaller home loans are also treated as priority loans. Buying back such loans from HDFC helps the bank meet the priority loan target.

The bank also gets virtually risk-free income on the loans it has bought back as HDFC is a servicing and collections agent. By being a single-product company, HDFC has expertise and very low costs in processing, servicing and recovery of loans. The bank does not have this expertise or scale. Over 40 years, HDFC's total loan loss, or the money written off, has been only 0.04% of its mortgage portfolio.

Till 2014, HDFC was making money by keeping a 1.25 percentage point margin on the loans sold. The bank too makes money—if it was buying the loans at 9.75%, minus the cost of fund, the difference was its profit. A home loan customer is not in any way concerned about this internal arrangement.

Whose Brand is Bigger?

Yet another area of hush-hush discussions in the corridors of the parent and the offspring is about whose brand is bigger. Everyone in the bank agrees that it wouldn't have been successful had it not got the 'HDFC' name. But that was in 1994. Now the 25-year-old seems to be adding to the umbrella brand and is not a parasite any more. In valuation parlance, this phenomenon is called equity migration.

Renu feels the bank has a positive rub-off on the HDFC brand as it has followed the basic tenets of integrity, transparency and customer service in line with the HDFC philosophy.

In private, many in the bank say it is contributing significantly to the HDFC brand compared to the promoter.

It could be true. How many times does one deal with HDFC? One may take a home loan or two and instruct one's bank to transfer money from the account every month to repay the loan. But one is dealing with the bank frequently at different service points—for keeping deposits, taking loans, using credit and debit cards, ATMs, buying mutual funds and insurance. "Frequent interaction of customers with the bank leads to a high recall and enhances the overall brand recall," Renu says.

The HDFC brand is responsible for the success of the bank but the incremental value is being created more by the bank than by HDFC. Use of one brand across the spectrum is always risky. If any one of the entities does not do well, the overarching brand suffers. The HDFC brand hasn't suffered despite minor loss of reputation by the bank on a few occasions—it was penalized by the regulator. The bank has been solidly contributing to it.

The late Ranjan Kapur, former Country Head of WPP India, the parent of well-known advertising agencies such as J. Walter Thompson USA Inc. (commonly called JWT), Young & Rubicam and Ogilvy & Mather, spoke about the brand: "What is a brand? It's an asset whose transfer takes place at an emotional level. Initially, it had got transferred from HDFC to the bank—the parent's value, integrity and so on. Then the child grew up, stood on its feet and became equal to its parent. Now it is a brand in its own rights—it is neither dependent on HDFC nor confused of its identity. Each one is now equally strong a brand and transferring assets back and forth. One is lifting the other. It's unfair to compare who is bigger as they are in different spaces, banking and mortgage. In future anyone can become a liability or an asset to the other but at this point both are equally strong."

Ranjan was on the board of HDFC Bank for two years—between January 2004–March 2006. "I admire the bank for its governance and ability to grow without being aggressive. I used to call [Aditya] Puri 'Mr 31%' as he would always grow at 31%—not half a per cent less or more," Ranjan told me.

Ramanujam Sridhar, CEO of Integrated Brand Comm Pvt.

Ltd., a communications consulting company headquartered in Bengaluru, says HDFC is the leader in performance and imagery: "Newer, more aggressive players like ICICI Bank have entered the market but haven't been able to match the service quality of HDFC which has been a strong financial services brand. The key thing to be remembered is the equity of the HDFC brand which the bank has used to great advantage."

He admits that the mother brand continues to be strong and each feeds on the other's equity and success. He refers to the Japanese principle of 'stretching' a brand. Companies such as the Mitsubishi Group and Yamaha Corporation straddle industries and verticals with varied degrees of success in the respective industries though the overarching brand is crucial to success. Virgin is yet another diversified brand.

Ramesh Jude Thomas, President and Chief Knowledge Officer of Equitor Management Consulting Pvt. Ltd., a brand value advisory, believes HDFC Bank has outgrown the parent primarily because a banking licence opens up opportunities far beyond mortgage business. However, mortgage finance is such a universal need that a strong pedigree in this area can easily extend itself to almost any financial services undertaking.

The first example that comes to Ramesh's mind is Caterpillar Inc. The company has exploited the gene of 'providing a firm foothold' to move into more consumer-driven businesses, including footwear. These, in turn, strengthen the mother business by maintaining integrity of the original DNA.

Another example is Samsung Electronic Company's Mobile Handset Division—it's a recent business line of the company, and does account for a hefty portion of its revenues, but handsets are what the company is known by. Similarly, Disney's theme park revenue is about 28% of its overall revenue. The media networks, films and merchandise have outgrown the theme parks but they were incubated by the theme park pedigree. Now it is running in the opposite direction—a Disney game influences park traffic.

The diversified Tata Group companies pay a licensing fee to Tata Sons Ltd., the holding company, for using the 'Tata' brand but other Indian business groups are wary of even discussing a licensing fee for fear of pushback from powerful CEOs. Ramesh says the Tata licensing programme is meant to get business heads to recognize two significant realities—the Tata brand is an arm's length asset belonging to Tata Sons and not to any individual listed entity; and the mere absence of the right to use this name will impair performance and valuations of many of the group companies by several dollars.

HDFC doesn't have any agreement to charge royalty for lending its brand to the bank but it does have an agreement with the bank that if HDFC's shareholding falls below a certain level, the bank would have to change its name. Keki says they haven't done any study on this. There have been informal internal discussions on licensing fees, but Deepak, insiders say, always puts his foot down.

"Will you charge your son? You set up HDFC Bank, haven't you? So, where is the question of collecting money for it?" he asks.

"Deepak is a giver; he is not a taker," Satwalekar says.

"Who will charge royalty to whom?" Ranjan of WPP asked. "Both brands are equally strong and they are adding value to each other."

Here is what Deepak has to say on the brand issue: "All the HDFC Group companies need to contribute towards enhancement of the mother brand to make it resilient, which will benefit everyone during rough periods. They should be careful or refrain from doing anything that will eat into the mother brand."

Incidentally, in September 2018, HDFC Bank was ranked as India's Most Valuable Brand for the fifth consecutive year. A survey conducted by Kantar Millward Brown, a group company of WPP, which announced the raking, values HDFC Bank brand at $21.7 billion.

Merger on the Cards, Forever

The market has been speculating on a possible merger of HDFC with the bank ever since ICICI, the project finance institution, merged with ICICI Bank in 2002. The context of that merger is different though. ICICI was crumbling under huge asset–liability mismatches. Survival in a changing environment was becoming increasingly difficult for it as the inherent cost advantage that such institutions were enjoying by virtue of their access to long-term cheap funds was disappearing and commercial banks were getting into project financing in an aggressive way. The regulator was pulling down the wall that separated financial institutions from banks.

Two years later, in 2004, IDBI too merged with IDBI Bank, for similar reasons.

But HDFC is a highly successful housing finance company. Most commercial banks that entered the mortgage business have a distinctive cost advantage over HDFC by virtue of their access to low-cost savings and no-cost current accounts, but HDFC continues to be profitable in an expanding mortgage market in Asia's third largest economy. The merger is not imperative for its survival.

"We have a large balance sheet. If we were to merge with a bank, then we would need huge regulatory reserve requirement. That's the biggest issue," says Keki, who has been a director on the HDFC Bank board since its inception. In June 2018, HDFC's asset base was ₹4.16 trillion.

In December 2018, under RBI norms, banks were to invest 19.5% of their deposits in government bonds or SLR and keep 4% of their deposits with RBI in the form of CRR, on which they do not earn any interest. Besides, they need to have 40% of their loan exposure to the priority sector—where the size of loans is smaller and hence the transaction cost is higher and return is relatively lower.

"If the regulator excuses us from these pre-emptions

for five years or allows us to maintain SLR and CRR on incremental deposits and not on the existing balance sheet, it would make tremendous sense for both HDFC and the bank," Keki told me.

Aditya says Deepak and he enjoy an excellent professional relationship and if they think that the merger is value accretive for the entire group, they will go ahead with it. However, at the moment, they feel that HDFC is well managed and is trading well above its book value and the return on equity will reduce significantly if the merger were to take place.

Holding Company

Can HDFC become a holding company? Keki feels the holding company concept makes immense sense but it requires a number of legislative changes, particularly from the fiscal side. HDFC is a housing finance company and it also holds equity in the bank, life insurance and general insurance companies, an asset management company and a venture capital fund. It is playing a dual role but technically it's not a holding company.

Conceptually, in a holding company structure, the holding company does not have any function except for owning the equity in group companies. This means, the mortgage business has to be separated from the holding company and made a subsidiary.

HDFC makes money in the mortgage business and re-invests that in the bank, insurance and asset management businesses. If it becomes a holding company by spinning off the mortgage business into a subsidiary, then the profit will get crystallized in that subsidiary and the holding company will get only dividends. At the time of paying dividend, the subsidiary will have to pay dividend distribution tax.

If HDFC as a holding company used that dividend to pay dividend to its own shareholders then the dividend distribution tax paid by the subsidiary to the holding company can be set-off against the dividend paid by the holding company to its own shareholders. However, in case the dividend received by the holding company is used for further investment in other subsidiaries, then no such set-off is permitted. So, there is tax leakage in the holding company.

"If the law is changed and tax exemptions are given when a holding company pays dividends to its shareholders and invests in its subsidiaries, the holding company structure makes sense," Keki says.

At the moment, all options are open, depending on how the regulations frame out. The bank can become bigger overnight through a reverse merger with HDFC if the RBI relaxes the reserve requirements. HDFC can also become a holding company if the tax issues are sorted out.

Such a structure also has implications for public sector banks. They always need capital to grow business as well as maintain the floor for the government's holding. For every loan of ₹100, a bank needs a capital of at least ₹9, and the government holding cannot come down below 51% under banking laws.

Some of the public sector banks have their own subsidiaries and many of them are capital guzzlers.

And of course, many of these banks are also capital starved as they need to set aside money for bad assets.

The Committee to Review Governance of Boards of Banks, headed by former Axis Bank Chairman, P.J. Naya, in its report in May 2014 suggested that the government should set up a Bank Investment Company (BIC) to hold equity stakes in these banks. While the BIC would be constituted as a core investment company under RBI registration and regulation, the character of its business would make it resemble a passive sovereign wealth fund for the government's banks. This committee was constituted by former RBI Governor Raghuram Rajan. Its mandate included a review of the Indian central bank's regulatory guidelines on bank ownership, ownership concentration and representation in the board, among other things.

This makes sense, particularly when the government is cash-starved and struggling to bridge its fiscal deficit. However, nothing has happened as yet.

Aditya or Deepak?

Who has built HDFC Bank—Deepak who had the vision and chose Aditya to fulfil it or Aditya who got together the team and runs the business?

"It's Aditya's bank. Would it have been possible without Mr Parekh? No. This is because every leader or CEO who builds an enterprise needs an understanding head. Deepak may not have been the chairman of the bank but as Chairman of HDFC, his influence is enormous. What is required of such a leader is to give space to the CEO to grow and develop and that space Deepak has definitely given Aditya. But if you look at purely building this bank, it certainly is Aditya's bank," Kamath told me.

Shirish of Citibank thinks Deepak and Aditya in equal measure were absolutely critical for the success. "I don't think any other two people could have taken HDFC Bank to this level.... Deepak's credibility and ability to connect with the business sector and Aditya's phenomenal managerial skill are a deadly combination. Aditya has a unique ability of being above and yet being very involved."

In 1977, HDFC started in virgin territory. The mortgage business did not exist in India before the housing finance company came into being: Hasmukh-bhai created the industry. But banking did exist when HDFC Bank set up shop. In fact, the entire Indian banking industry was privately run till July 1969, when then Prime Minister, Indira Gandhi nationalized

14 banks despite stiff opposition by her Finance Minister, Morarji Desai.

It wasn't an easy task for HDFC Bank. But it succeeded because the timing was correct. Could this bank have happened in 1960 or 1970? No, it couldn't. After the economy opened up in 1991, the canvas for a bank got broader and there was a vast open space to function in. When it came into being, there wasn't another HDFC Bank in India. It had to be created. And the best two people to create it were Deepak and Aditya.

The combination was able to take competition in a crowded sector and create a space for itself. It's one of the three banks in Asia that stands out in a crowd, the other two being Mizuho Corporate Bank (Malaysia) Berhad and Hang Seng Bank Ltd. of Hong Kong. "It has been able to ride the growth of the Indian economy in a very disciplined way without any of the excesses that some banks tend to get into," Piyush of DBS says.

Renu attributes the bank's success to its excellent team built by Aditya who, she says, "is a great leader and has the capacity to innovate and think about new products and businesses ahead of others. HDFC being a trusted brand also provided huge goodwill and comfort which is fundamental to the bank's success".

"How do we have an institution which is world class, privately owned and functioning as a corporate entity subjected to the best governance and international regulatory standards?" asks Bimal Jalan, former RBI governor, who was on the board of HDFC for more than a decade till July 2018. It can be done if there is no interference in day-to-day management and operations of a bank by regulatory authorities or government.

Earlier, Indian psychology was that in a developing country and protective market, one can't compete. But instances such as the creation of HDFC Bank have dismembered this belief and proved that one can compete in the Indian scenario, provided one allows the institution to be run by professional managers under the guidance of a competent board.

Who chose HDFC Bank's CEO Aditya, who has contributed substantially to the bank's growth and credit-worthiness? He was chosen and appointed by the board of the bank on merit, after careful consideration, and given full management responsibility for running the bank as per best international standards. This management freedom, subject to accountability, is critical for excellence.

Bimal cites the example of the Election Commission and the Comptroller and Auditor General of India (CAG). The Election Commission gives India the largest free and fair election in human history because it is not controlled by the Home Ministry. The CAG couldn't have been objective had it been reporting to the Finance Ministry. Would HDFC Bank have been so successful if its managing director had been selected through a bureaucratic process? Could it have performed so well had its board been interfering in day-to-day management?

A Foreign-Owned Bank?

Aditya is a highly competent banker, and he could succeed because he had a free hand to run the bank, with accountability for performance, but without any interference. HDFC, the promoter, holds a 21.4% stake in the bank; the foreign stakeholders a little more than 50%. The ADS holders, a sub-set of the foreign shareholders, about 20%, but they have no voting rights. Neither HDFC nor others interfere in any way. They keep an eye on the performance and nothing else. They don't enjoy power without responsibility the way ministers and bureaucrats do with respect to public sector banks.

Many in the financial sector say HDFC Bank is a foreign-owned bank because the foreign ownership is close to 74% allowed by FDI regulations—almost 52% direct foreign ownership and little more than 21% indirect, through its promoter HDFC which itself is 77% foreign owned.

But there is a difference between ownership and control. Although the bank's ownership is largely foreign, the control is based in India. India is still a developing country and needs foreign capital. Except for enjoying dividend, the foreign shareholders earn nothing—they don't control the bank. It is managed by Indian professionals, serves Indian customers and the bank doesn't repatriate funds overseas, except by way of dividends.

HDFC Bank has one branch each in Hong Kong, Bahrain and Dubai and representative offices in Abu Dhabi and Nairobi. It also has a presence in International Financial Service Centre at Gujarat International Finance Tech or GIFT City in Gandhinagar, Gujarat—India's first smart city and an international financial services centre.

It wants to go big wherever it goes but most global markets such as US are over-banked and the regulations are strict, restricting the entry of the foreign banks. Besides, India is growing. There is a large underpenetrated financial market and growth is never an issue. So, why would the bank go abroad? Aditya is not convinced on going global unless there is a shift in world regulations.

No Celebrations

The bank never celebrates even after winning awards. That's the culture of HDFC Bank. There isn't a single meeting or party to acknowledge what it has achieved. The question is always what next and where it has gone wrong. It believes that the awards are for the past but the bank needs to focus on the future to make the present meaningful.

The RBI has given it the tag of too big to fail along with SBI and ICICI Bank. Given the runway of opportunities and its positioning, HDFC Bank has a long way to go. It now roughly has 7% market share of banking assets, one-third of SBI, and equivalent of all foreign banks.

There are two ways to look at its growth trajectory in the future—nibbling away share from the public sector banks and creating new markets. A little less than 70% of the Indian banking assets are with the government-owned banks in 2018. Assuming that top five of them retain their market share, the balance is up for grabs.

Even if we assume that HDFC Bank will capture one-fourth of the balance, there is still about 8–10% of the bankable business it can capture. The bank has gained 7% market share in 25 years but it can be doubled quickly. Beside the pain that the bad loans-laden government-owned banking sector is undergoing, at least one large private bank is not in the best of health and two larger ones have been trying hard to get out of a troubled phase. They are not growing as aggressively as they were used to. Not to speak of another 11 state-owned banks which till recently were restrained by the RBI from normal banking activities because of their ill health. This gives a tremendous opportunity to HDFC Bank.

Yet another dimension is the opportunity in semi-urban or rural India where 60% of the nation lives. As India's economy grows, per capita GDP in this geography is bound to grow. With that will grow the aspiration of consumers, leading to demands in consumer goods, providing the bank an opportunity to expand business.

HDFC Bank is making inroads in rural India and there is tremendous opportunity to scale up business in that segment. Today 53% of its branches are in rural areas and it has been growing its branch presence in past seven years. The bank's business mix mirrors India's GDP with a 55% retail portfolio matching with the share of consumption in GDP, the remaining being wholesale. It does not want to overstretch and go down the risk ladder.

The Next Phase: Digital

The next phase of growth will be driven by digital strategy. Uninterrupted existence, proven track record, investment in advanced technology to understand consumer behaviour, the ability to invest in innovations and right platforms, and the willingness to partner with bigger players to be able to offer every product under one umbrella will help HDFC Bank leap forward and compete with the likes of Amazon, Google and Apple. From a life cycle bank, it is transforming itself into a lifestyle bank.

The biggest lesson from the HDFC Bank story is that once the market is opened to competition, people must be allowed the freedom. They are capable of delivering the best globally. Promoters of the new set of private banks and small finance and payments banks that have opened shops should also take note of this. A few new banks that were peers of HDFC Bank did not survive because they did not respect corporate governance or the freedom they enjoyed and because they did not work for the benefit of their customers and investors.

The HDFC Bank story is not merely one of entrepreneurship. It is a testimony to what new India can do—what can happen when passion for excellence merges with high corporate governance. It has not done anything unique. Doing very ordinary things with extraordinary execution and redefining the distinction between real risks and perceived risks are what make HDFC Bank different from the rest. Going digital is the logical path at this juncture

This bank, a child of economic liberalisation, strives to reinvent itself periodically while many others either remain where they are or become a throwback to old times, an anachronism that painfully survives the passing years.

Abbreviations

ADS	American Depositary Shares
AI	Artificial Intelligence
AIIMS	All India Institute of Medical Sciences
AMCs	Asset Management Companies
AML	Anti-Money Laundering
API	Application Programming Interface
APMC	Agricultural Produce Marketing Committee
ATMs	Automated Teller Machines
BHIM	Bharat Interface for Money
BoB	Bank of Baroda
BoP	Bank of Punjab
BPO	Business Process Outsourcing
BSE	Bombay Stock Exchange Ltd.
CAG	Comptroller and Auditor General of India
CAGR	Compounded Annual Growth Rate
CAMS	Computer Age Management Series
CASA	Current Account and Savings Account
CBDT	Central Board of Direct Taxes
CBI	Central Bureau of Investigation
CDSL	Central Depository Services Ltd.
CEO	Chief Executive Officer
CFO	Chief Financial Officer
CGA	Controller General of Accounts
CITIL	Citicorp Information Technology Industries Ltd.
CRM	Customer Relationship Management
CRR	Cash Reserve Ratio

CTRs	Cash Transaction Reports
CUI	Conversational User Interface
DBS	Development Bank of Singapore Ltd.
DPs	Depository Participants
ECH	Electronic Clearing House
ED	Enforcement Directorate
EMI	Equated Monthly Instalments
EVA	Electronic Virtual Assistant
ERP	Enterprise Resource Planning
FERA	Foreign Exchange Regulation Act
FIU	Financial Intelligence Unit
Fincon	Financial Control Unit
FMCG	Fast-Moving Consumer Goods
GAAP	Generally Accepted Accounting Principles
GST	Goods and Services Tax
GSTN	Goods and Services Tax Network
HBR	*Harvard Business Review*
HDFC	Housing Development Finance Corporation Ltd.
HFC	Housing Finance Company
HSBC	Hongkong and Shanghai Banking Corporation
I-Sec	ICICI Securities Ltd.
ICICI	Industrial Credit and Investment Corporation of India Ltd.
IDBI	Industrial Development Bank of India
IDFC	Infrastructure Development Finance Co. Ltd.
IFC	International Finance Corporation
IIM-A	Indian Institute of Management-Ahmedabad
IIT	Indian Institute of Technology
IMPS	Immediate Payment Service
IPO	Initial Public Offering
IRA	Interactive Robot Assistant
IT	Information Technology
JLG	Joint Liability Group
KDVK	Kisan Dhan Vikas Kendra
KGC	Kissan Gold Card

KYC	Know Your Customer
LAMF	Loans Against Mutual Funds
LAS	Loans Against Shares
M2M	Milk to Money
MD	Managing Director
MFIs	Micro Finance Institutions
MIS	Management Information System
MNC	Multinational Company
NABARD	National Bank for Agriculture and Rural Development
NACH	National Automated Clearing House
NatWest	National Westminster Bank PLC
NBFCs	Non-Banking Finance Companies
NEFT	National Electronic Funds Transfer
NGOs	Non-Government Organizations
NIM	Net Interest Margin
NPAs	Non-Performing Assets
NPCI	National Payments Corporation of India
NRIs	Non-Resident Indians
NRO	Non-Resident Ordinary
NSDL	National Securities Depository Ltd.
NSE	National Stock Exchange Ltd.
NYSE	New York Stock Exchange
OCI	Overseas Citizenship of India
OTT	Over the Top
P27	Power of 27
PDR2	Protect, Detect, Respond and Recover
PKI	Public Key Infrastructure
PNB	Punjab National Bank
PoS	Point of Sale
QR	Quick Response
RBI	Reserve Bank of India
RPA	Robotics Process Automation
RTA	Registrar and Transfer Agent
RTGS	Real Time Gross Settlement
Samba	Saudi American Bank

SBI	State Bank of India
SBICI	State Bank of India Commercial & International Bank Ltd.
SCM	Supply Chain Management
SEBI	Securities and Exchange Board of India
SEC	Securities and Exchange Commission
SHG	Self-Help Group
SLR	Statutory Liquidity Ratio
SMAC	Social, Mobile, Analytics and Cloud
SME	Small and Medium Enterprise
SOA	Service-Oriented Architecture
STP	Straight through Processing
SWIFT	Society for Worldwide Interbank Financial Telecommunication
TCS	Tata Consultancy Services Ltd.
TELCO	Tata Engineering and Locomotive Co. Ltd.
TISCO	Tata Iron and Steel Co. Ltd.
TTD	Through-the-Door
UBS	United Bank of Switzerland AG
UI	User Interface
UPI	Unified Payments Interface
UTI	Unit Trust of India
UX	User Experience
VRM	Virtual Relationship Manager
YMCA	Young Men's Christian Association

Glossary

accretive merger: An acquisition that results in a rise in the price-to-earnings ratio of the acquiring company.

ambulance chasers: A derogatory phrase that typically refers to attorneys in the United States who solicit business from accident victims or their families.

American Depositary Share (ADS): A US-dollar-denominated equity share of an overseas company available for purchase on an American stock exchange. An ADS is issued by depository banks in the United States under agreement with the issuing foreign company; the entire issuance is called an American Depositary Receipt (ADR) and an individual share is referred to as an ADS.

articles of association: The regulations governing the relationships between shareholders and directors of a company.

Artificial Intelligence (AI): The theory and development of computer systems able to perform tasks normally requiring human intelligence, such as visual perception, speech recognition, decision-making, and translation between languages.

Application Programming Interface (API): A set of programming code that queries data, parses responses, and sends instructions between one software platform and another.

asset classification norms: Norms introduced by the Reserve Bank of India (RBI) in the mid-1990s as a prudential measure to strengthen the banks' balance sheets by setting aside money not only for their bad assets but also for their standard assets, marginally though for the latter.

asset management company: A company that invests its clients' pooled fund into securities that match its declared financial objectives. Such companies are called mutual funds in India and they run different schemes for investments in debt and equities.

asset–liability mismatch: A mismatch that occurs when an institution's assets and liabilities do not match. They should match in terms of tenure as well as amount.

Audit and Compliance Committee: An operating committee of the board of directors charged with oversight of financial reporting and disclosure.

back office: The section of a company that provides administrative and support services. A financial services company is typically broken up into three parts: the front office, which includes sales personnel and corporate finance; the middle office, which manages risk and information technology resources; and the back office.

bad assets: Assets on which a bank does not earn any interest. Additionally, it needs to set aside money to provide for such assets. An illiquid asset is also called a bad asset when its secondary market disappears.

balance-of-payment crisis: Also called a currency crisis, this occurs when a nation is unable to pay for essential imports and/or service its debt repayments.

bank guarantee: A guarantee that enables the customer (debtor) to acquire goods, buy equipment or draw down loans, and thereby expand business activity. Banks offer such a guarantee for a fee.

Bankex: An equity index traded on the Bombay Stock Exchange that tracks the performance of the leading banking sector stocks. It consists of 10 stocks (eight private banks and two public sector banks).

Banking Regulation Act: The 1949 Act enacted to safeguard the interest of depositors and prevent abuse of power by promoters of banks. It has been amended many times to make the laws contemporary. This Act, however, does not supersede the Companies Act. This means that a listed banking entity is governed both by the Banking Regulation Act as well as by the Companies Act.

bellwether equity index: A security or indicator that signals the market's direction. The Sensex is BSE's bellwether equity index.

bill discounting: The process by which a bank buys the bill—a bill of exchange or a promissory note—before it is due and credits the value of the bill after a discount charged to the customer's account. The transaction is practically an advance against the security of the bill and the discount represents the interest on the advance from the date of purchase of the bill until it is due for payment.

black swan phenomenon: A concept derived from the 'black swan' event or theory, a metaphor that describes an event that is a surprise (to the observer) and has a major impact. The theory was developed by Nassim Nicholas Taleb to explain the disproportionate role of high-impact, hard-to-predict, and rare events that are beyond the realm of normal expectations in history, science, finance and technology.

blue chip: A nationally recognized, well-established and financially sound company. Blue chips generally sell high-quality, widely accepted products and services.

bonus share: A free share given to current shareholders in a company.

book building: The process of generating, capturing and recording investor demand for shares during an initial public offer.

book runner: The main underwriter or lead manager in the issuance of new equity, debt or securities instruments.

bulk deposit: Any single rupee term deposit of Rs 20 million and above is a bulk deposit. Banks have the freedom to offer differential interest rates on such deposits.

business correspondent: A financial organization such as a securities company or a bank that regularly performs services for another company that does not have the requisite facilities or the access to perform the services directly. Business correspondents earn commission for their services.

business process outsourcing: The process of hiring another company to handle one's business activities.

business process re-engineering: The analysis and redesign of workflow within and between enterprises.

CASA: Low-cost current and savings accounts. Banks do not pay any interest on current accounts (CA) and pay relatively low interest on savings accounts (SA). Till 2011, interest on savings accounts was mandated. The higher the CASA, the lower the cost of fund for a bank.

cash management: Functions for processing receipts and payments, that is, managing the cash flow between a company and its suppliers. For example, a Mumbai-based company selling its products across India gets a payment as a cheque drawn on some bank's branch in Ludhiana, Punjab. When the Mumbai company deposits the cheque in its account, the cheque goes back to Ludhiana for clearing and the money could take up to a week to be credited. In a cash management system, the company deposits the cheque with the bank's branch or a partner bank in Ludhiana and gets the money almost immediately. The bank either charges a commission, or gets to keep the money for a day or two.

Cash Reserve Ratio (CRR): The portion of deposits a bank needs to keep with the Reserve Bank of India (RBI), on which it does not earn any interest. Currently it is pegged at 4 per cent.

certificate of deposits: A savings certificate entitling the bearer to receive interest. It bears a maturity date, a specified fixed interest rate and can be issued in any denomination.

chatbot: A computer program that simulates human conversation through voice commands or text chats or both. Chatbot, short for chatterbot is also known as 'talkbot', 'bot', 'IM bot' 'interactive agent' or 'artificial conversation entity'.

circuit breaker: Any measure used by stock exchanges during large sell-offs to avert panic selling. It works the other way too, when a stock price rises too much.

circular trading: A scheme that creates artificial trading activity by passing shares among a closed group.

clearing corporation: An organization associated with an exchange to handle the confirmation, settlement and delivery of transactions, fulfilling the main obligation of ensuring that the transactions are made in a prompt and efficient manner. It is also referred to as a 'clearing company/firm' or 'clearing house'.

cloud: A network of remote servers hosted on the internet and used to store, manage, and process data in place of local servers or personal computers.

collateral: A borrower's pledge (in a lending agreement) of specific property to a lender, to secure repayment of a loan.

collection agent: A person who contacts debtors on behalf of a client.

compensation committee: Also known as remuneration committee, it is a committee of the board of directors that sets appropriate and supportable pay programmes in the organization's best interests and aligned with its business mission and strategy.

Compounded Annual Growth Rate (CAGR): The year-on-year growth rate of an investment over a specified period of time. It is calculated by taking the nth root of the total percentage growth rate, where n is the number of years in the period being considered.

compromise settlement: The resolution of a dispute between a lender and a borrower by mutual agreement to avoid a lawsuit.

consent process: A process by which a company or an individual involved in an alleged wrongdoing settles a dispute with the capital market regulator by paying some money. Such a settlement neither establishes the guilt of the company involved nor does it say the company has not done anything wrong.

control premium: An amount that a buyer is willing to pay over the current market price of a publicly traded company to gain control over it.

Controller General of Accounts (CGA): The principal accounts advisor to the Government of India, responsible for establishing and maintaining a technically sound management accounting system.

Corporate Social Responsibility(CSR): The continuing commitment by a business to behave ethically and contribute to economic development while improving the quality of life of the workforce and their families as well as of the local community and society at large. Companies with a turnover of at least ₹1 billion, it is compulsory to have a CSR initiative according to the Companies Act.

cost-to-income ratio: An efficiency measure, similar to the operating margin, defined by operating expenses divided by operating income. Unlike the operating margin, lower the cost-to-income ratio is the better. The cost-to-income ratio is most commonly used in the financial sector, and can be used for benchmarking by a bank when reviewing its operational efficiency.

credit score: A number representing the creditworthiness of a person, that is, the likelihood that a person will pay his or her debts.

credit scoring model: A model based on credit scores used by lenders, such as banks and credit card companies, to evaluate the potential risk posed by lending money to consumers.

cross-selling: The practice of selling among or between established clients, markets and traders, or selling an additional product or service to an existing customer. For an instance, a bank can sell an auto loan to an existing home-loan buyer.

currency swap: A foreign-exchange agreement between two parties to exchange aspects (the principal and/or interest payments) of a loan in one currency for equivalent aspects of an equal in net present value loan in another currency.

current account: A current account in a bank is a form of demand deposit from which withdrawals are allowed any number of times. Generally, such accounts do not offer any interest and carry an overdraft facility.

data warehouse: A database used for reporting and data analysis. The data stored in the warehouse are uploaded from the operational systems (such as marketing, sales etc.). The data may pass through an operational data store before being used in the data warehouse for reporting.

death-backed bond: A security backed by life insurance which is derived by pooling together a number of transferable life insurance policies. Similar to mortgage-backed securities, the life insurance policies are pooled and repackaged into bonds to be sold to investors.

delinquency: A default in repaying bank loans. A loan becomes 'delinquent' when the borrower fails to pay interest/principal. For failure to pay for three months, such a loan becomes bad or a Non-Performing Asset(NPA).

demat: A dematerialized account for Indian citizens to trade in listed stocks or debentures in electronic form rather than on paper. The Securities and Exchange Board of India (SEBI) has made a demat account mandatory in order to trade in stocks.

depositaries: Organizations where the securities of an investor are held in electronic form.

derivative product: A contract between two parties that specifies conditions (especially the dates, resulting values of the underlying variables and notional amounts) under which payments are to be made between the parties.

direct sales agents: Individual sales agents who reach out to and deal directly with clients. Typically, private and foreign banks employ such agents to sell loans.

direct tax: A tax paid directly to the government by the persons on whom it is imposed (such as income tax).

dividend distribution tax: The tax levied by the Government of India on a company on the dividend paid to its shareholders.

dotcom: A company that embraces the internet as the key component in its business. They are so named because of the URL customers visit to do business with the company. The .com at the end of the URL stands for commercial; by contrast, websites run by companies whose primary motivations are not commercial, such as nonprofit companies, often have domain names ending in .org, which is short for organization.

due diligence: An investigation or audit of a potential investment. Due diligence serves to confirm all material facts with regard to a sale.

'eat well, sleep well' dilemma: An adage that refers to the risk/return trade-off—the type of security an investor chooses depends on whether he or she wants to eat well or sleep well.

economic liberalization: On-going economic reforms in India that started on 24 July 1991.

face value: The nominal value of a security stated by the issuer. For stocks, it is the original cost of the stock. For bonds, it is the amount paid to the holder at maturity.

financial inclusion: The delivery of banking services at an affordable cost to vast sections of disadvantaged and low-income groups.

fintech: A portmanteau word combining financial and technology, it describes new technology that seeks to improve and automate the delivery and use of financial services. The term originally referred to computer technology applied to the back office of banks or trading firms. With the internet revolution and the mobile internet/smartphone revolution, financial technology has developed and has expanded to include any technological innovation in — and automation of — the financial sector, such as money transfers, depositing a check with your smartphone, bypassing a bank branch to apply for credit, raising money for a business start-up, or managing your investments, generally without the assistance of a person. Fintech also includes the development and use of crypto-currencies such as bitcoin.

fiscal deficit: The shortfall created when a government's total expenditure exceeds the revenue that it generates in a fiscal year. This deficit or gap is taken care of by borrowing money from the market.

fiscal stimulus: The proposition that by borrowing money and spending it, the government can raise the overall state of the economy, raising output and lowering unemployment. The Government of India did this in 2009 in the wake of an unprecedented credit crunch following the collapse of US investment bank Lehman Brothers Holdings Inc.

float money: The money that a bank enjoys for a short period without paying interest on it. For instance, the money that remains with the bank between the time a bank draft is made and the time it is encashed, on which the bank pays no interest. Smart banks do business that ensures a steady flow of float money.

Foreign Exchange Management Act (FEMA): The Act passed in the 1999 winter session of the Indian Parliament to replace the Foreign Exchange Regulation Act. This Act seeks to make offences related to foreign exchange civil offences.

Foreign Exchange Regulation Act: The 1973 legislation passed by the Indian Parliament, under the Indira Gandhi government, that came into force with effect from 1 January 1974. The Act imposed stringent regulations on certain kinds of payments, such as dealings in foreign exchange and securities and transactions that had an indirect impact on foreign exchange and the import and export of currency.

gala: An industrial shed. Typically, small and medium enterprises operate in a gala which is nothing more than an industrial floor where heavy-duty machinery works.

gamification: Real-world activities are made game-like in order to motivate people to achieve their goals. Frequent-flyer programs, loyalty rewards points, and frequent shopper points are examples of the everyday use of gamification.

Generally Accepted Accounting Principles(GAAP): The standard framework of guidelines for financial accounting used in any given jurisdiction, generally known as accounting standards.

greenfield project: A new project that is not constrained by prior work (metaphorically, creating a business opportunity where none existed before). In construction, greenfield projects refer to construction on unused land where there is no need to remodel or demolish an existing structure. Such projects are often coveted by engineers.

gross NPAs: The bad assets of a bank which have not been provided for. See net NPAs; non-performing assets (NPAs).

growth outlier: A company whose growth is abnormally higher than that of its peers.

gurukul system: An ancient Indian system of education where the 'shishya' (student) resides with the 'guru' (teacher) for the duration of learning; thus, knowledge was imparted in the natural environment of the guru's home and its surroundings.

heaven and hell bond: A bond with principal redemption related to the change in the spot exchange rate from issuance to maturity.

high-net-worth customer: A classification used by the financial services industry to denote an individual or a family with high net worth (wealth).

high-value cheque: A cheques with a high denomination; they get cleared on the same day, if deposited before 11 a.m.

holding company: A parent corporation that owns enough voting stock in another corporation to control its board of directors (and, therefore, its policies and management).

'in the money': A state where one's stock option is worth money and one can sell or exercise it.

Indian Contract Act: The Act relating to contracts in India, passed in 1872. Based on the principles of English Common Law, it is applicable to all Indian states except for Jammu & Kashmir. The law determines the circumstances in which an agreement made by the parties to a contract shall be legally binding on them.

Initial Public Offering (IPO): A stock market launch where shares of a company are sold to the general public, on a securities exchange, for the first time. Through this process, a private company transforms into a public company.

inter-corporate deposit: An unsecured loan extended by one company to another.

interest rate derivative: A financial instrument based on an underlying financial security whose value is affected by changes in interest rates. Interest rate derivatives are hedges used by institutional investors such as banks to take care of the changes in market interest rates.

interest rate swap: The exchange of one set of cash flows (based on interest rate specifications) for another.

internet banking: A facility that allows customers (of a financial institution or individuals) to conduct financial transactions on a secure website operated by banks.

Internet of Things (IoT): The interconnection via the internet of computing devices embedded in everyday objects, enabling them to send and receive data.

IPO scam: A well-structured game played by the absolute opportunists consisting of intermediaries, financiers and bank employees, who make money by controlling shares meant for retail investors in an initial public offer. The IPO scam, unearthed in April 2006, involved depositaries, depositary participants and many market operators who allegedly used or abetted certain entities in creating 59,000 fictitious demat accounts to corner shares of many IPOs meant for small investors. Apparently, in 105 IPOs between 2003–2005, scamsters cornered shares meant for retail investors by creating multiple identities.

Joint Liability Group (JLG): An informal group consisting of preferably four to ten individuals, but can be up to 20 members, coming together to get bank loans either singly or through the group mechanism against mutual guarantee.

'knock-in': A financial option contract that is valid only when a certain price is met; so if a price is never reached, the contract is considered to have never existed.

'knock-out': A financial option contract with a built-in mechanism to expire worthless should a specified price level be exceeded.

Know Your Customer (KYC): A norm enforced by all regulatory authorities in financial services. Banks, mutual funds and all other intermediaries should 'know' the customers whose money they deal with. A customer's identity can be established by his or her driving licence, passport and/or permanent account number (PAN), among other documents.

lead manager: An investment banker appointed by companies going public. For bigger public issues, companies appoint more than one lead manager. The main responsibilities of a lead manager are to initiate the offer processing, help the company in road shows, create the draft offer document and get it approved by the capital market regulator and stock exchanges, and list shares at the stock market.

market capitalization: The market value of a company's outstanding shares. Market capitalization is calculated by multiplying a company's outstanding shares by the current market price of one share.

Micro Finance Institutions (MFIs): Organizations that offer tiny loans to micro entrepreneurs, small businesses and poor people who lack access to banking and related services. Such loans are relatively expensive because of high transaction costs associated with serving these client categories.

multi-channel banking: The concept of multiple or alternative modes of banking. Banking via bank branches is the first, and perhaps most conventional, channel of banking. Increasingly, banks are offering multi-channel banking facilities such as internet banking, telephone banking, automated teller machines and even doorstep banking where a banker goes to a client's house with products. Typically, high-net-worth customers have the privilege of banking in their homes.

nationalized bank: A government controlled bank that is governed by the Nationalization Act. The first set of banks was nationalized in 1969.

Net Interest Margin (NIM): The difference between the interest income generated by banks or other financial institutions from loans and the amount of interest paid out to the depositors.

net NPAs: When a loan turns bad, a bank has to set aside or provide for it. Net NPAs are bad assets not of such provision. A profitable bank can provide handsomely to bring down its net NPAs. See gross NPAs; non-performing assets (NPAs).

net open position limit: An aggregate limit of a bank's currency risk exposure.

non-banking finance company: A financial institution that provides banking services without meeting the legal definition of a bank, that is, one that does not hold a banking licence. In India, non-banking finance companies are typically not allowed to mobilize deposits from the public.

Non-Government Organizations (NGOs): Legally constituted organizations created by natural or legal persons which operate independently from any form of government.

Non-Performing Assets (NPAs): Credit facilities or loans for which the interest and/or instalment of principal has remained 'past due' for at least a quarter or 90 days. See gross NPAs; net NPAs.

open offer: A secondary market offering that is similar to a 'rights' issue in which a shareholder is given the opportunity to purchase stocks. The pricing of an open offer is determined by a formula of market regulators. Any entity that wants to buy at least 25% in a listed company is required to make an open offer.

over-the-counter derivatives: Contracts that are traded (and privately negotiated) directly between two parties, without going through an exchange or other intermediary. Products such as swaps, forward rate agreements, exotic options—and other exotic derivatives—are almost always traded in this way.

overdraft: A deficit in a bank account caused by drawing more money than the account holds. An overdraft facility allows money to be withdrawn even when the available account balance goes below zero.

overnight indexed swap: An interest rate swap involving the overnight rate being exchanged for a fixed interest rate. Overnight indexed swaps are popular among financial institutions for the reason that the overnight index is considered to be a good indicator of the inter-bank credit market and less risky than other traditional interest rate spreads.

Overseas Citizenship of India (OCI): A scheme by which a person of Indian origin in a foreign country who was (or was eligible to become) a citizen of India on 26 January 1950 or thereafter, except who is or has been a citizen of Pakistan and Bangladesh, can register as an 'overseas citizen of India'. Foreigners of Indian origin whose present nationality is such that their country of nationality allows dual citizenship in some form or other are eligible to apply and if accepted are provided with an OCI card. The status provides no political rights, but travel benefits and parity with non-resident Indians in financial, economic and educational fields.

par issue: A public issue where shares are offered at their face value without any premium.

pay-ins: A pay-in of securities refers to the transfer of stocks from a client's demat account to a broker's/clearing member's account; a pay-in of funds is the transfer of money by a broker to an exchange towards settlement dues for that particular day.

pay-outs: A pay-out of securities is the transfer of stocks from a broker's pool account to a client's demat account; a payout of funds is the transfer of money from an exchange to a broker towards settlement dues for that particular day.

personal loan: A consumer loan granted for personal use as opposed to business or commercial use. Typically, such loans are not backed by collaterals.

platformification: A business model that allows multiple participants (producers and consumers) to connect to it, interact with each other, and create and exchange value.

Point of Sale (PoS) terminal: A computerized replacement for a cash register.

price-to-book: A ratio used to compare a stock's market value to its book value.

priority loan: A loan given to the priority sector of farmers (agriculture) and small-scale industries among others. Under RBI norms, banks are required to give 40% of their loans to such segments and people from socially backward classes.

private equity: Equity capital (or shares) of a company not quoted on the market or publicly traded on an exchange.

private equity company: Investors and funds that make investments directly into private companies and even listed entities. Typically, they cash out by selling their stakes in the market when the private company goes for a public issue. Private equity firms characteristically make longer-hold investments in target industry sectors or specific investment areas where they have expertise.

project finance institution: An institution that gives project loans. The erstwhile Industrial Credit and Investment Corporation of India Ltd. and Industrial Development Bank of India were such institutions.

prudential regulation: A regulation of deposit-taking institutions and supervision of the conduct of these institutions that limit their risk-taking. The aim of prudential regulations is to ensure the safety of depositors' funds and keep the financial system stable.

public equity: Stocks and shares of a company that are traded on a public exchange.

public float: The portion of a company's outstanding shares that is in the hands of public investors, as opposed to company officers, directors or controlling-interest investors.

real-time gross settlement: A fund transfer system where transfer of money or securities takes place from one bank to another on the basis of 'real time' and 'gross' amounts.

receivables: Receivables, also referred to as accounts receivable, are debts owed to a company by its customers for goods or services that have been delivered or used but not yet paid for.

relationship manager: A professional who works to improve a company's relationships with partner companies and customers. They play a key role in banks, particularly for getting business from high-net-worth customers.

reputation risk: A type of risk related to the trustworthiness of business. When a bank is penalized by the banking regulator and a company is penalized by the market regulator, they suffer from reputation risk.

retail banking: Banking in which institutions execute transactions directly with individual consumers, rather than with corporations or other banks. Home loans and auto loans are part of retail banking.

return on equity: The amount of net income returned as a percentage of shareholders' equity. Return on equity measures a corporation's profitability by revealing how much profit a company generates with the money shareholders have invested.

risk appetite: The level of risk that an organization is prepared to accept. It represents a balance between the potential benefits of innovation and the threats that change inevitably brings on.

risk–reward trade-off: The principle that potential return rises with an increase in risk. Low levels of uncertainty (low risks) are associated with low potential returns, whereas high levels of uncertainty (high risks) are associated with high potential returns.

run on the bank: A rapid loss of deposits that occurs when a large number of customers (rush/'run' to) withdraw their deposits from a bank at the same time as they believe that the bank might become insolvent. A run on the bank is also known as a 'bank run'.

S&P/CNX Nifty Index: The Standard & Poor's CRISIL NSE Index 50, popularly called Nifty, is a stock market index, and one of several leading indices for large companies listed on the National Stock Exchange of India Ltd., index-based derivatives and index funds. It consists of 50 stocks. All Sensex stocks are part of Nifty stocks.

savings account: A bank account that offers the account holder a cheque facility and pays interest on money deposited.

securitization: The financial practice of pooling various types of contractual debts such as residential mortgages, commercial mortgages, auto loans or credit card debt obligations and selling these consolidated debts as bonds, pass-through securities or collateralized mortgage obligation to various investors.

Self-Help Group (SHG): A financial intermediary usually composed of 10–20 local women. Most SHGs are located in India, though they can also be found in other countries, especially in South Asia and Southeast Asia. SHG members make small regular savings contributions over a few months until there is enough capital in the group to begin lending.

Sensex: A free-float market capitalization weighted stock market index of 30 well-established and financially sound companies listed on the BSE Ltd., Asia's oldest bourse.

settlement fund: The transferable assets available to meet obligations or debts of a transaction or trade. The Securities and Exchange Board of India requires stock exchanges to have a system of guaranteeing settlement of trades or set up a clearing corporation to ensure that the market equilibrium is not disturbed in case of payment default by members of the exchanges. Typically, exchanges have a trade guarantee fund (or a settlement fund) to ensure timely completion of settlements of contracts. Members of the exchanges contribute to the settlement fund.

small and medium enterprises (SMEs): Companies whose personnel numbers as well as turnover fall below certain limits. In India, a micro enterprise is one where a company's investment in plant and machinery does not exceed ₹2.5 million; a small enterprise is one where the investment is ₹2.5 million–₹50 million; and a medium enterprise is one where the investment is ₹50 million–₹100 million.

Statutory Liquidity Ratio (SLR): A ratio of the amount that a commercial bank is required to maintain in the form of cash or gold or government bonds before providing credit to its customers. As of April 2019, the SLR is 19% of bank deposits in India.

stock options: A benefit in the form of an option given by a company to an employee to buy shares in the company at a discount or at a stated fixed price.

strategic partner: A party with which a strategic partnership is reached. A strategic partnership is a formal alliance between two commercial enterprises, usually formalized by one or more business contracts but falls short of forming a legal partnership or agency or corporate affiliate relationship.

Supply Chain Management (SCM): The management of a network of interconnected businesses involved in the provision of product and service packages required by the end-customers in a supply chain.

sweep facility: The facility of automatically transferring money from a customer's savings bank account or even a current account to a term deposit once it crosses a certain limit, say ₹5,000. This way, customers earn higher interest while banks earn customers' loyalty by offering a facility to earn more. Not all banks, however, offer this facility.

teller: An employee of a bank, or similar institution, whose job includes helping the bank's customers with their banking needs, such as depositing a cheque or making a withdrawal.

three-in-one: A facility that links savings and demat accounts to online trading accounts.

trade finance: International trade transactions involving exports and imports. While a seller (the exporter) can require the purchaser (an importer) to pre-pay for goods shipped, the purchaser may wish to reduce risk by requiring the seller to document the goods that have been shipped. Banks may assist by providing various forms of support such as by offering letters of credit.

transactional banking: A banking process that allows for the safe and efficient movement (transaction) of cash securities in the global financial system.

turnaround time: The time required to complete a task; in the context of this book, from the date (time) a transaction is submitted (received by the bank) to the date (time) it is completed.

Unified Payment Interface (UPI): A smartphone application which allows users to transfer money between bank accounts. It is a single-window mobile payment system developed by the National Payments Corporation of India (NPCI), which eliminates the need to enter bank

TAMAL BANDYOPADHYAY 417

details or other sensitive information each time a customer initiates a transaction.

unsecured loan: A loan that is issued and supported only by the borrower's creditworthiness, and not by any collateral.

wagering: A sort of gambling; betting on the outcome of an external event.

warrant: A derivative security that gives the holder the right to purchase securities (usually equity) from the issuer at a specific price within a certain time frame.

white label product: A product or service produced by one company (the producer) that other companies (the marketers) rebrand to make their own.

wholesale banking: The provision of services by banks to large corporate clients, mid-sized companies, real-estate developers and investors, international trade finance businesses, institutional customers (such as pension funds and government entities/agencies) and other banks or other financial institutions as opposed to retail banking that involves products such as home loans and auto loans given to individuals.

yield: The return on an investment. This refers to the interest or dividend received from a security and is usually expressed annually as a percentage based on the investment's cost, its current market value or its face value.

Index

Individuals

Institutions / Groups /Locations

225, 379
HDFC Group 98, 344, 373, 389
HDFC Securities Ltd. 226, 379
HDFC Standard Life Insurance
Co. Ltd. 337
Helios Capital Management Pte
Ltd. 176
Hero Group 190
Hexaware Technology Ltd. 309
Himatsingka Seide Ltd. 314
Hindujas' Group Firms 95
Hindustan Unilever Ltd. 86, 224
Home Ministry, Government of
India 395
Hongkong and Shanghai Banking
Corporation (HSBC) 123
Housing Development Finance
Corporation Ltd. (HDFC) 73
HP [Hewlett-Packard
Development Co. L. P.] 353

i-Flex Solutions Ltd. (now Oracle
Financial Services Software
Ltd.) 26, 50, 161, 222, 299
ICICI Bank Ltd. xi, 83, 86, 101,
115, 125, 178, 218, 226,
230–31, 235–37, 281, 308,
322, 344, 370, 378, 390, 396
ICICI Prudential Life Insurance
Co. Ltd. 344
ICICI Securities Ltd. (I-Sec) 101
ICICI Venture Funds
Management Co. Ltd. 244
IDBI Bank 286–87, 390
Ind Global Financial Trust Ltd.
177
Indian Air Force 133
Indian Hotels Co. Ltd. 86
Indian Institute of Management,
Ahmedabad (IIM-A) 104
Indian Institute of Technology
(IIT) 119
Indian Overseas Bank 165
IndusInd Bank Ltd. 83, 95
Industrial Development Bank of

India (IDBI) 84, 94, 95, 237,
286, 390
Industry House 193
Infosys Ltd. 157–60
Infrastructure Development
Finance Co. Ltd. (IDFC) 294
ING Vysya Bank Ltd. 124
Institute of Chartered
Accountants of India 336
International Business Machines
Corporation (IBM) 160, 353
International Civil Services 17
International Finance
Corporation (IFC) 78
International Monetary Fund 94
International Swap Dealer
Association 312
ITC Ltd. 192

Jamnalal Bajaj Institute of
Management Studies, Mumbai
125
Jawaharlal Nehru University 134
J. P. Morgan & Co. 101
J. Sagar Associates 309–10
Jumbo Group 81
J. Walter Thompson USA Inc.
(JWT) 387

Kalyani Steels Ltd. 81
Kamala Mills Ltd. 22, 39,
150–53, 284
Keppel Group 291
Kewal Industrial Estate, Lower
Parel, Mumbai 153, 161
Khattar Holding Pte Ltd. 170
KhattarWong & Partners 170
Kingfisher Airlines Ltd. 243
Kodaikanal International School,
Kodaikanal 223
Kotak Mahindra Bank Ltd. xi,
198, 308, 378
Kotak Mahindra Group 101
KPMG 309, 310

About the Author

Tamal Bandyopadhyay, a keen observer of the Indian banking sector for over two decades, is a bestselling author and an award-winning columnist. His weekly column 'Banker's Trust', which dates back to when he was part of founding team at *Mint*, is widely read for its incisive analysis and informed opinion.

A Consulting Editor with *Business Standard* and Senior Advisor to Jana Small Finance Bank Ltd., Tamal was previously an advisor on strategy at Bandhan Bank Ltd., the first microfinance company to transform itself into a universal bank in India.

Author of *From Lehman to Demonetization: A Decade of Disruptions, Reforms and Misadventures, Bandhan: The Making of a Bank, Sahara: The Untold Story* and *A Bank for The Buck*, Tamal is one of the contributors to the *Oxford Handbook on Indian Economy*, edited by Kaushik Basu, and *Making of New India: Transformation Under Modi Government*, edited by Bibek Debroy.

In 2018, Linkedin, the global professional network, nominated him as the second most influential voice in India. A year earlier, he was conferred the Ramnath Goenka Award for Excellence in Journalism (commentary and interpretative writing).

When he is not weighing in on financial matters, Tamal writes poetry in Bengali.

He lives in Mumbai with his family that includes his canine son Gogol.

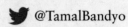 @TamalBandyo

bankerstrust.in